The Wanderer

The Last American Slave Ship and the Conspiracy That Set Its Sails

ERIK CALONIUS

St. Martin's Griffin ⚊ New York

www.stmartins.com

973.7
Cal

Design by Sarah Maya Gubkin

Library of Congress Cataloging-in-Publication Data

Calonius, Erik.
    The Wanderer : the last American slave ship and the conspiracy that set its sails / Erik Calonius.
        p. cm.
    ISBN-13: 978-0-312-34348-4
    ISBN-10: 0-312-34348-5
    1. Slave trade—United States—History—19th century.   2. Slave traders—United States—History—19th century.   3. Wanderer (Schooner).   4. Slave trade—Georgia—Savannah—History—19th century.   5. Slave traders—Georgia—Savannah—History—19th century.   I. Title.

E438.C35 2006
973.7'11—dc22

2006005454

First St. Martin's Griffin Edition: February 2008

10   9   8   7   6   5   4   3   2   1

2009 / 11 gift

Additional Praise for *The Wanderer*

"A compelling and heartrending record of a journey that helped push the nation to the brink of the Civil War."   —*The Washington Times*

"Historical reporting at its best."   —*Tuscon Citizen*

"A spell-binding page turner, opening with a shipwreck and never letting up . . . Narrative history rarely rises to these heights."
—Eileen Mackevich, executive director,
Abraham Lincoln Bicentennial Commission

"A fast-paced narrative . . . Calonius has a terrific eye for atmospheric details."
—*Publishers Weekly*

"Written in a style more reminiscent of thrillers than history books, the highly accessible text digs deep into the motivations of the Civil War and illuminates some of the darkest corners of our nation's past."
—*School Library Journal*

"This is a beautifully written book, full of imagery . . . I have reacted as positively and enthusiastically only one time before—that being to Nathaniel Philbrick's *In the Heart of the Sea*."
—Donald Thompson, coauthor of *The Civil War Research Guide*

"*The Wanderer* is a must-read for anyone interested in the causes of the Civil War."   —Eric Wittenberg, CivilWarCavalry.com

To my mother and father,

and for Nancy,

Michelle, and Matthew

Contents

Author's Note

JEKYLL ISLAND, off the coast of Georgia, was once the private wintering grounds of America's wealthiest businessmen—the Carnegies, the Rockefellers, the Vanderbilts, the Morgans, the Macys, the Pulitzers, and the Goulds, among others. Even today, the winter "cottages" of these tycoons, which have been fully restored, and especially their wonderfully turreted clubhouse (now the gracious Jekyll Island Club Hotel), are well worth the visit.

At the center of Jekyll Island sits a small museum. As you walk through it you see photographs of happy millionaires, reclining in their white linen suits, their wives smiling from beneath floppy hats and their children riding bicycles, dressed in knickers and soft caps. You learn that the Federal Reserve was founded at Jekyll by the magnates-in-residence in 1910, and that America's first transcontinental phone call was made from Jekyll to the West Coast, principally because AT&T president Theodore Vail was vacationing on Jekyll Island at the time.

I was strolling to the end of the exhibit a few years ago, not far from the exit, in fact, when I saw the ghostly image of a sailing ship on the wall. It was tucked into a dark corner. Its sails were huge—and they spread like gray wings. (The image, from a painting by Warren Sheppard, appears on the jacket of this book.) The caption beneath the grainy photo reproduction read: "In 1858, 50 years after the importation of slaves was prohibited by Congress, the Wanderer delivered a cargo of African slaves to the coast of Jekyll. This action caused a scandal, and charges were brought against many people, including the ship's crew and its owner, Charles Lamar of Savannah. All of the defendants were found innocent, or charges against them were dropped." That was all it said.

How strange, I thought, that a shipload of slaves would be brought here, to this place of pleasure. Later, when I did a bit of research, I discovered that while some of the conspirators were from Savannah, others were from the North. And the ship itself had been built on Long Island, New York. What kind of voyage was this, then? The question stuck with me for two years. I had to find out. And hence came this book.

In writing this book, I have learned a lesson about history: Although history may appear as a quiet pond, reflecting its light back serenely, a wonderful world opens up once one sinks one's head beneath the surface. It is populated by hundreds of long-gone people, their voices, as clear today as they were back then, arguing a hundred points of view, telling a hundred stories, expressing a hundred shades of emotion. It is noisy down there, beneath the surface of history, and a fascinating place to gather information to bring home. My first acknowledgment, then, is to those long-ago writers—the journalists, the essayists, the letter-writers, and the authors of the 1800s—who left their piquant words behind for me to find.

This book owes a special debt to several other writers. One of them is Winfield M. Thompson. In 1904 Thompson wrote a three-part series about the *Wanderer* for the magazine *The Rudder,* and created a story that, for the first time, drew together the many newspaper accounts of the incident. Thompson's account was not only elegantly written, it benefited from interviews with the families of some of the *Wanderer* participants. For instance, John Eugene du Bignon, whose late uncle, John du Bignon, had helped Corrie unload the Africans onto Jekyll, was still around, and Thompson interviewed him. Thompson also found the families of the late Captain Rowland, who designed the *Wanderer;* the family of the late Thomas B. Hawkins, who fitted the yacht with water tanks in preparation for the slave voyage; and the family of the late S. S. Norton, the inspector at Port Jefferson who blew the whistle on the group.

Building on the work of Thompson is Tom Henderson Wells. In the early 1960s, Wells wrote articles about Charles and Gazaway Lamar for the *Georgia Historical Quarterly,* and then a master's thesis about the *Wanderer* incident itself. This was made into a book, *The Slave Ship Wanderer,* which was published by the University of Georgia Press in 1967. To the tale told by Thompson, Wells added the skills of a probing academic researcher, carefully footnoting the *Wanderer* story and exploring its legal implications. As a graduate of the U.S. Naval Academy (1940) and an authority on naval history, he also brought to the story the eye of an experienced maritime historian. His work served as some of the stepping-stones for this book. Although I went through thousands of pages of primary documents, I never found a single error in his meticulously written account.

In terms of framing this story in its political context, I owe a debt of gratitude to Dr. Ronald T. Takaki, whose superb book *A Pro-Slavery Crusade* opened my eyes to the larger issues surrounding the voyage of the *Wanderer*—and in particular to the composition of that group of radicals known as the fire-eaters, including the notorious Leonidas Spratt. To anyone who wants to know more about the fire-eaters, in exquisite detail, Takaki's book is one to read. Second, I want to cite Manisha Sinha's excellent work, *The Counterrevolution of Slavery.* Sinha's writings once again awakened me to the conspiracy behind the voyage, and particularly to the plan to use the reopening of the African slave trade to split the nation. In addition, I owe a great debt to Michael P. Johnson for *Toward a Patriarchal Republic;* John McCardell for *The Idea of a Southern Nation;* Avery O. Craven for *The Growth of Southern Nationalism;* and George Fort Milton for *The Eve of Conflict*—books that again made me see the ultimate ambitions of the radical leaders.

For information about the African Squadron and the story of Commanders Totten and Conver, I am indebted to Warren S. Howard's superb *American Slavers and the Federal Law.* I'm also indebted to Hugh Soulsby's *The Right of Search and the Slave Trade in Anglo-American Relations.* In terms of setting the economic stage I am indebted to Robert R. Russell's *Economic Aspects of Southern Sectionalism.*

Finally, for the account of the sinking of *Pulaski,* I am grateful for the beautiful, anguished accounts of the tragedy written by Rebecca Lamar and James Hamilton Couper.

I want to give my sincere thanks to Ceceile Kay Richter, my primary researcher. From her perch in Washington, D.C., Ceceile dove into the recesses of the National Archives, the Library of Congress, the Georgetown University Library, and other repositories, extracting thousands of pages of pertinent materials that arrived at my door in streams of envelopes and boxes. Ceceile not only executed my instructions, but found her own path to a wealth of materials that were unexpected and essential. I also want to thank Lynn Watson-Powers, based in Atlanta, for her great research at the National Archives, Southeast (East Point, Georgia), the University of Georgia, and Emory University. Thanks also to Anne Dodenhoff for her research in Charleston, South Carolina.

I also want to thank Dan Kelly and Bill Blundell, two *Wall Street Journal* legends, for reading several chapters and offering their extremely helpful comments. Thanks also to Glenn Ruffenach, another great *Wall Street Journal* editor, who likewise tackled several chapters, and, through his suggestions, made them much better. In terms of reading parts and iterations of this book, I'd also like to thank Ed Weathers, Larry Pritchard, Wes Evans, David Holman, and Richard Conner.

I want to thank the staff of the Georgia Historical Society Library who assisted me in my research and who copied reams of documents; and the fine folks at the Forsyth Park Inn in Savannah, which was my home during my research trips. I also want to thank the Rollins College Library in Winter Park, Florida, for the use of their microfilm machine, and the staff of the Winter Park Public Library.

I want to thank my agent, Dan Greenberg, for helping me land a contract; Vicki Lame, editorial assistant at St. Martin's Press, for her great assistance and patience in helping me put this book together; and most of all, my editor at St. Martin's Press, Michael Flamini, for believing in this book in the first place and guiding it to its successful completion.

Last, I want to thank my wife, Nancy, for her unceasing support, even in the dark hours of this endeavor; my mother and Michelle and Paul, for encouraging me from afar; and especially my son, Matthew, who would sense my car lights flashing past his bedroom window in the dark of early morning, and know that I was off again, to see what I could find beneath the placid face of history.

The *Wanderer* left a great amount of evidence behind in its wake, in terms of newspaper accounts, letters, and legal documents. But there were a few places where the evidence ran thin, and even disappeared. This was particularly so in the description of the African "factory" and of the slave market from which the *Wanderer* captives were taken. Little evidence also remains of the brief tour the *Wanderer* crew took into Africa, and of the *Wanderer's* final voyage back to Jekyll Island.

In these few cases I have tried to reconstruct what the crew of the *Wanderer* probably saw and experienced. Fortunately, at least for the purposes of this book, the slave trade created many eyewitness accounts, with which one can paint a very clear picture. For the sections on the factory, I dug into eyewitness accounts appearing in George Dow's *Slave Ships and Slaving*, particularly a narrative in that book entitled "The Recollections of a Slave Trader." I also found useful material in Daniel Mannix's *Black Cargoes;* and a striking description of the "factory," which was written by Robert W. Shufeldt, an African Squadron commander, in *The Journal of Negro History*.

J. Egbert Farnum had bragged about viewing "African nature in all its originality" and "native princes in their palaces" during a brief trip into the continent. To describe this excursion in further detail, I relied on *Travels in West Africa* by Mary Kingsley. Kingsley traveled about 200 miles north of where the *Wanderer* must have gone, and forty years later, but the conditions and people were probably very similar. Other useful eyewitness accounts included "Slave Smuggling a Hundred Years Ago," which appeared in *Slave Ships and Slaving*. In terms of the *Wanderer's* return trip, little is known but that some eighty Africans died along the way and that the yacht suffered through a violent storm. To illustrate what this voyage was probably like, I relied heavily on several eyewitness accounts chronicled in George Dow's *Slave Ships and Slaving*, and particularly an account of life aboard a slaver from that book in "Six Months on a Slaver in 1860."

Finally, most of the dialogue in this book is drawn directly from newspaper transcriptions, letters, and memoirs. In only a few cases, as in the presidential conversation in the White House and the initial meeting of William C. Corrie with William Edgar, the commander of the New York Yacht Club, did I feel it necessary to create a few sentences of dialogue, and some internal thought, to move the narrative along. My intention, in every case, was to tell the tale of the *Wanderer* based on the facts, with only as much reconstruction of events and occasional touches of color as was required to bring the story to life.

Charting the *Wanderer*'s Course in Modern-Day Savannah

Savannah River

1. U.S. Custom House (where *Wanderer* auction and trial were held)
2. Lamar residence (44 E. Broughton)
3. Lamar's Bank of Commerce (4 Drayton St.)
4. Price's Clothing Store (1 Bull St.)
5. City Hotel (157 Bay St., where defendants were arrested)
6. Prosecutor Joseph Ganahl's residence (223 E. Charlton St.)
7. Prosecutor Henry Jackson's residence (450 Bull St.)
8. Defense attorney John Owen's office (119 Bay St.)
9. Supreme Court Justice Wayne's residence (10 E. Oglethorpe St.)
10. Slave quarters of George Wylly (from which African was stolen)
11. Pulaski Hotel (Bull and Bryan Sts.)
12. Claghorn & Cunningham ship chandlers (where *Lamar*'s captain was found)
13. Model of the *Wanderer* (Ships of the Sea Museum, 41 M.L.K. Jr. Blvd.)
14. Plaque at the entrance of Savannah's City Hall honoring Gazaway Lamar and the steamship *John Randolph*

The Wanderer

INTRODUCTION

CHARLES LAMAR should have done better than to have ended up flat on his back with a bullet in his chest.

His family, after all, included some of the most distinguished individuals in the nation. His father was one of the most successful businessmen in the South, a visionary with offices in Savannah and on Wall Street. His cousin, Mirabeau Bonaparte Lamar, was the second president of the Republic of Texas; another cousin was Lucius Quintus Cincinnatus Lamar, a U.S. senator and later a U.S. Supreme Court justice. His aunt, Mary Ann Lamar Cobb, was wife of U.S. Treasury Secretary Howell Cobb. When Charles Lamar was baptized, no less a man than the Marquis de Lafayette, the Revolutionary War companion of George Washington and Thomas Jefferson, held Lamar, red and wiggling, in his arms while the holy water was applied. Hence, the full name: Charles Augustus *Lafayette* Lamar.

Lamar's accomplishments were many. He was a director of the Savannah, Albany and Gulf Railroad, as well as the Savannah Bank of Commerce. Lamar owned warehouses and cotton presses, and a sprawling cotton plantation as well. He was lionized by the *Savannah Daily*

Morning News, and with his drive and pedigree could have become a state governor, a U.S. senator, or even a statesman on the order of a Washington or a Jefferson . . . if only he had so desired.

Yet, as Lamar came into his own in the 1850s, and the nation raced toward civil war, another group of advocates caught his attention. Racist, paranoid, fiery, exploitive, brutal, and domineering, these were the "fire-eaters." They were radicals who urged the South to expand slavery at home and across the territories, and, failing to do that, break up the union and form a new southern nation. Like radicals of their kind throughout history, they were mocked at first, both in the North and the South. But they gradually gained power, sowing their seeds of fear.

It happened that Charles Lamar fell in with their lot. He would join the fire-eaters in arguing for more slavery, not less, and most important, for a reopening of the African slave trade. But Lamar was a man of action, not words. He knew that hot words alone would not get the agenda done. But he had a plan that might.

It all centered on a little sailing yacht, 114 feet long, a glistening, gorgeous schooner with billowing sails and softly glowing brass work. She had been built on Long Island, New York, to be one of the most luxurious and fastest yachts ever—and she was. Beloved by the press, celebrated by other yachtsmen, whispered to be the successor to the famous yacht *America,* she was admitted immediately into the prestigious New York Yacht Club. From then on, the NYYC pennant flew proudly from the peak of her mainmast. Her name was the *Wanderer.*

No one would have imagined that a year later, the *Wanderer* would embark on one of the most notorious voyages in the nation's history, one that would cause alarm in Congress, force the president to ponder the survival of his party, and, in a nationally publicized trial, challenge the federal laws of the nation. Unimaginable, too, would be the proposed duel between Charles Lamar and the editor of the *New York Times,* and a duel at dawn between Lamar and Edwin Moore, the naval commander of the Republic of Texas. In the end, the voyage of the *Wanderer* was more than a notorious cruise. It was an incident that rocked the nation, pushed the country closer to war, and established Lamar as one of the most cunning radicals of his time.

What ended with a bullet began in the summer of 1838, with a catastrophe that would shape the character of Charles Lamar forevermore. In that year Savannah was still a soft, sleepy place, and Charles's father, Gazaway, with all the success in the world behind him, could not imagine the tragedy that was yet to come.

1

EARLY SAVANNAH

THE SUN was shining brightly as Gazaway Lamar, vibrant and hand-some, stood on the top step to the entrance of his home at 44 East Broughton Street, the finest address in Savannah. Lamar was one of the city's leading citizens, and certainly one of the South's most successful and wealthiest businessmen. And now, as he hurried down to the river-front to catch up with his eldest son, Charles, and the rest of his family, he felt his life was about to reach its peak of satisfaction.

In 1838, Savannah was even then a city of trees and squares, large opulent homes, and an indelible sense of history. James Oglethorpe had planned the town around a series of squares, leaving two sides for pub-lic buildings and two for private homes. From this came the fundamen-tal symmetry upon which the beauty of Savannah was based.

For years following Oglethorpe, Savannah retained the rustic char-acter of its colonial past. Even in 1838, the squares were enclosed with split-rail fences. Cows lolled in the lanes. The streets were lit, if at all, by oil-burning lamps. The city market bustled with customers and produce of all kinds, which was brought into town on creaking wooden carts from the country. And everyone paid with English coins—mostly shillings and pence. The only U.S. currency available at the time was a big copper one-cent coin.

At the east end of Bay Street, on the bluff that became Emmet Park, people would gather to see the ships departing, carrying cotton and rice, and arriving, bearing with them the commercial treasures of the world. Some fifty feet beneath the bluff was the riverfront, where all was alive with activity: horses and mules, carts and buggies, men carrying sacks in every direction, bales of cotton creeping to the edge of the wharf, awaiting the hooks that would lift them, swinging slowly, into the ship's holds.

Hand-pulled fire wagons were sometimes seen dashing about as well. Savannah was still built mostly of wood, and had suffered a disastrous fire eighteen years earlier. At the sight of a fire, the watchman at the top of the City Exchange would ring his bell furiously, and, if night had fallen, thrust a lantern on a pole in the direction of the blaze. Then the citizens would tumble out of their homes, their shadows leaping off the walls, grab the leather buckets by the handles, form a double-line brigade, and pass the water from the cisterns to the flames and then back again to the well.

The roads were unpaved, of course, and the carriages rolled softly across the tawny sand. "The first thing that struck me on landing was the absence of noise. Everything seemed so quiet," Sara Hathaway, a visitor from New York, remarked in 1833. "Even the carriage we rode in, as well as the others which were about us, gave us no sound, for their wheels sank into the sand, which appeared to be bottomless."

Harsh sound was also softened by an abundance of trees, creating the impression of a city tucked into a forest. South Broad Street, in particular, was lined by towering chinaberry trees, many of them with limbs extending thirty or forty feet, creating more than a half mile of elegant shade. "Long limbs were thrown out on every side," recalled Charles Hardee, who was a boy in Savannah in the 1830s, "some of them interlocking with the limbs of trees on the other side, furnishing a dense shade, which was a very pleasant protection from the midsummer heat." The flowers, which grew in clusters from the tips of the branches, were of a lilac color, and their perfume filled the air.

To be sure, a remarkable sight rose above this rich canopy: the Grecian pediments of theaters and banks, the spires of churches, white towers with bells ringing, and along the bluff, warehouses and offices that stretched from one end of town to the other. Still, the quiet beauty of the place, with its heavy perfume, overhanging branches, and omnipresent mid-summer heat was almost sleep-inducing. Perhaps this was why "South-ern people have one marked peculiarity—they almost always move slowly," as one visitor marveled. "The ladies have a natural loveliness and grace, an ease of manner and self-possession, soft and gentle ways. And the gentlemen: They are so courteous and chivalrous in their bear-ing, so deferential to the ladies."

However dreamy that impression may have been, by 1838, Savannah was beginning to awaken from its slumber. Something new was afoot. Its presence was causing old salts to cuss, horses to rear in alarm, and men to start dreaming of bigger and bigger things: paddle wheelers, rail-roads, factories—*steam*! After falling behind the North for at least twenty years, the South's entrepreneurs were beginning to awaken to the roar of the Industrial Revolution.

In the 1820s, Savannah's cotton planters began to produce their own hemp bagging, which saved them considerable expense over Northern-made bags. Then, in 1828, a group from Savannah purchased the latest textile-making machinery in Philadelphia, shipped it south, and estab-lished a mill. That worked out so well that they added a dye house to the complex, and were soon making denims in stripes and plaids. In 1834, a factory in Augusta began manufacturing its own spindle frames, which had previously been imported from the North. By 1840, when the Georgia census listed nineteen cotton mills in the state, with 42,589 spindles, 779 employees, and two dye-houses, there was no doubt any longer: The South had crossed the threshold from a mere picker of cot-ton to a maker of cotton goods as well.

Meanwhile, railroads began to catch the eye of the Southern indus-trialists. The North had two experimental lines, the Rocket and the Tom Thumb. But Charleston snatched the lead with what was dubbed the nation's first regularly scheduled line, the South Carolina Rail Road, which ran from Charleston to Hamburg, South Carolina. Pulling the passenger cars was the first American-made locomotive, the "Best Friend," soon to be equipped with a very useful embellishment, thanks to inventor Isaac Dripps—the cowcatcher.

Challenged by Charleston's leap into the railroad business, Savannah laid the first rails for its Central of Georgia Railroad in 1836. The locomotive was an ungainly looking contraption that belched smoke and covered the wagons rattling behind with black soot. But you couldn't convince anyone in Savannah that their railroad was anything short of a technological miracle. "As the people were coming in from the Commons, where they laid the *first rail*," the wife of Savannah's mayor wrote ecstatically, "it was more like Broadway than anything I have ever seen . . . from Broughton Street all the way to our house both sides of the street were crowded." At 10 P.M., she added, "they came before our door and called out distinctly, 'Nine cheers for the railroad and Mayor Gordon!' And they gave the full number, for I counted to see if they did."

Nine cheers were about right, for in this progress the South saw new economic life. Georgia's banks "will bear an honorable comparison with those of similar institutions in perhaps any state of the Union," Georgia governor Wilson Lumpkin declared in 1834. Her schools of higher education were destined "in no distant day . . . to be justly considered a rival of the best literary institutions in our widely extended country." Lumpkin had a similar confidence in the railroads. "The superior advantages of rail road, over every other description of expensive works of internal improvement seems now scarcely to be questioned," he stated. "The day is not far distant when the commercial advantages and disadvantages of all the principal Atlantic cities will approximate much nearer than they do at the present."

In all this excitement, an even bigger, even more complex possibility began to glimmer. "Having a day or two since visited the plantation of the Honorable L. Cheves," a reader informed the *Savannah Daily Georgian* in 1838, "my attention was called to the operation of a newly constructed engine known as Avery's Rotary Steam Engine. This engine propels two threshers, two fans, and two rakes . . . Mr. Richardson, the overseer of the plantation, informed me that the straw alone would generate all the steam and more that could be used, and with the labor of just one Negro man. Rice planters would do well to examine this marvel for themselves!"

If the South was about to embrace the Industrial Revolution, and the evidence showed that she was, this was a radical shift in thinking. Thomas Jefferson had counseled his fellow Southerners to adhere to the "Agrarian Ideal," which emphasized a life of farming and agriculture over that of industrialization. Georgia's founder, James Oglethorpe, preached the same message: There would be no manufacturing in his Georgia colony, he declared, no industrial class to be downtrodden like those poor souls in England. What should Georgians do then? Be happy. Make wine, silk, and oil, he replied.

For many years following Oglethorpe's remarks, adherence to the Agrarian Ideal was not difficult to achieve. Following the War of 1812, cotton prices rose, and continued to do so, with a few twists and turns, for the next twenty years. With cotton booming, the South was rich. Concert halls and plantation homes were her style. Let the North play the industrial giant, with all the social ills and miserable mill towns that industrialization entailed.

But when cotton prices slumped in 1833, tumbling even harder in 1839, the South was stricken with remorse. The South had allowed itself to become a one-crop economy. Facing possible bankruptcy, the region's financiers and businessmen began to reconsider the merits of "progress." It might not be such a bad thing after all. In fact, they realized, factories might make them even more money than they could make from cotton alone.

In Savannah, the city's citizens had always considered their town a worldly, cosmopolitan place—a leafy little Athens, a seaport city where commerce and the arts commingled. But now they dreamed that Savannah might become bigger still, a nexus of commerce and culture—on the scale of New York City itself.

After all, New York and Savannah were already partners in business. Savannah's cotton row was filled with New York businessmen, who, from their brick offices overlooking the Savannah River, could see the ships crowding in below. New York's best hotels, meanwhile—the Astor, the St. Nicolas, the Clarendon, the Metropolitan—were always booked with Savannah's merchants and planters, and, in the sultry months of July and August, their families as well. The social links between the two seaports were extensive, and would remain so right up until the Civil War. As the *Savannah Daily Morning News* reported:

> The *"gay season"* in New York, according to some of our ex-changes from that great metropolis, promises to be particularly bril-liant this winter . . . This year a gala opera season led off, any number of weddings followed, and now the party and ball season is commencing with vigor . . . A great many invitations are said to be out for entertainments to be given during the present month, many of them large private balls, and others, where amateur theatricals, music and acting charades are to be the principal amusements of-fered . . . the initiatory steps have also been taken for periodical soirees, by some of the leading ladies in New York society, which are partly literary, partly musical, and wholly delightful . . .

Indeed, they had *so much* in common. One could find the best Tenerife wines or Irish linens in New York City, and buy them in Sa-vannah as well. One could read the latest dispatches about the possible marriage between the Duke d'Aumale and the infant queen of Spain (or of the expedition from Toulon to Antarctica) in the New York dailies, and find them in the Savannah newspapers as well. And if one had missed the luminaries of the stage—Edwin Booth, Charlotte Cushman, and Edwin Forrest—in New York, you could always catch their perfor-mances in Savannah instead.

In 1838, then, it took no great stretch of the imagination to see Sa-vannah catching up—a social equal, a cultural equal, a mercantile equal to the great Gotham. That idea soon caught on among the Georgia newspapers, and before long they had hatched a new moniker for their state, "Georgia, the *Empire State* of the South."

Ever since colonial days, of course, the North and South had found points of contention and places of dispute. They had quarreled over the expansion of slavery, and its place in the Constitution; over the placement of the nation's capital—Virginia or Philadelphia; over federal tarriffs; over the removal of the Indians. But in 1838, the nation seemed to take a breather: Americans were more interested in speculating in railroads, steamboats, canals, roads—and fighting Indians—for a change, than fighting each other.

In fact, when a conclave of Southern businessmen finished their meeting in Savannah in 1837, they offered a series of toasts—to railroads, to steamboats, to free trade, and, of course, to the ladies of the city. Then one delegate stood. Raising his glass, he proclaimed, "To the Northern states! Let us show that in honorable enterprise, brothers may compete—and be brothers still!" The whole room cheered.

Sitting in their clubhouse on the banks of the Savannah River, all this talk of sporting competition gave the members of the Aquatic Club of Georgia an idea. Since Savannah and New York were such gracious competitors, why not a friendly race to extend relations even further? Henry du Bignon and Charles Floyd, the club's secretaries, immediately penned a challenge to the Knickerbocker Club, a Manhattan sporting society, and placed it in one of New York City's newspapers:

> *Gentlemen, The Aquatic Club of Georgia, having frequently heard of the fitness of your Boats and skill of your Oarsmen, are desirous of comparing the speed of one of their Boats with the speed of one of yours, on the following terms: We propose to run the four-oared Canoe Boat "Lizard" one straight mile opposite the city of Savannah, in fair and calm weather, against any four Oaked Plank Boats built in the City of New York, not over 27 feet 3 inches on the keel (which is the length of the Lizard's) for Ten thousand dollars a side—Two thousand forfeit . . . Should those terms proposed be acceptable, address Cas. Ro. Floyd, Jeffersonton, Camden County, Ga., and particulars can be arranged by correspondence.*

Competition, fair and square, with big stakes. That was the kind of challenge that attracted the southern scullers, and it was the kind of challenge that excited Gazaway Lamar as well. In fact, it was exactly the kind of challenge that made him quicken his pace as he hurried down the steps of his house, across Broughton Street, and into a carriage that would take him down to the wharves on the Savannah River.

If the embodiment of all the excitement and energy that was coursing through Savannah could be found in one man, that man would have been Gazaway Lamar. Gazaway was born on October 2, 1798. He was the third of twelve children born to Basil and Rebecca Lamar, whose great-grandparents, French Huguenots, had fled France in 1660. Gazaway was married to Jane Meek Cresswell, and by 1838, had six children. Gazaway had made his first fortune in banking and cotton in Augusta. In 1833, he moved the family to Savannah, placed his eldest son, Charles, in Reverend White's prestigious Chatham Academy, and set about enlarging his fortunes. It didn't take long.

Gazaway bought one warehouse on the river, then another, and soon had a row of brick buildings collected under the inscription, in big white letters, LAMAR'S WHARF. At the east end of Broad Street he added a cotton press to the enterprise, an operation employing steam presses to compact loose cotton into bales. But this was just the beginning. Lamar also founded the Bank of Commerce, situated on Drayton Street. The Bank of Commerce soon became Savannah's second largest bank.

Yet Gazaway was more than a mere merchant. *The Dictionary of American Biography* (New York, 1933) described Gazaway Lamar as being "quick to discern the trends of the time." Indeed, he was a visionary. When steam locomotives were making their first appearances in America, for instance—as strange and irritating an object as anyone had ever seen—Lamar immediately recognized their potential. Savannah needed a "rail road," he argued, one that would run from the city to the vast new cotton fields near Macon. At the time that Lamar was promoting the idea of this "iron horse"—in 1836— Savannah was nearly broke, having been battered by a recession. When the mayor balked, Lamar offered to finance the downtown spur of the line himself.

But railroads weren't the only new technology that fascinated Lamar. Steamboats were another. At the time, Savannah's steamboat traffic was ruled by Laurel Howard, an entrepreneur who had sewn up the rights to steam navigation on the river from 1814 to 1834. But now that Howard's franchise was finished, Gazaway decided to put the monopoly to the test. Howard's stern-wheelers were bulky vessels. When the Savannah River drew itself down in the dry season, Howard's steamboats couldn't get all the way upriver to retrieve the bales of cotton waiting inland, leaving them to rot.

But Lamar had an idea. He knew of an English inventor, John Laird, who had built a new kind of steamboat: Its hull had been crafted from iron plates, less than a half-inch thick, rather than the traditional wood. Not only was the hull stronger than one of wood, but lighter. And since it was lighter, it could float in shallower waters. The Englishman's first iron-hulled ship, the *Alburka,* had been used to take explorers far up the Niger River, to areas that had never been navigated before. The second ship, the *Lady Lansdowne,* had a similar iron hull, but was exceptional in another manner: She had been built modularly, so that she could be shipped in parts from Liverpool to Dublin—and then reassembled by workmen there.

If an iron-hulled steamship could be sent across the North Sea, why couldn't one be sent across the Atlantic as well? Most people at the time would have hesitated at the notion of a cast-iron boat, let alone one that would be built in pieces in England and reassembled thousands of miles away. But Lamar snapped his fingers in delight. He ordered the ship, had it sent across the Atlantic on a sailing brig—all 100 tons of it—and then reassembled it in Savannah. A few British workmen came over with the steamship to help with the assembly. But Lamar declined their assistance: *Southern* workmen could do the job just as well, he insisted—and they did.

The *John Randolph,* as she was named, was remarkable in every way. She was 100 feet in length, 22 feet in beam across the hull, and had two paddle wheels. Her bottom and lower strakes were of the best English-rolled boilerplate iron, $\frac{5}{16}$th of an inch thick. Above that, the skin plates were a ¼-inch thick. She was powered by a condensing engine, the cylinders of which were 30 inches in diameter. The piston itself had a five-foot stroke. The total weight of the machinery was seventeen tons.

On her maiden voyage on July 15, 1834, she created a sensation. "As might have been expected, the novelty of a boat constructed of iron, which had generally been considered too heavy even to *float,* attracted very considerable attention and curiosity," the *Augusta Daily Constitutionalist* exclaimed. The *John Randolph* not only floated through the shallows on her maiden voyage, she pulled two heavily loaded barges. Her paddle wheels, turning at eighteen revolutions per minute, set her speed at a remarkable five miles an hour, *upstream.*

Augusta's city dignitaries boarded the *John Randolph* that evening to celebrate. As she passed the Citadel, in nearby Hamburg, the cadets fired off the school's cannons in salute. The crowd aboard the *John Randolph* cheered in reply. "We entertain a high sense of respect and regard for Mr. Lamar—who indeed ran a great risk in this enterprise, and has rendered a great service to the country in general by this experiment," the *Augusta Chronicle* said the next day. "We sincerely hope that it may prove a successful and profitable one . . ." It did. The *John Randolph* went down in the history books as America's first commercially successful, iron-hulled vessel. Not surprisingly, Lamar soon expanded the Iron Steamboat Company of Augusta to include six iron-hulled steamboats, including one that he named the *Lamar.*

The *John Randolph* was a commercial success, but it was a mere inland waterway vessel. What Lamar dreamed of next was an oceangoing steamer, one to compete with the Northern steamers that went up and down the East Coast, collecting riches in passengers and freight. She would be a grand ship, with the greatest technology—a ship that would bring honor and wealth to Savannah and the South. And her name would be the *Pulaski.*

2

THE *PULASKI*

THE *PULASKI,* named for the Revolutionary War hero Count Pulaski, was a big side-wheeler, 203 feet long and weighing 687 tons. Her wooden scrollwork was painted white, her roof red, and her wheel-house was decorated in gold leaf. Her brass, buffed so brightly that the faces of the smiling passengers glowed as they swept by, blazed in the southern sun. Above this wedding cake of ornamentation and detail rose twin smokestacks, casting their black plumes far to the rear. But she was not a thing of beauty alone: Her twin paddle wheels, each six stories high, were integrated into the body of the ship, covered with gently curving cowlings, adding to her ornamentation a sleek muscular appearance.

"No expense has been spared to have a vessel to answer the purpose she is intended to accomplish," a notice in the *Savannah Daily Georgian* declared. "Her engine—one of the best ever made in this country, is of 225 horsepower. Her boilers are of the best copper, and great strength. Her qualities as a sea vessel for ease, safety and speed are superior to any steamer that ever floated on American waters."

Gazaway Lamar was proud of this marvelous machine. But his excitement was more profound than that. Back in 1819, William Scarbrough, a wealthy Savannah businessman, had put his prestige into the *Savannah,* a sailing ship that had been fitted out with a single boiler and two paddle wheels. The *Savannah,* carrying the pride of the city with her, was supposed to be the first steamship to transverse the Atlantic.

The *Savannah*'s efforts began auspiciously. In May 1819, President James Monroe rode the SS *Savannah* out to Tybee Island and back on a maiden voyage, the vessel compliantly belching smoke and slapping her paddle wheels as crowds cheered from the shore. The following month the *Savannah* set off, making a 10,000-mile transatlantic journey that took her to Liverpool, Stockholm, St. Petersburg, Copenhagen, Arendal (Norway), and back. But since her paddle wheels turned a mere eighty hours of the twenty-seven days at sea, many maritime authorities refused to acknowledge her as America's first transatlantic steamer. Rebuffed, and abandoned by her financial supporters, the *Savannah* was stripped of her boilers and paddle wheels and returned to sea as an ordinary sailing vessel. Scarbrough, meanwhile, was driven into financial ruin.

Now, Lamar was convinced, the *Pulaski* would win back some of the South's honor. She wouldn't make a transatlantic crossing, but rather accomplish something more important: She would challenge the monopoly that New York City had on coastal transportation, and teach the nation that the South was on the rise again.

In June 1838, the following ad appeared in the *Savannah Daily Georgian*:

FOR BALTIMORE VIA CHARLESTON

Only one night at sea, and passing Cape Hatteras by daylight. The new steamer PULASKI, Captain Dubois, is now receiving engagements for passengers to Charleston and Baltimore—also to Philadelphia, as an arrangement has been made with the Philadelphia, Wilmington & Baltimore Rail Road Company, to carry passengers of that boat in the cars that leave Baltimore daily at half past 6 and half past 9 in the morning, and arrive at Philadelphia in six hours. The PULASKI will leave here precisely at 8 o'clock tomorrow.

Passengers will please send their baggage on board as early on that day as possible.

It was for this occasion that Gazaway Lamar had hurried through the streets of Savannah and now bounded up the gangplank to the *Pulaski*. On this trip, he would be taking his entire family along. There was his wife, Jane, the quiet dynamo behind much of his success, her curls bouncing beneath her silk bonnet; and there was his beloved sister Rebecca—Aunt Rebecca to the children—who, with her soft hands and ready shoulder was as much a mother to the children as Jane herself. And then there were the children: Martha, William, Thomas, George, Eliza, and, of course, his firstborn son—Charles Augustus Lafayette Lamar.

While the rest of the family members settled into their cabins, Gazaway took Charles below to see the heartbeat of the ship—the engine room. As they descended the stairway, Charles felt the blast of flames raging within the fireboxes beneath the boilers. Gazaway pointed out the sturdy glass tube, five feet long and filled with a thin line of mercury, that measured the pressure. He showed his son how the steam ran from the top of the twin boilers, along shiny copper pipes to the vertically pitched "walking beam" engines, whose flywheels would soon be spinning, and whose mighty piston would soon rise and fall.

The boy's face glowed attentively in the flickering yellow light. "The engines were built by Watchman and Bratt of Baltimore," Gazaway exclaimed over the roaring fires. "The pistons have an eight-foot throw!" Gazaway looked up with equal pride at the boilers, studded with rivets and as shiny as mirrors. "Twelve tons each," he cried. "Made of the best-grade copper." Gazaway put his hands in his pockets and ran his eyes appreciably over all the machinery. "Son," he said, looking down again. "*This* is the future of the South."

By now, the *Pulaski* was filling up with additional passengers. "Many of the most respectable families of Georgia had passage in her on their annual visit to the North," wrote James Hamilton Couper, a prominent attorney and highly regarded amateur architect. "Of these were Mrs. Nightingale, wife of my friend P.M. Nightingale of Cumberland Island, with his infant and servant, and my sister in law, Mrs. Fraser, with a little boy five years old. Mrs. Nightingale was going to spend the summer with her father's family at Jamaica, Long Island, and Mrs. Fraser to visit her three eldest boys at school in Connecticut."

The *Pulaski* left Savannah on the morning of June 13, and by late afternoon had arrived in Charleston. There, other passengers boarded. "The passengers, both from Savannah and Charleston, were mostly acquainted with each other," Couper continued, "and as we went over Charleston bar that next morning at 8 o'clock, the weather fine and with all our colors flying, friends were congratulating each other upon meetings, and on the prospect of a pleasant voyage, exclaiming that this was a party of pleasure."

Later that night, many of the passengers gathered on their promenade deck, dressed in their light sweaters. In their midst the great piston-shaft of the *Pulaski* rose through a break in the deck, connecting twenty feet above to a horizontal bar that transferred its power through twin drive shafts to the paddle wheels below. It was a mechanical marvel, the passengers exclaimed, watching its rhythmic movement—a steam-breathing testament to the ingenuity of man.

The sky was so dark and velvety that night that the stars seemed close at hand. One of the men pointed out Ursa Major, with the North Star embedded brightly in the constellation, and remarked that he had never seen it so distinct and diamondlike. James Couper looked up. Indeed, the ship seemed to be sailing in its own lovely galaxy, with beautiful people and beautiful shining stars all around.

Down below, where Gazaway and his family had taken several of the cabins and large staterooms, Aunt Rebecca was busy putting two of the children to bed. "Eliza came in, and then Martha," Rebecca wrote later. "I heard Eliza say her prayers and as she lifted her eyes, I remember how beautiful she looked as she knelt before me. We went to sleep, free from anxiety, to wake in Baltimore!"

Couper had also retired to his berth. The light from his cabinmate's bunk kept him from sleep, however, and so he lay there thinking. It was just before 11 o'clock at night. The *Pulaski* was about 45 miles south of Cape Lookout, North Carolina, some 30 miles from the nearest land.

———

Solomon, a black waiter, was just leaving the engine room when he heard the second engineer frantically turning the water cock on the starboard steam boiler. As it turned out, the engineer had inadvertently left the blow cock open, draining the boiler and turning it red-hot. As soon as the second engineer realized this, he shut the blow cock and tried to refill the boiler. Every drop of water went skittering and dancing across the hot metal, however, turning itself instantaneously into steam. The valves screamed; the mercury in the pressure gauge shot to the top of its glass tube.

When the boiler exploded, it drove itself up through the promenade deck, splintering the wood, tossing lounge chairs into the sea, shattering the starboard side of the vessel midship. Simultaneously, the bulkhead between the boilers and the forward cabin caved in. The port boiler was still full, and now the ship rolled in that direction. Seawater rushed in.

As the *Pulaski* began to sink, water from the aft end pushed itself forward to the promenade deck. She hung like that for about forty minutes, and then there was another enormous crash: She snapped in half, freeing the extreme bow and stern portion to rise above the ocean. The promenade deck separated from the hull in three parts, and the keel separated from the main structure and came to the surface, bottom upward.

Rebecca recalled hearing a sound like thunder crashing nearby, and then the "trembling and careening of the steamer." She leapt from bed and held her two nieces near. She tried to open the cabin door, and finding it jammed, she tried to go out through a gap in the transom. "My head and shoulders were through the opening when the steamer gave a tremendous lurch," she recalled. "The berth flew under in a flash, and the door opened with tremendous violence. The china and glass fell in the closets with a crash, and every light went out."

Forcing her way out of the cabin, Rebecca found Mrs. Lamar with her nurse and three of the children at the stateroom door. "I heard groans proceeding from the now darkened passage," said Rebecca. "I stepped a few paces and found a Negro man on his hands and knees, in agony. I said, 'Daddy, what is the matter?' 'Oh, missus, my feet done burnt off!'" Her heart was full of sympathy, but there was nothing she could do.

Now Charles Lamar came stumbling down the passageway, herding his brothers and sisters before him. They needed to get up the stairway to the promenade deck. "It was characteristic of Charles—the most obliging and most grateful of children," Rebecca would later write. "Charles collected their clothing, put them in his arms, and made the children precede him up the stairs. He was fourteen years old."

By now James Couper was on deck. His bare feet slashed by broken glass, he found Mrs. Nightingale and her infant son, and took them to where he had seen the lifeboat. It was dangling some twelve feet below, hardly visible. Mrs. Nightingale gave Couper her boy and jumped into the boat. Couper jumped next, but caught his foot on the gunwale and fell headlong into the sea. He came up, gasping for breath but with his grip still tight on the infant, and climbed aboard. Mrs. Fraser next threw her little boy to Couper, who caught the lad, and then jumped into the boat herself.

As Charles Lamar was helping his brothers up the stairs, Gazaway suddenly appeared, pale and trembling. "The boiler has burst, the boat is sinking, and we shall be lost in five minutes!" he cried. There was stunned silence. "Could we not get on the upper deck?" Rebecca replied. They moved slowly, as a group, herding the children before them. As they proceeded through the darkness and the screaming of the desperate, a voice called out, "Mr. Lamar, save my children and Mr. Mackay will bless you!" Gazaway replied, "I will do all that I can for you, but I have no hope for any of us."

Reaching the upper deck, the family found a lifeboat. "I got in with Eliza, with my arms around her. I sat facing seaward," Rebecca recalled. "Instantly I felt a blow on my chest, and the sensation that I was drowning." The steamer had suddenly parted; the machinery had gone to the bottom, and the two ends rose up in the water. Rebecca had been knocked backward out of the boat. But she fought her way to the surface. "I rose upon the waves, and I could catch a gleam of the struggling, drowning people around me," she recalled. She was grasping for wreckage when a piece of timber floated into her arms. "I folded them back over it as it lay across my chest," she recalled, "floated on my back, seeing only the sky."

Gazaway came swimming over. Then Martha and William appeared. Charles swam over next. They found the ship's stern and climbed the inclined plane to the ship's wheel. Each grabbed a brass spoke. The ship continued to rise and level itself. They could see that the windows of the ladies' cabins were now horizontal again. It was a good sign. Then, the ship shuddered violently again, and they were all thrown again into the ocean. This time Rebecca came up grasping a life preserver. Then she felt her feet touch something solid. It was the stern of the ship, now resting just beneath the waves. Now she, Gazaway, and Thomas were together, but the rest of the children were gone.

"I gained the wreck near me and I saw a solitary man near one end," wrote Rebecca. "His back was turned toward me, in one hand a carpet-bag and the other hand in his pocket from whence he drew a key, fitted it to the lock, and opened it while I still approached. My brother, swimming, came on board between me and the unknown person. He cried out: 'Oh sister, do we meet again once more?' and opening his arms, embraced me. His voice attracted the attention of the gentleman, who turning, recognized my brother, and they shook hands, and I was introduced to Mr. Hutchinson, of Savannah."

James Couper and his boatload of survivors had just pushed off from the ship when, looking back, they heard a crash, and a multitude of screams. The lights were extinguished, one after another. A final wave slapped over the bow of the ship and she was gone. All around them people were thrashing around in the darkness. The seas were rough now, and their lifeboat, leaking badly, was tossed about. Shortly they ran into another lifeboat. Realizing that neither boat could take any more passengers, they decided to strike out for the coastline. Between the two boats they had three oars, one to use as a rudder; no hats; no food; no water. But they did have the North Star, still shining brightly above, and with that, they headed west toward the North Carolina coast.

By 3 o'clock the next afternoon, they could hear the breakers crashing at New Inlet, North Carolina. Just as the sun was setting, they reached the first line of rollers. The first boat capsized; five passengers drowned and six made it to the beach. The second boat crossed the first breaker, but spun around at the second and capsized upon the third. Miraculously, all crawled ashore. The men buried the women and children in the lee side of a sand dune to keep them warm, and then ran for help. They found a house some miles away, and finally returned with rescuers, food, blankets, and water.

The Lamars would not be as lucky. Gazaway, Rebecca, and Thomas floated along all night. At one point a man swam aboard with a little girl in tow. "Whose child is this?" he asked. At first, Gazaway and Rebecca hoped the bedraggled form would be one of theirs, but she wasn't. Instead, the little girl recognized one of the men at the far end of the wreckage. "Papa, Papa!" she exclaimed, holding out her arms. "Connie, Connie, my child!" the man cried. "She was only three years old, and beautiful," Rebecca recalled. "She had only a night slip on, and it was wet. The breeze was fresh and chilly."

Fortunately a brown camlet cloak had floated on with the carpetbag, and the child was wrapped in it. "She seemed to feel the situation, and adapting herself to her strange circumstances, did not ask for her mother, her nurse, or any of her family," wrote Rebecca. "Seeing her father's emotion, she tried to divert his attention by pointing to the stars: 'Papa, Papa, see the beautiful stars!'"

By the next morning, the survivors were huddled at one corner of the wreckage, which protruded from the sea. They put up two small sails and tried to lash the flotsam more tightly together. There was also a lifeboat aboard the wreckage as well, still lashed down and never used. The group made sure it was securely tied, for it might be their means of escape in the hours ahead.

Later that day, a basket floated by and from it the group retrieved two bottles of wine and two vials, one of peppermint and the other of opium. A body was found on the wreck and turned over. It was Mr. S. B. Parkman, the prominent Savannah citizen. A man and a young woman drifted by as well, clinging to two settees lashed together. The man was laid on the cover of the ship's hold, and soon died. The woman was wearing a fashionably low-cut silk dress. Her white skin was deeply sunburned and blistered. She was given a taste of the peppermint, and revived enough to raise her head and say:

"Mr. Lamar, I saw your little boy this morning."

"Charles?"

"Yes, Charles. I called to him and told him not to give up."

"When did you see him?"

"He was floating in a little box," she said, closing her eyes. "Charles and I went to the same school together in Savannah . . . Reverend White's." Her eyelids fluttered. "You must keep an eye out for him, as he will be coming along soon."

Soon they discerned a speck on the ocean. It was not a box but a piece of the floating wreckage, upon which were clinging a man, a woman, and a boy. The boy was supporting the lady, who was leaning on his shoulders.

Gazaway staggered to his feet.

"We must get the boat to them!" he exclaimed to a man lying at his feet.

"Oh, I am so tired," the man complained.

"Mr. Smith, it is my son!" Gazaway replied.

The two men launched the small boat and brought Charles and the other two to the floating wreckage. Charles fell into the arms of Rebecca, sobbing, finally falling asleep in her lap.

Night came, and a cold breeze. "Dear Papa," three-year-old Caroline said, "when we get to New York won't you give me three cups of tea?" He replied, "Yes, my darling, as many as you want, I will give you."

Rebecca put her arms around Charles on one side, and Thomas on the other. Though she felt that her back might break, she propped them against her so that they could sleep. Finally she leaned against Mauma, one of the slaves aboard. All that night, Mauma prayed and sang in a low, soothing tone that lay richly beneath the cold stars.

The following day, Gazaway agreed to be one of six men to take the lifeboat and attempt a run to shore for help.

After Gazaway and the others had departed, the survivors distributed what little they had left. What was left of the wine and peppermint were reserved for the children. But one man, his tongue extended and as hard and brown as a piece of leather, begged tearfully for just a drop. "Aunt Rebecca, give it to him," said Charles. Recalled Rebecca: "The man laid his hand on Charles' head and said, 'You are a noble boy!'"

On the second night two of the men imagined they were in Florida and decided to take a stroll. They stepped off the wreckage and plunged into the sea. Struggling back, they decided to do it again, and this time disappeared. Another man swore that a beacon was shining on the horizon. He lashed together a few sticks to make a raft and set off to investigate it. He never was seen again.

Then Thomas Lamar suddenly let out a groan. "I called him. He did not reply. I leaned over, and pressed him too heavily. 'You hurt me!' I looked at his hands, and the nails were blue. I was now alarmed," Rebecca said. "I chafed his hands, but the blood would not circulate. He was unconscious. It did no good, and I was in despair. I knew he was dying."

Charles then leaped to his feet. Pointing to the horizon in great excitement he cried, "See, Aunt Rebecca, Boatswain is drowning!" Boatswain was his dog. He moved two or three steps toward the edge of the raft and stumbled. Mr. Hutchinson picked Charles up and brought him back to Rebecca. No sooner had he done so, then Charles was on his feet again. The vision of the dog drowning was repeated, and each time Rebecca had to ask Mr. Hutchinson to pick him up. At last, Charles became totally unconscious, she recalled, but remained sitting, perfectly quiet.

Thomas now began to jerk and thrash in Rebecca's lap. She would gather him up again, and he would throw himself again dangerously near the edge of the raft. Each time became more difficult for her, until, exhausted, she fell unconscious.

When she awoke she asked Mr. Hutchinson when the carriage would come to take them to Savannah. "Soon," he replied weakly. "*How* can I go to Savannah like this?" Rebecca replied despondantly, looking down at her wet gown and bare feet. "I am *not* dressed!" Then she gazed around at the wreckage and the bodies and began to scream—scream for her carriage to take her away again.

She was screaming when Mr. Hutchinson grabbed her by the shoulders and forced her to look, to see the shape on the horizon. "I saw a vessel, her sails spread and filled, her hull painted black, and a dazzling sun shining on her canvas," she later recalled. "I explained, 'Oh, how beautiful! Oh, how beautiful!!' "

The ship that arrived at sunrise was the schooner *Henry Cameron* from Philadelphia, on its way to Wilmington, Delaware. Once the captain found that there were other survivors, he set sail and found them as well. Then he made haste to bring them in to Wilmington, Delaware, the nearest port.

"Awful Steamboat Disaster," cried out the *Charleston Courier,* as the first news arrived of the sinking. "The Pulaski, a gallant boat, which but a few days ago danced like a thing of life upon the waters of our harbor, and under the mighty impulse of steam, boomed away from our port on her northward voyage . . . was literally torn in pieces by the explosive power of that mysterious agent, which propelled her on her course, and she sank beneath the ocean with her precious burden, leaving but a hardy rescued few to tell the melancholy tale . . . Our sister city, Savannah, has suffered dreadfully, losing in one fell swoop no less than four in the Parkman and ten in the Lamar families, besides numerous others."

Indeed, Savannah was in shock. Flags were drawn down to half-staff, the citizens donned black armbands; only the doors of the churches and synagogues remained open. People could not eat, sleep, or work. "We confess that we have been in no frame of mind necessary for the discharge of political duties incumbent on the conduct of a press," the *Savannah Daily Georgian* said in its grief. "For ten days only have passed since we were appalled by the intelligence that many of the experienced minds and beautiful youth of our city had been cast upon the waste of waters, never more to see, in this life, those who were dearer than existence itself. . . ."

A week later, on the Fourth of July, there were none of the usual parades and celebrations. A regiment of local militamen donned their uniforms, raised their arms, and fired a lonesome salute. Then they went home. "The gloom consequent on the late dreadful catastrophe forbade the usual rejoicings," noted the *Georgian.*

There was considerable anger, as well, which Savannah's representatives took to Washington. On July 7, Congress enacted legislation that required regular inspections of steam boilers. Experienced engineers had to be aboard all steamships as well. In the event of an explosion, the owner of the vessel and the ship's master would be fully responsible for the damages.

In the end, of the *Pulaski*'s 131 passengers and crew, 77 were lost and 54 survived.

When Rebecca regained consciousness aboard the *Henry Cameron,* she asked immediately for Charles. The physician pointed to the berth next to hers, where Charles lay, breathing but unconscious. "There was a smaller boy—what about him?" she asked. Before the doctor could reply, Rebecca saw an image of him in her mind, lying at her feet in the water on the wreck, and she knew he was dead.

Gazaway survived. He and the five others in the boat made it to shore at New River Inlet, 40 miles north of Wilmington. They were eventually taken in by Mr. John Wilings and his wife and given food and shelter. A man was hired to ride express to Wilmington for help.

Charles lay still the first night, barely breathing, his face burned red by the sun and blackened with sores. He was better the next day, however, and out of danger the third. Gazaway was spent by the ordeal and distraught. Gazaway's brother suggested that he and his wife take Charles to live with them in Wilmington until the boy recovered. Gazaway gratefully agreed.

On July 13, 1838, a month after the *Pulaski* had departed, the bell atop the City Exchange in Savannah tolled mournfully, as did a dozen other church bells in the town. Beneath the Grecian portico of Christ Episcopal Church on Bull Street, the crowd gathered for the final memorial service. The citizens knew death well—death by yellow fever, by consumption, by cholera, in childbirth. But nothing had struck the city like this.

Beneath the beating bells, the crowd moved slowly into the church. In came the judges from the circuit and high courts, the officers of the army and navy. Children from the local Sunday schools arrived, accompanied by their teachers; then representatives from the Union Society, the Medical Society, the Hibernian Society, the British consul, the German and French consuls. On each side of the gallery the front pews were reserved for the relatives of the deceased, and they slowly came forward, a line of bent mourners dressed in black suits and dresses, black hats and gloves, carrying black handkerchiefs weary of absorbing their tears.

A funeral dirge led the service, followed by a prayer that echoed in the vast vault of the church, and a reading from the scriptures. There was another hymn and prayer, a sermon by the Reverend W. Presson, another prayer, and finally, the benediction. Bagpipes cried that morning and throughout the day. Into the night one could feel the somber beating of the drums.

Gazaway left Savannah following the *Pulaski* disaster, moving to Alexandria, Virginia. Within a year he had married Harriet Cazenove, the daughter of an influential banker. She was twenty years his junior, and just six years older than Charles. Gazaway and his new bride would have six children together.

Gazaway was not driven out of Savannah. The official inquest assigned the *Pulaski* tragedy to the second engineer, who drained the starboard boiler and then attempted to refill it. Still, many people felt that Lamar had been too ambitious, too obsessed with building wealth. "Gazaway is apparently tranquil and resigned," one relative wrote. "But probably an altered man—a serious and thoughtful cast of countenance, and satisfied, I believe, to abate his pursuit of wealth . . ." Said another: Gazaway had "seen the error of his ways."

And so, for a while at least, Gazaway stepped away from Savannah. Now it was time for his son, Charles, to make his mark on the city.

3

LATER SAVANNAH

BY MAY of 1857, a fresh set of eyes—gray, impatient eyes—was scanning Savannah, and a new set of boots strode confidently through its streets. They belonged to Charles Lamar, now thirty-four, who had returned to Savannah to take over his father's sprawling business empire. Charles Lamar was not only a player in Savannah; he was a kingpin, a man of enormous power and wealth.

By now, an inventory of Charles Lamar's holdings would have included the big cotton presses on the eastern wharves on River Street, the 5,000-bale warehouse nearby, a lumberyard, a 11,500-acre pine forest, and the Cold Spring Plantation in Merriweather County, Georgia. Lamar was a director of the Bank of Commerce, which his father had founded, and a director of the Savannah, Albany and Gulf Railroad, which was pushing its tracks ever deeper into Georgia. Looking seventeen miles in toward Savannah from the ocean, two tall structures rose above all others: One was Savannah's City Exchange building, and the other was Lamar's six-story rice mill.

If that were not enough, Charles Lamar headed the Savannah Jockey Club, acted as a judge for the Savannah Aquatic Club, and had served for several years as Captain of the Georgia Hussars, the local militia that had guarded Savannah since the War of 1812.

"I remember well seeing him riding through our streets on his famous horse Black Cloud," one neighbor recalled of Lamar, "both horse and rider presenting a magnificent appearance." Black Cloud was more than magnificent. Black Cloud was such a wild and willful horse that few men dared mount him.

That alone said a great deal about the man that Lamar had become. Lamar was powerfully built. But more impressive than his physical presence was the toughness of his character. He had weathered all the adversity a person could endure. He had lost his mother, his siblings, and nearly his own life by the time he was fourteen. He needn't reflect any further. He knew what he wanted, and in most cases, he simply took it.

By 1857, Savannah had grown from twenty wards in 1838 to thirty-six wards. New streets had been added, and new squares—Pulaski, Madison, and Lafayette, among others. While Greek revival mansions and neo-Gothic homes rose from the perimeter of every pretty square, new public buildings added importance to the city's charm. Among them: the new U.S. Custom House on Bay Street; the St. John's Episcopal Church, designed by Calvin Otis; and the plush Pulaski House Hotel. In the finer neighborhoods, dinner parties and balls brightened the nights, and picnics and parades dominated the days. "The most charming of cities," declared Swedish traveler Fredrika Bremer, in her *Homes of the New World: Impressions of America*.

Charles Lamar could have chosen any of the finer addresses in Savannah for his home. But he remained at his father's house at 44 East Broughton Street, where he grew up, and where he could still gaze with misted eyes down the sidewalk and see his mother and his five siblings smiling at him as they drew near. It was still a fashionable place: A few houses from Lamar lived two of Savannah's famous jurists, Judge John M. Berrien and Judge William B. Fleming. Dr. William Elliott and Dr. William H. Cuyler, the city's finest physicians, lived on Broughton as well. It was here that Lamar would bring his wife, the daughter of one of the most illustrious men in town, U.S. Circuit Court Judge John C. Nicoll, and eventually raise his four children.

Lamar was at ease with the ruling elite, and they seemed to respect and like him as well. He had the strong, handsome face of his father, and the open, expressive, and almost luminous eyes of his cousin, Mirabeau B. Lamar, the second president of the Republic of Texas. Lamar could be the sprightly, cheerful, and bold student that his classmates at Dr. White's school recalled. He could be the "noble boy" who had given the last drop of peppermint to the parched man on the wreck of the *Pulaski,* and the brother who selflessly helped his brothers and sisters up the staircase as the ship began to sink.

He was, after all, the godson of the great Marquis de Lafayette—the confidant of George Washington and Thomas Jefferson—who, during his triumphant return to Savannah in 1825, had held the infant Lamar at the sprinkling of the holy water, giving the lad the name Charles Augustus *Lafayette* Lamar.

And yet, as Lamar moved into adulthood, few of his neighbors realized that Lamar had developed a darker, moodier side to his personality as well, one that drove him increasingly into shadows and activities that, had they known, would have filled them with alarm. Few of them realized it at first, but deep inside the psyche of Charles Lamar, something had snapped.

By 1858, the push for progress that had begun in the mid-1830s seemed to be paying off. Nine steam locomotives a day arrived in Savannah now, each pulling twenty or thirty cars piled "mountain high" with fluffy white cotton. In the long row of brick buildings that rose four and five stories high between River and Bay Streets, hundreds of men worked feverishly, weighing, marking, receiving, and shipping the cotton, rendering bills and collecting money. Industry was flourishing in other ways: Savannah had several new textile mills, iron factories, and brickyards. In 1858, the city was building half of its freight cars locally, rather than importing them from the North. Three years later, it added a machine shop, coppersmith's shop, boilermaker's shop, and a pattern shop to its railroad depot. Henceforth, Savannah made *all* its own railroad cars—and had laid plans to build its own steam locomotives as well.

Likewise, throughout the South "progress" was beginning to take hold. In the South the manufacture of woolens increased some 140 percent in just ten years, from 1848 to 1858; the value of men's clothing produced in the South rose 65 percent; the value of boots and shoes, about 89 percent and 70 percent, respectively. The production of paper increased almost threefold, and printing, more than sevenfold. Railroad spikes and nails, sashes and doors, carriages and coaches, the South was making them all.

It seemed, then, that the South was fulfilling its dreams. A bit of euphoria was in the air. Success was at hand! Exclaimed the *Savannah Evening Journal*: "Awake! Arise! She has awoke—she has arisen—the spirit of the age has caught—ONWARD is her motto—PROGRESS her policy—GREATNESS her destiny!"

Yet for all of the appearance of progress, the South was slipping further and further behind the achievements of the North. In 1810, the South had surpassed New England in its manufacturing might, according to the census of that year. Georgia alone had manufactured more yards of cloth than Rhode Island. But by 1860, New England was manufacturing *three times* as much as the South. Taken from another perspective, the South had about 35 percent of the nation's population in 1860, yet the region employed only 8.4 percent of its workers in industry and was producing only about 8 percent of the nation's manufactured goods.

In fact, the capital invested in manufacturing in the South actually *declined* between 1840 and 1860, from 13.6 percent to 9.5 percent of that invested in manufacturing nationwide. One after another of the Southern factories failed or was forced along in a sickly existence, poorly managed and even more poorly capitalized. Even Southerners stopped buying southern-made products, preferring the cheaper and better constructed goods "just in from New York."

What had happened to the great promise of the South? It was lost to poor planning, poor management, and a lack of Southern money to sustain it. By 1860, Savannah ranked sixty-fifth among all U.S. cities in terms of manufacturing and Charleston, eighty-fifth—hardly the industrial dominance of their expectations.

The greatest failure, however, was that the South had been unable to forge a direct trade route, back and forth, with Europe. Rather, the North, and particularly, New York City, had seized coastal and Atlantic commerce in what was an iron grip. "New York's businessmen, many of them originally hailing from Connecticut, penetrated every nook and cranny of the field where a dollar could be made," maritime historian Robert Greenhalgh Albion observed. "They settled as factors in the inland towns, advancing money to the planters and handling their cotton bales as they appeared . . . meanwhile, Yankee representatives of New York concerns, backed with adequate capital to make loans, swarmed into the southern ports and, provided they survived the yellow fever, found it a simple matter to absorb the lion's share of the business."

The pattern of commerce that formed was called the "cotton triangle": At the southern ports, the cotton was sent in Northern ships directly to Europe, returning to New York, and then turning south with their holds filled with manufactured goods. Along the way, fees, in the form of freight levees, insurance, commissions, and interest, were imposed. Cotton was the grand prize of American commerce in the 1850s—the nation's greatest export—and in the fees and financing, the North had figured out how to extract 20 to 30 cents of each cotton dollar.

In 1857, when a financial crisis suddenly stopped the sale of cotton, Southerners began to realize how beholden they were to the financiers of the North. "With plenty of money in assets," wrote one Southern businessman, "it is locked up one way or another in cotton and until that begins to move there is no 'Balm in Gilead' for us . . . we cannot help ourselves . . . Unless cotton sells we and all here must be submerged."

For Charles Lamar, living under the heel of the Northern capitalists was intolerable. But what made it worse was that his father had joined their ranks. Following the sinking of the *Pulaski,* Gazaway had moved to Alexandria, Virginia. Shortly thereafter, Gazaway moved his new and growing family to New York, purchasing a grand home at 170 Atlantic Avenue, in Brooklyn.

Gazaway had moved his energy and ambition as well, founding the Bank of the Republic, which he headquartered at the northeast corner of Broadway and Wall Street. Before long, Lamar had forged interlocking directorates and operations between his bank and the New York–based Great Western Marine Insurance Company, one of the most powerful financial institutions in the city. Once again, Gazaway had placed himself in the midst of a fertile crescent. This time the South needed capital; Wall Street had plenty of it, and Gazaway was willing to handle the spread with all the aplomb of the shrewdest Connecticut Yankee.

But what Gazaway saw as a great opportunity began to fill his son with disgust. Charles had seen how the New York newspapers were filled with advertisements, addressed specifically to Southerners, urging them to visit this or that store, to inspect the latest assortments of dry goods, hardware, boots, and shoes, and other types of merchandise. He had seen the New York firms elbowing into Southern commerce with their branch offices. He saw how New Yorkers were eager to pump capital into Southern roadways and mines, railroads and shipping ventures, at exorbitant rates. He even saw how New York creditors often took possession of plantations and slaves as they changed hands, becoming for a short time slave owners themselves.

He had watched the South eat hungrily from the trough of Northern merchandise—slave clothing, boots and shoes, harnesses, saddlery, fine furniture, and even Northern-built locomotives—and the foreign goods sent south through New York's shipping agents: Yorkshire woolens, Lancashire cotton goods, Birmingham hardware, and Sheffield cutlery. He knew that the packet ships that brought passengers and cargo up and down the coast were owned by Yankees, such as the Phelps, Morgans, and Suttons, were built in Northern ports, and were captained by Northern seamen.

Southerners not only gave all their business gladly to the Yankee ships, Lamar fumed, they flocked eagerly aboard them in the hot summer months, when Yellow Fever flared, sucking lemons and popping the Rev. B. Hibbard's Vegetable Anti-Bilious Pills to forestall seasickness. It made *him* ill.

"New York City, like a mighty queen of commerce, sits proudly upon her island throne sparkling with jewels," the *Vicksburg Daily Whig* complained angrily, "waving an undisputed commercial scepter over the South. By means of her railways and navigable streams, she sends out her long arms to the extreme South; and with avidity rarely equaled, grasps our gains and transfers them to herself—taxing us at every stop and depleting us as extensively as possible without actually destroying us."

Added Lamar's friend, journalist James DeBow:

> *Who conducts our commerce, builds for us our ships, and navigates them on the high seas? The North! Who spins and weaves, for our domestic use (and grows rich in doing it)? . . . The North. Who supplies the material and the engineers for our railroads where we have any, gives to us books and periodicals, newspapers and authors, without any limit or end? The North. Who educates our children, and affably receives the annual millions we have to expend in travel and in luxury? The North. Is there a bale of cotton to leave our ports for Liverpool, shall not a Northern ship transport it? Is there a package of broadcloths or a chest of tea to be landed at our warehouses? There is a tribute, first to Boston or New York. We look on and admire the growth of the tremendous power there, scarcely admitting any excellence in ourselves or willing to make any effort to secure such excellence. Yet we expect to be respected in our rights, and deferentially bowed to by the rulers of the North. Vain hope if history be credited!*

Lamar resented the economic dominance of the North. But nothing angered him more than the North's attack on the slavery of the South.

Lamar had felt the sting of Yankee reprobation before. Twenty years earlier, Henry du Bignon had laid down a friendly wager before the New York rowing clubs to beat the Savannah teams. On the appointed day, the Southern oarsmen wore crisp white shirts and trousers. Spectators by the thousands brought their picnic baskets to the edge of the Savannah River. Cheers went up as the sleek boats flashed by. In the end, Henry du Bignon's *Lizard,* which he had brought from Jekyll Island, won.

The day was spoiled, however, by the absence of the New York teams. Du Bignon had run his ad in the New York papers for weeks, but in the end, not a single team appeared. Du Bignon finally learned why: "We have no *desire* to row against *black servants,*" the New Yorkers sniffed. Du Bignon was stunned. Yes, he replied, the Southern rowers *were* black slaves. But that could be fixed. "The Lizard shall be manned by *gentlemen,* who, we warrant, shall be the equals of the Knickerbockers in bone and muscle, blood and breeding," he shot back. But the New Yorkers never replied.

Now the attack from the North was even greater than before. In the modern world, slavery was an anachronism. In a moral world, it was a disgrace. The European nations had washed their hands of it. In America, its opponents, mostly in the form of the new Republican Party, were gaining power fast. And yet here was the South, with three million slaves, demanding even more of it. The South had painted itself into a corner. Most Southerners knew it. It was the odor that clung to their clothes even as they attended the grand parties and events in the North, evoking dark whispers and furtive glances.

Yes, yes, Lamar once felt like shouting, slavery was the biceps that lifted the cotton bales in the South; it was the strong fingers that plucked and sewed, hammered and pulled; the arms that chopped, and washed, combed cotton; that groomed horses, tied little girls' hair with bows, and dropped little boys into the tub; dusted the gentleman's hat and adjusted the lady's gown; dug the ditches, shoveled the coal, and hauled the wood and water. Black men, women, boys, and girls—more than three million of them, worth some $4 billion in the currency of the 1850s—were the lumps of coal thrown into the firebox every morning, just so the wheels of the Southern economy would turn.

It was why you could find a theater review in the Savannah papers praising the "intelligent discrimination and good taste of our Savannah audience" during the performance of *Madelaine* in the Athenaeum Theater—and an advertisement next to it proclaiming, "FOR SALE . . . A GANG OF 460 Negroes . . . Accustomed to the culture of Rice and Provisions . . . One-third cash; remainder by bond."

Or why you would see in the advertisements: "Arthur Napoleon . . . IN CONCERT! . . . On this occasion assisted by Signorina Cairoli, Prima Donna Soprano, from the Academy of Music, New York . . . ," and in the adjacent column: "FOR SALE . . . Will be sold at the Court House in Chatham County . . . the following property of the estate of

Henry Haupt, deceased, One Negro slave Jonas, about 45 years old; One Negro slave Dedlia, about 18 years old; One four wheel buggy and harness; One chestnut horse, saddle and bridle . . ."

It was why you could buy Shakespeare's collected works, Carlyle's biography of Frederick the Great, "Great Men of Science," Byron, Fielding, and the Bible—and in the same newspaper consider: "$100 REWARD . . . For the delivery to me at Savannah or to J.S. Montmollin's, or to George W. Wylly's office or to the Savannah Jail, so that I can get him, my boy TONEY, about 22 years old, five feet six or seven inches high, weighs about one hundred thirty or forty pounds, dark complexion. When spoken to generally smiles, shows a good set of teeth, flat face, with little beard on his face. Fifty dollars will be paid for the said boy, and fifty dollars for proof to convict any person of harboring him . . ."

Yes, the South was chained to slavery. But what right had the North to pass judgment? Hadn't New York enriched itself on the Southern-grown cotton, taking its thirty cents on every dollar? "What would New York's maritime greatness be without slavery?" Lamar's friend DeBow had proclaimed. "The shops would rot at her docks; grass would grow in Wall Street and Broadway, and the glory of New York, like that of Babylon and Rome, would be numbered with the things of the past."

Lamar was angry. He was tired of apologizing to his Northern hosts for the "peculiar institution" of the South, as they condescendingly called it. He was sick of the fact that the Republican Party, based on radical abolitionism, had garnered a million votes in the elections of 1856; that *Uncle Tom's Cabin* had stereotyped Southerners, and still sold 300,000 copies in its first year and a million since; that a fanatic named John Brown had murdered five proslavery men in Kansas three years earlier, and was still roaming free.

It was no secret that one-third of the city clerks and shopkeepers in Savannah and half its engineers had recently arrived from the North; that more than half of the Savannah's lodging facilities, food, and clothing stores, were owned by foreign-born men.

It was no secret as well that the populist tendencies of the North were seeping into the South and changing it—that free Negroes, seamen, and Irish laborers were cavorting and causing trouble in the back streets; that the Negroes were getting increasingly out of hand: smoking in public, against all the ordinances; riding their horses on Sundays without permits; visiting their friends after the ring of the night bell without tickets; testing their marksmanship with pistols in the streets; using increasingly boisterous language around town. It all had to stop.

Forget the North, Lamar muttered. Forget its vile, smoking industry—the boilers bulging, the whistles shrieking, the steam-valves seeking release. Forget its cacophonous, populist democracy as well. What Lamar wanted was the Old South, the Plantation South, a Slave Republic governed by the enlightened elite—men, in fact, just like himself.

Given all this, it is perhaps understandable that Lamar found himself joining a group of men who had already decided that a revolution was in order, one that would secure the South as a Plantation Aristocracy. Most of these rebels fancied themselves patriots, men on the same plane as the patriots of the Boston Tea Party. But in their case, they were an entirely different kind of revolutionary.

4

THE FIRE-EATERS

ANYONE WHO had ever faced the frightening visage of John C. Calhoun in his final years would never forget what they had experienced— the tight yellow skin pulled across the bony face, the blazing eyes, the stiff hair parted severely, falling to the shoulders on either side. Alive, Calhoun looked just as shocking as he did in his coffin.

But Calhoun's physical appearance was nothing compared to the spirit that seethed inside. When the federal government tried to slap a steep tariff on many imported goods—a tax that would have benefited Northern manufacturers and burdened Southern consumers—Calhoun led a Southern rebellion that had South Carolina, his home state, threatening to break from the Union. This was in 1832—twenty-nine years before the start of the Civil War. At the time, Calhoun was not only the fiery leader of a new proslavery, pro–Southern Rights rebellion, he was also vice president of the United States.

In the end, the government reduced the tariff, and the tensions abated. But the conflict set a precedent: From then on, many Southerners felt it was their right to nullify unappealing federal laws. And if the North didn't like it, then the South would simply pack up her bags and secede.

Now, as the economic pressures from the North descended again on the South, politicians of Calhoun's ilk rose again. They were men who could clutch a podium, with torches flaming around them, the bonfire lit, and harangue a crowd into a frenzy. They could incite riots with the words that they poured onto the page. They were masters of logic—and illogic—and understood the persuasive powers of rhetoric as well as Cicero himself. The English traveler Lieutenant Francis Hall classified the various brands of Southern orators at the time as: the Political Spouters; the Fourth of July Orators; the Orators of the Human Race; and the tobacco-spitting Stump Orators. But as the rhetoric of this group of demagogues grew hotter—as their demands grew more insistent and their logic grew more perverse—there was only one name for them: the fire-eaters.

The fire-eaters were led by William L. Yancey, who was 44 in 1858; James DeBow, 40; Edmund Ruffin, 64; Leonidas W. Spratt, 40; Henry Hughes, 24; and Robert Barnwell Rhett, 58. Yancey was called the best orator of the group, a velvety-voiced, Yale-educated radical whose rhetoric could turn any audience his way. "At the conclusion of the speech several thousand of his audience sprang to their feet as one man," one observer noted. "Yells, shouts, cries filled the air; men announced their change of vote, as if they had been converted by an evangelist."

James DeBow was the editor and publisher of *DeBow's Review,* the literary mouthpiece of the proslavery movement. He was also the founder of the Southern Commercial Conventions, which evolved over the years into the leading platform for radical Southern politics. Edmund Ruffin, meanwhile, was a disheveled expert on soil chemistry, whose "Essay on Calcareous Manures"—in which he expounded on the gospel of marl—was called "the most thorough piece of work on a special agricultural subject ever published in the English language." Beyond his soil studies, Ruffin was a fanatical and early proponent of secession. Ruffin was accorded the honor of firing the first shot into Fort Sumter and subsequently, when he learned that Lee had surrendered at Appomattox, of firing his last shot into his brain.

Spratt was the editor of the radical *Charleston Standard*, which praised slavery as a social paradigm; Hughes, a sociologist, was the author of treatises defending the subjugation of blacks based on biology. Rhett was the editor of the *Charleston Mercury*, the fire-eaters' favorite fiery journal, and the newspaper that Northern radicals liked most to quote as the general opinion of the South (although its total circulation in the South was but a mere 500 copies). Hovering over them—or below, depending on one's point of view—was always Calhoun, their wild, driving chieftain.

The fire-eaters were not monolithic in their opinions. But in general, they all hated "Yankee Rule," painting dark pictures of life chained to the Northern mercantile machine, and even more horrific images of life after emancipation—economic ruin, anarchy, murder, and rape. The fire-eaters called upon the South to defend her honor, rebuild her confidence, rekindle her pride, and maintain her social traditions. Most important, they urged the South to celebrate slavery.

Slavery was not "a necessary evil," as Washington, Jefferson, Madison, Monroe, Whyte, and other of the Rousseau-reading Southern forefathers had proclaimed; they were wrong, said the fire-eaters. Slavery was *good*. It was *right*. You had to *believe* in slavery—to celebrate it every day. That was the message of the fire-eaters to the South: You have no reason to feel guilty anymore.

To support that premise, the fire-eaters propounded racism. Slavery was much more defensible, after all, if the slave was fundamentally inferior to the master. In one purportedly scientific essay in *DeBow's Review*, for instance, a physician noted that Africans were intellectually inferior due to the habit of sleeping with blankets and arms over their heads, which caused them to breath "heated air, loaded with carbonic acid and aqueous vapor." "Negroes," he added, "resemble children in the activity of the liver and in their strong assimilating powers . . . hence they are difficult to bleed, owing to the smallness of their veins."

There was no doubt that the fire-eaters were well-read. Most of them could spout Homer, Gibbon, and Shakespeare as though they were chatting with a neighbor over the backyard fence. But their intelligence was overwhelmed with personal problems. Yancey was an alcoholic who didn't know how to stop talking once he was lit; DeBow, a notorious womanizer whose parents begged him to find a girl and settle down. Henry Hughes worshipped fame: "I love Glory, Power, Fame," he wrote in his diary. "She is my Soul's Idol. To her, I, with a lover's hot devotion, kneel." Ruffin was generally depressed. Even Calhoun was tortured by a continuous quest for the presidency, an office that eluded him due to his increasing radicalism. Overall, the fire-eaters were extremely sensitive. Hot tempers, depressed spirits, and theatrics predominated. As children, many of them had lost a parent or had been socially ostracized, one scholar noted. In radical politics, perhaps, they were seeking attention and psychic repair.

Their strangest obsession, though, may have been with chivalric tales, particularly those of Sir Walter Scott. Here they found fair maidens in distress and heroes riding to their rescue in shining armor. Honor, shame, revenge, vengeance, the slap in the face, the demand for "satisfaction," and the ultimate thrill, the duel—the fire-eaters absorbed them all, and filled their lives with them. While Scott was their favorite author, there were others. They particularly liked the fourteenth-century French poet Froissart, and, for homegrown talent, the romantic musings of Mirabeau Buonaparte Lamar, who, before leaving for glory in Texas, had transformed his father's cotton plantation near Milledgeville, Georgia, into a kingdom—and found in the local girls the inspiration for "The Rose of Sharon" and "The Blue Eyed Queen."

All this could have been dismissed as harmless romanticism, except that the chivalric code allowed a "man of honor" to ignore federal and even local laws when they fell at odds with his own moral compass. Even trials by jury became a test of the validity of the law itself—not the guilt or innocence of the honorable defendant. Under this code of conduct, the nullification of federal laws was appropriate, and secession, merely pragmatic. Charles Lamar knew it well. "That is the advantage of a small place," he once boasted to a friend. "A man of influence can do as he pleases."

At first, most Southerners laughed off the fire-eaters. They were a ridiculous group of misfits. But as the 1850s advanced, the citizens began to fear them. And, in the end, the South marched over the cliff into war with them. An observer once noted that the final memorial to

John C. Calhoun should not be the marble monument that stands in Charleston, but the graves of all the Southern soldiers that followed his spirit into battle. As Georgia governor Howell Cobb noted in 1849, "Calhoun is our evil genius."

Of all the fire-eaters, the demagogue that most attracted Charles Lamar was Leonidas Spratt. Spratt was a tall South Carolinian, with black hair that swung across his angular face in the style of Calhoun. Lamar marveled at Spratt's ability to spring gracefully onto a stage, and, with a dramatic sweep of his fingers through his mane, captivate an audience. Spratt was the best orator the fire-eaters had, next to Yancey. He was a star.

Spratt graduated from South Carolina College in Charleston, which, since Calhoun's time, had been the wellspring of radical Southern politics. He then served in the South Carolina House of Representatives, his eloquence boosting him to house leader. In 1853, Spratt wrote *The Destiny of the Slave State,* the first major work that encouraged Southerners to celebrate slavery, rather than apologize for it. Wrote Spratt: "The American Revolution vindicated the great truth that all men are born free and equal. But society in its secret movements vindicated a still greater truth: That inequality was necessary to man's progress." The book sent shock waves through the nation. Shortly thereafter, Spratt started his own newspaper, the *Charleston Spectator,* into which he poured thousands of words devoted to slavery and sedition.

Spratt had another great accomplishment: the transformation of the South's Southern Commercial Conventions from an economic forum into a platform for radical politics. The conventions began in the 1830s, to help Southerners compete with the North, in terms of economics and business. The 1837 Commercial Convention, for instance, advocated direct trade between the South and Europe, greater railroad construction, and the building of better levees on the Mississippi. It was here that one of the delegates declared, "To our country—the whole must prosper when every part takes care of itself," followed by, "the Northern states—Let us show them that in honorable enterprise brothers may compete and be brothers still."

But that generous toast was raised before Spratt had arrived. In 1854, Spratt attended the convention and tried to turn its agenda toward slavery and secession. He was rebuffed. In 1855, he tried again, with little success. But in 1856, when the convention was held in Savannah, he was received more cordially—and in 1857, in Knoxville, he got some of his proslavery resolutions on the agenda. Finally, in the 1858 meeting, held in Montgomery, Alabama, and attended by Spratt, Yancey, Ruffin, and several other fire-eaters, the radicals finally took control of the proceedings. Like wolves that had crept up in the sheep's clothing, the fire-eaters had taken over the Southern Commercial Convention. It had become theirs. "When the South gets ready to dissolve the Union," the *Milledgeville Federal Union* stated in 1858, "all she had to do is to reassemble the Southern Commercial Convention."

Spratt had successfully preached slavery and secession, but now he realized that there was another issue that needed to be raised. In 1808, the U.S. Congress had banned the transportation of African slaves to the shores of America. With that measure, a brutal trade, one that had brought a million Africans to American in chains, had ended. The measure banning the trade was supported as strongly in the South as in the North: President James Monroe of Virginia was a chief proponent of the 1808 bill, as were the Southern members of his cabinet, including William Crawford of Georgia and even the fiery proponent of slavery itself, John C. Calhoun of South Carolina.

But now, said Spratt, the African slave trade should be reopened. Why? Simple economics, he explained: The South was running out of slaves. Especially with the Western territories opening, the domestic supply could not meet the demand. Already, he complained, the prices of slaves were higher than ever: In one sale, a 16-year-old boy sold for $1,410; seven children, ages 6, 7, 8, 9, and 10 years old, brought $581, $750, $850, $910, $1,000, and $1,130. As the *Savannah Daily Morning News* had exclaimed, "How much longer can Southern men *afford* to buy Negroes at such prices?"

More slaves would not only increase the supply, Spratt argued, but also moderate the price. Spratt offered a political consideration as well:

The South needed more slaves to balance the millions of European immigrants flooding into the North. More slaves would not only balance out the respective workforces, North and South, he said, but ensure that the South maintained its political power and representation in Congress.

But Spratt had more Machiávellian reasons for wanting to reopen the slave trade. For one, the fire-eaters needed to make Southerners feel comfortable with slavery. But how could slavery be good when the African slave trade was a crime? This imbalance had to be addressed. The equation had to be changed. Slave trading had to be made right, otherwise slavery itself was imperiled.

For another, Spratt was a disunionist. He wanted the North and South to part ways. But in the 1850s, the slavery issue was *not* proving to be the divisive wedge that would split the country. Most Northerners were willing to leave slavery in the South alone. Even Abraham Lincoln had said that he expected slavery to last in the South for a long time, before flickering out. But suppose the Southern radicals put African slave trading on the table? Suppose they demanded it. The North would never agree! It would never cross that line. The issue would split the nation, and possibly, to the delight of Spratt and many of the other fire-eaters, start a civil war.

As Spratt's proposal for reopening the African slave trade reached the public, politicians in the North and South condemned it. Newspapers responded with outrage. The churches nearly unanimously called it an immoral idea. But rejection only fueled Spratt's passion. Taking his new argument from town to town, standing atop soapboxes, filling the front page of his newspaper with tightly reasoned arguments, Spratt slowly began to make an impression.

His first success came in November 1856, when South Carolina governor James H. Adams supported Spratt's tract. The South needed more slaves to protect its cotton monopoly from growers in the East Indies, Egypt, and Brazil, said Adams. A few months later the U.S. House of Representatives considered the issue. Of that body, 152 congressmen voted against the reopening of the slave trade. But a surprising number, 57, voted their support (and most of those were from the South). And so the African slave trade movement began to gain ground.

But Spratt was an idea man, an idealogue. What the fire-eaters needed was a man of action, someone to pull the trigger. Charles Lamar was just the man.

5

THE *RAWLINS* AND *COBDEN*

WILLIAM POSTELL held a length of rope in his hand, and was pulling a lead weight out of the sea. It came up dripping, glistening with the warm water of the Wassaw Sound, near Savannah's Tybee Island.

Postell was once a rising star in the navy of the Republic of Texas, until he was charged in a plot to steal one of the republic's ships. Since then he had been the captain of a leaky steamer, the master of a schooner transporting oranges, and most recent, a surveyor mapping the seabed for the Lighthouse and Buoy Service. Even there he'd run into trouble: A recent pay raise had been rescinded due to "disobedience of orders and continued hard drinking." Postell was running out of options; so one evening in May of 1857, when Charles Lamar suggested an opening in the near future that would replace tedium with adventure, he was all ears.

At the time, the fire-eaters were in the midst of their latest Southern Commercial Convention, this time sweating out their ideology in a dirt-floored cotton warehouse in Montgomery, Alabama. By now the convention had become so radicalized that the *fifth* item on the agenda was direct trade with Europe; the *fourth,* a Southern system of literature, schools, and colleges; the *third*, the Kansas conflict; the *second*, filibustering expeditions to broaden the territory of the South. And the number-*one* concern: reviving the African slave trade.

But while Spratt, Yancey, Rhett, and the other fire-eaters were there, sweating and swaying beneath the warehouse roof, Charles Lamar was ensconced in a meeting with a friend, a sallow-faced individual by the name of Nelson Trowbridge. Trowbridge was a domestic slave trader, with an office in Edgefield, South Carolina, where he bought and sold slaves. Like a vulture, Trowbridge appeared at funerals and estate settlements, always eager to buy the remaining slaves of the deceased and redistribute them. He was also the first to knock on the door of any planter who could not pay his debts, and needed to offload his assets. Trowbridge was a necessary part of Southern society, and rich as well, but he was not the kind who was pursued for his pleasant company.

Trowbridge had met Lamar a few years earlier, but only recently had Lamar asked him to lunch. Trowbridge was flattered, but before long saw that Lamar had an ulterior motive. After they had eaten, Lamar announced that he had decided to defy the federal law: He would send a ship to Africa from the Port of Savannah, fill her decks with slaves, and then bring her back home. Trowbridge narrowed his eyes with interest. If Trowbridge would front the money for the voyage, Lamar continued, Lamar would name him as the agent in the ensuing sales transactions. Trowbridge rubbed his chin thoughtfully, and then extended a bony hand to Lamar. The deal was done.

The first attempt came in July of 1857. Lamar purchased a sturdy schooner, the *E. A. Rawlins,* and prepared her for the voyage. Tied to the wharf near the Lamar cotton press, the vessel was soon loaded with what was required: pilot bread, cowpeas, rice, cooking pots, and tanks for extra water. When she was ready to go, Lamar requested a clearance from the port's inspector, John Boston. But Boston had already heard rumors about the *Rawlins*'s possible mission. The items put aboard the ship were certainly of a suspicious nature. Boston, therefore, refused to stamp the vessel's papers.

Lamar was astounded. Immediately, he sent an indignant letter off to Howell Cobb. Cobb, the former governor of Georgia, was now the U.S. secretary of the treasury, responsible for the federal surveillance of the nation's ports, among other things. But more important, to Lamar at least, was the fact that Cobb had sold Georgia bonds through Gazaway Lamar's bank in the past, and, in fact, was married to Gazaway's sister, Caroline.

"I am loathe to trouble you," Charles Lamar wrote sourly, "but your damned sap-head of a collector refuses to do anything . . . He detained my vessel eight days after she was ready for sea, and after she had applied for her clearance papers. Mr. Boston said she was not 'seized,' but merely 'detained.'" Lamar was so incensed that he attached a bill: "Eight days' detention at $150 per day . . . $1200; wharfage, landing, shipping and storage . . . $120; total, $1,820."

When Secretary Cobb received the letter, he telegraphed Collector Boston, requesting further details. He also consulted his legal staff. After some discussion, Cobb ruled that the vessel could not be held.

And so, the *Rawlins* sailed away. But if Lamar had high hopes for the completion of his scheme, they were soon dashed: The captain of the *Rawlins* took the ship to the African coast, as ordered. But once there, he spotted a British warship cruising nearby. Losing his courage, the captain decided to head for a safer port, where he sold the ship's provisions, pocketed $1,800 of Lamar and Trowbridge's gold, and eventually meandered home with an empty ship. Lamar was livid. "What excuse does (Captain) Grant make?" Lamar wrote to Trowbridge. "Why did he not go to the Coast? He knew, before he undertook the command, that there were armed vessels on the Coast, and a number of them." Lamar was disgusted. "Discharge him—pay him nothing," Lamar fumed, "and hope with me that he will land speedily in hell."

The second attempt was no better. On December 26, 1857, Lamar dispatched a letter to L. Viana of 158 Pearl Street, the notorious Manhattan slave trader. "I am anxious to have you interested in the next expedition," Lamar wrote solicitously, "and would be pleased to have you say what interest you would like, and give your views generally as to the manner the whole matter should be conducted." Viana obviously offered some advice, for this time the *Rawlins* sailed out of Savannah without any provisions at all. Instead, with Captain C. W. Gilley in charge and surveyor William Postell aboard as chief commercial officer, the vessel went directly to Mobile, Alabama. There the appropriate bribes were paid, and the requisite supplies were obtained, along with forged clearance papers.

Leaving Mobile, the *Rawlins* sailed directly to the Portuguese island of St. Thomas, which lay about 400 miles from the Congo River.

On June 18, Gilley went ashore with the ship's papers, ostensibly to receive clearance from the Portuguese authorities. While ashore—at least by Postell's later account—the captain tried to sell off not only the ship's provisions, but the ship itself. Postell discovered this, he claimed, when he rowed ashore, argued with Captain Gilley, and found himself pursued back to the beach by Gilley and a band of cutthroats. Holding them still at the point of his Bowie knife, Postell leapt into a dingy, reached the *Rawlins,* ordered the sails hiked, and sailed away—leaving Captain Gilley, some of the crew, and all the ship's papers behind.

While this was happening, Cobb learned that the *Rawlins* had cleared Mobile with faked papers, was heading for Africa, and would return to the same vicinity again with slaves. On March 2, 1858, he sent an urgent notice to the customs collector in New Orleans:

> *Sir: I informed you by telegraph yesterday that information has reached this department that a slaver, with a cargo of Africans, will attempt to land the same very soon on the southwest coast of Louisiana or on the Texas coast—probably the latter. You will send the cutter at your port in search, and give directions to use every exertion possible to intercept the landing of the vessel. I have telegraphed to the collector at Mobile to place the cutter at his port under your charge, which you will also use for the same purpose.*
>
> *The name of the bark suspected is the E. A. Rawlins, which sailed from Mobile in July last. Communicate in the most expedient manner the information sent to you to the collector at Galveston, and direct him to do everything in his power to intercept the vessel. You will consult with the district attorney in regard to the proper legal proceedings in the event of the arrest of the vessel, and inform the department by telegraph and by mail of the result of your exertions. I am, & etc. Howell Cobb.*

Three revenue cutters and a naval steamer were sent out to intercept the *Rawlins.* But they never found her. Instead, following a five-month cruise that never went near the slave coast, the *Rawlins* turned up unexpectedly off Tybee Island, a few miles from Savannah, tattered and worn, and without clearance stamps or papers.

In a letter to the *New York Times,* a "Traveller" reported what happened next:

> *When it was known that the Rawlins had actually anchored off Tybee bar, all kinds of rumors were at once put in circulation. One report was that she had actually landed her cargo of Africans; another, that she had 500 on board. The owners were in high glee. They immediately went down in a small steamer duly armed with sundry baskets of Champagne, bottles of brandy and quantities of ice, intending to have a grand jollification over their good luck, when lo! They found that they were "sold." The ship had come back empty and the self-made captain had come ahead of the ship to the city.*
>
> *Back the owners posted and found Captain Postell. They were furiously mad, and cursed him for a fool in not having crossed over to the coast of Africa and taken on board a cargo of slaves, as they had some 700 awaiting the ship; and their curses knew no bounds when they learned that he saw no men-of-war of any nation, and could have taken off the slaves had he possessed the nerve to have gone after them.*

Next, the curious writer climbed aboard the vessel:

> *On board the Rawlins was a tall, wiry-looking fellow, with a huge steeple crowned hat, having an immense broad brim. He says he merely went to Africa as a "passenger" but forgets to tell that he is chief clerk to one of the largest Negro traders in the city of New Orleans. I presume that the Rawlins will be off again as soon as she can refit, and manage a small matter with Uncle Sam about a new set of papers, which is now endeavoring to be done.*

Finally, the Traveller located Charles Lamar himself:

> *One of the owners of the E.A. Rawlins swears that he will carry on the slave trade openly, and he does not deny the object for*

*which the Rawlins was sent to Africa. This gentleman is a son of
Mr. G.B.L., who formerly resided in your city and was President
of a bank. He is considered a "fast young man." There are associ-
ated with him in this business two or three Negro traders of this
place, and several other parties . . .*

As news filtered back about the voyage of the *Rawlins,* the Lamar
family wondered whether Charles Lamar had lost his mind. "You remember our conversations about the Lamars—and the prospect of some
of them getting in the penitentiary?" John B. Lamar, Gazaway's brother,
confided to his sister, Caroline. "The way Charlie is going on I fear he
will lead off that way."

"While on that score let me tell you that I am not on Charley's side
in the controversy with Mr. Cobb," Gazaway Lamar wrote to his brother,
John. "I have repeatedly told him his errors—but he is too impulsive and
so crazy on that Negro question—that I can make no impression on
him."

Gazaway tried to hammer some sense into his son. But his efforts
were angrily repelled. Wrote Charles:

*I was astonished at some of the remarks in your letter; they
show that you have been imbued with something more than the
"panic" by your associations in the North and with Mrs.—. For
example, you say that, "An expedition to the moon would be
equally sensible, and no more contrary to the laws of Providence.
May God forgive you for all your attempts to violate His will and
His laws." Following on the same train of thought, where would it
land the whole Southern community? Did not the Negroes all come
originally from the coast of Africa? What is the difference between
going to Africa and Virginia for Negroes? And, if there is a difference, is not that difference in favor of going to Africa?*

Charles added:

*You need not reproach yourself for not interposing with a
stronger power—than argument and persuasion—to prevent the
expedition. There was nothing you or the Government could have*

*done to prevent it. Let all the sin be on me. I am willing to assume
it all . . ."*

Indeed, Lamar was determined. Even before the *Rawlins* had reappeared
off Tybee Island that August, he had a new ship, the 750-ton *Richard
Cobden,* preparing for a run to the African coast. This time Lamar tried
a new tack: Through his shipping agent, Lafitte & Co., he requested
clearance "for the purpose of taking on board African *emigrants,* in ac-
cordance with the United States passenger laws, and returning with the
same to a port in the United States."

By now Cobb was up to Lamar's tricks. Lamar was *not* planning to
introduce Africans with all the rights and privileges of free men, Cobb
replied, but slaves or persons held to service or labor. And since neither
slaves nor persons held to service or labor could be brought into the
country, under U.S. law, the request was denied. Lamar stepped back
and coyly made a second request, this for clearance to board a shipload
of African *apprentices,* returning them to a port in Cuba. This, added
Lamar, would not be in violation of any law, and in fact was the current
practice in France, which had recently begun shipping "apprentices" to
its own island possessions.

Cobb's patience was wearing thin. "I have no hesitation in saying
that the clearance should *not* be granted," he replied sharply. "To believe, under the circumstances, that there is a bona fide purpose on the
part of Messrs. Lafitte and Co., to bring African emigrants to this country, to enjoy the rights and privileges of freemen, would require an
amount of credulity that would justly subject the person so believing to
the charge of *mental imbecility."*

When he read that, Lamar shuddered with excitement. Cobb had
branded him not only a liar, but an idiot! At last he had what he needed.
An insult! Requisitioning his best purple prose, Lamar fired off a ran-
corous seven-page letter to Cobb.

"I have been abridged of my proper right," Lamar bleated angrily. "It
was my right to have sent the ship to Africa or the depths of the ocean, as
either may have pleased me; and for an officer of this Government, without law, to prevent me, was as much a wrong, and, I will add, as much an
outrage to my nature as a man, as though he had set his hostile foot upon

my hearthstone." In the next few thousand words, Lamar accused his fellow Georgian of "grasping the powers of legislation"; of being "a tool" of the North; of "helping plant an iron heel upon the *bosom* of that very land that gave you birth!" Finally, in the clearest words possible, Lamar threw down the gauntlet:

> . . . *Under ordinary circumstances I would not violate the laws . . . But this law prohibiting the slave trade is a badge of servitude, a brand of reprobation, and not only would I not sustain it, but as I have told you, frankly, from the first,* I intend to violate it. *If that shall be the only way by which the South can come to right upon this question, I will re-open the trade in slaves to foreign countries*—let your cruisers catch me if they can.

With that, Lamar knew he had wounded Cobb. After all, Cobb had presidential ambitions, and needed Southern support to win the nomination in the upcoming Democratic National Convention in Charleston. Now Lamar had labeled him a tool of the North. "He is a gone sucker in this state," Lamar gloated in a letter to Spratt. "His chance for the Presidency is gone—certain."

Now Lamar made a new plan. Once again he wrote to the slave agent Viana. This time his letter prophesied the events that were soon to come. "I can show you, when we meet, the place or places I propose to land them, where you can go in and out by one tide, the bar straight and deep and no persons about, and the men, both in reference to their standing in the community and reliability in case of difficulty, who own the place," Lamar confided. "One thing is certain. Nothing can be done in the way of conviction. If the worst should happen, we could only lose the cargo . . ."

Yes, Lamar had a new plan. But for it to be successful, he would have to stay far behind the scenes. He had a new ship for the task as well, and its name was the *Wanderer.*

6

JOHNSON'S *WANDERER*

THE HANDS of William J. Rowland, worn by twenty-five years in the shipbuilding business, lay on his lap, and the old man slept in a yellowed armchair by the window. In his dreams there were the wings of seagulls, shaped to the wind, and the tails of striped bass, disappearing into the sea.

Outside, a willow tree, its branch tips leafless and coated in ice, clattered gently against the glass. Rowland awoke. Dawn was breaking over East Setauket harbor. From the window he could see the workmen below, bundled up in their woolen coats and flat caps, trudging silently to the shipyards below.

Before him on his desk lay a carving knife, a brass lamp with its oil nearly depleted, and next to it, the replica of a ship's hull, carved from soft pine. Rowland leaned forward and gently lifted the hull from his desk. He put its shape between himself and the window and sighted down its length. The bow was sharp and long, the lines flowing to midship. There they flared briefly, then raced aft and leapt steeply at the stern. Rowland turned the wooden model over in his hands, caressing its lines with a stern paternal eye.

The hull of every fast ship he had ever seen—since a lad—passed through his mind: The pilot boats that raced 200 miles out to sea to win the business of ships making their way into New York Harbor; the fishing schooners racing down the coast from the Maritimes to reach the docks with their catch; even the privateers that sacked British merchant ships and ran from the Royal Navy's mighty men-o'-war. These were the fastest hulls that men had ever devised, slipping through the seas beneath clouds of canvas.

Now he closed his eyes. He placed his fingers on the bow and let them run along what would be the waterline. Below the waterline the hull gradually narrowed, as though it were a living thing that had inhaled, then swelled aft and rolled gently outward. He reached the stern of the model, and, pleased, repeated the motion, as though the lines had something important to say. He heard the hissing of a hull cutting through the water, the boil and ripple that is left behind by the rudder. His mind wandered and soon he was thinking again of the fish—the striped bass and giant tuna most of all—and the way they cut effortlessly through the water, leaving nothing in their wake but transparent green sea.

Rowland had arrived in East Setauket forty-five years earlier, a dark-haired boy who had watched ships passing Long Island for as long as he could remember. He had been hired on at his first shipyard at fourteen, as a saw-boy at the bottom of a six-foot-deep sawpit, handling the lower end of a long-bladed saw, whose chisel-pointed teeth would cut three inches farther into a piece of squared timber at every stroke, reducing a tree trunk in short order to a pile of two-inch planks.

Three years of that, sawdust raining down into his eyes and mouth, and he was made a journeyman. Then it was learning to trim wood with a sharp-bladed adze to within an eighth of an inch, boring straight through tight-grained oak with a hand-turned auger, cutting precise notches and grooves with a hand chisel and mallet, jackplaning the oak planks so that they were as smooth as skin, and sanding them until they were smoother than glass.

But the boy had more than perseverance. The master shipwright who ran the yard soon saw that Rowland had an eye. He not only recognized that the keel, the stem and stern, the ribs, and the planks must be perfectly squared and aligned, but that more than mechanics and measurements were required; it took an eye to shape the ribs and stretch the skin so that she flowed. Rowland had the eye; and so the young man was promoted again.

In 1855, Rowland bought a small shipyard in East Setauket from Isaiah Hand, one of Long Island's leading shipbuilders, who had several yards along East Setauket Bay. The yard he purchased had a sawpit for cutting planks, a hotbox and boiler for softening timbers, two 50-x-25-foot sheds for storing wood and tools, and a track for running a ship down the gentle slope into the bay. In his yard, Rowland had room to repair two ships and build another from the keel up. He was now the master shipwright.

One day in the fall of 1857, a Louisiana sugar baron by the name of John D. Johnson arrived at the shipyard, stepped out of a covered carriage, placed his silk stovetop hat upon his head, and looked around imperiously. He was a big man, his impressive belly secured behind a silk brocaded waistcoat and gold watch chain. Five years earlier Rowland had built a luxury yacht for Johnson, named the *Irene*. The *Irene* was 62 feet long, not a large boat by later standards, but with a distinct elegance in the shape of her hull. Johnson had joined the prestigious New York Yacht Club with her, and together, they had done splendidly: One afternoon off the north shore of Long Island, in fact, she had rendezvoused with two of the club's fastest yachts, and in a prearranged challenge, beat both of them. Over drinks later, the losers tried to call it a mere "trial of speed," not a club-sanctioned event, but Johnson knew better.

Now, as Rowland showed Johnson to a chair in his cluttered office, Johnson expressed his continued admiration for the *Irene*. She was certainly one of the best medium-sized, single-stick racers in the club's early fleets, he exclaimed. Rowland responded with humble thanks, and they discussed that yacht for a few minutes. Then Johnson drew himself up purposefully and explained that he had come up from Islip, where he had just built a new home, to see Rowland because he was ready to build a very special yacht. She would be much more than the *Irene*. She would be more remarkable in every way. In fact, Johnson wanted a racing machine that was bigger, faster, and more elegant than any yacht that had ever existed. He studied Rowland's face for a moment, the lines etched by the gray window light. There was one yacht, in fact, that might compare.

Even before Johnson uttered the name, Rowland knew it. The image swept through his mind. She was the *America,* the most famous yacht in the world. The *America* had been the creation of a young boat designer from New York named George Steers. Steers had first won recognition for his boat-building skills at age sixteen, when he won a race with the *Martin Van Buren,* a boat he built. By the time he was in his early thirties he had already built the *Gimcrack,* for New York Yacht Club founder John Cox Stephens, as well as the *Una,* the *Cygnet,* the *Cornelia,* and other fast yachts. His place in history, however, arrived in 1851, when he designed what would become the most famous yacht in the nation—the *America.*

The *America* was of middling size—170 tons displacement, overall length of 101 feet, beam of 22 feet and 6 inches, and sail area of 5,263 square feet. Her masts had a distinctive rake toward the stern of $2\frac{7}{8}$ inches per foot, giving her a sleek, fast look. She was luxuriously built as well: Below deck, her furnishings were upholstered in green velvet, her walls paneled richly and lighted with brass lamps. She had a kitchen with fresh water provided from two water tanks, a big ice box, and a convenience that most Americans could not have fathomed for their own homes: a bathtub. Her greatest glory, however, was her speed. This was the mark of Steers's special genius, for he had designed her with a revolutionary hull design, one that broke the sea with a sharp bow, swept it back with an undulating hull, and then cast it behind effortlessly with a broad and flat beam.

It was this splendid yacht that a group of investors from the New York Yacht Club took proudly to England. Her greatest glory arrived when she raced fourteen British schooners and cutters 51 miles around the Isle of Wight in August 1851, and won, sending home to New York an ornate silver chalice soon called "The America's Cup." Addressing the Massachusetts House of Representatives, Daniel Webster had declared in exultation, "Like Jupiter among the gods, America is first and there is no second!" The name George Steers was engraved on the cup along with the *America*'s owners, and subsequently his career skyrocketed.

Rowland knew that Johnson would have hired the great talents of George Steers, if he could have. Johnson was certainly rich enough to afford his fees, and would have had the full support of the New York Yacht Club to entice Steers into a contract. But there was one problem. On the afternoon of September 25, 1856, on his way home to his summer residence in Little Neck, Steers either fell or leapt from his open carriage. He was found lying unconscious on the toll road near Cyprus Hill Cemetery. His carriage and team of horses were stopped at a tollgate farther on. There was no evidence that they had bolted or even that the carriage had left the road. The mystery was never solved. But the premier yacht designer of his time had died that evening, at the age of thirty-seven.

Of course, the *America* herself had already been lost: Within nine days of winning what was now the America's Cup, she had been sold to an Irish lord, John de Blaquiere of the Royal Victoria Yacht Club. She returned to the United States years later, but never regained her glory.

Johnson's eyes searched Rowland's as the two men sat in the office in the darkening afternoon. *America* had been lost, Johnson explained, and Steers had died. But there could be a new *America,* and a new George Steers, in the form of Rowland himself.

Johnson took a piece of paper and began to sketch out the details. He wanted this new yacht to be 238 tons, which would make her not only the largest in the New York Yacht Club fleet, but the biggest racing yacht in the nation. She would be 114 feet long on deck, 95 length of keel, 10½ feet depth of hold, 26½ feet abeam, with a shallow draft of 9½ feet. She would be luxuriously appointed—rosewood, velvet, silk, gilt, crystal. She would have the best sails and equipment. But most of all she would be fast—Rowland would have to improve upon the lines he had created for the *Irene,* and best the lines of the *America* as well. The New York Yacht Club members had given Steers $20,000 to build the *America*. Johnson was willing to pay $25,000. He would name the yacht the *Wanderer*.

————

Two months later, with the January wind blowing sleet into his beard, Rowland stood out in the middle of his shipyard. By now the model that he had hand-carved had been transferred into a full-scale schematic of a ship. A series of wooden blocks had been secured to the ground in the shipyard, and now the keel timber—a single piece of tightly grained white oak, 95 feet long, and shaped with adzes—was bolted down to the blocks.

The stem of the ship, the second timber cut from the same massive oak, was now ready, the workmen yelling to one another as it was swung into place using block and tackle, and bolted securely to the keel so that it projected forward at a 45-degree angle. Following this came the stern, another piece of massive oak, this set into the keel so that it would rise at a steep 55-degree angle aft. With snow swirling around its golden form, the backbone of the *Wanderer,* handpicked by Rowland and hauled from a nearby grove to East Setauket, had been set in place.

The following week, the workmen assembled the ribs that would comprise the *Wanderer*'s structure. With block and tackle squealing, they hoisted each rib into place, securing each of them with ribbands of pine that ran horizontally around the ship. Thomas Hawkins, who Johnson had hired to supervise construction, kept a sharp eye on operations.

The *Wanderer* began to rise in her cradle. Her long, tapered bowsprit lofted high over the boatyard's fence, peering into her neighbor's yard. As her form grew, crowned by her 90-foot main mast and spars, boys and the men who worked in town gathered outside the yard and gazed up, as workers might gaze up at a church steeple, or as workers, just a few generations later, would gaze up at the metal framework of the first skyscrapers climbing into the American skies.

Now the long white oak planks that would serve as her skin were pulled from the steam box, where they had been softening in a bath of hot linseed oil and steam. Their ends were fitted into the slots that had been carved into the *Wanderer*'s stern and stem pieces. The planks were carefully shaped and beveled to fit snugly. Hand augers countersunk holes a half inch into the oak; smaller drills then put holes through the full 3-inch width of the planks; trunnels, sea-soaked wooden nails, were hammered through and secured. Next, the men took out their jack-planes, and with long strokes, curled the wood off the planks until they were smooth, then sanded the grain until it glowed. When the *Wanderer* had been clad with her golden skin, the caulkers arrived, a hard and sullen bunch who pounded long lines of tar-soaked hemp into the crevices with wedge-shaped irons and wooden mallets.

By now it was early May. The ice of winter had given way to a steady shower of cold spring rain. The workmen lived in perpetual dampness, their twill shirts, heavy woolen trousers, and leather boots continually wet and muddy. The older men would hobble home at nightfall, crippled by the rheumatism that the constant wet and hard labor had driven into their limbs; the younger men, exhausted, would go off and drink. Only the boys and young men had the energy, and the dreams remaining, to look back fondly at what the day's exertions had done.

Every few weeks a carriage would pull up, and Johnson and his New York Yacht Club friends would spill out, pop oilskin umbrellas against the rain, and walk eagerly around the ship, stepping over the discarded shavings and lengths of wood that littered the site. They would converse briefly with Rowland, laugh and chatter among themselves, and then leave.

Rowland had promised the ship to Johnson by late May, and now, as the deadline neared, he agonized over the final details. The masts had been stepped into place and dressed with standing rigging. The structural inner work was under way: the gunwales clamped into place, the deck beams placed in, braced with iron or oak to give them strength. The white spruce decking boards had been put down, and the finishing carpenters and cabinetmakers were busy down below. When these workers were finished, a new group arrived, driving their wagons and carriages from New York City: carpet merchants with fine Belgian carpeting; interior designers with velvets and silk; an artillery dealer, with two brass "6-pounders" that were mounted on deck; even a bookseller, bringing several loads of leather-bound books for the ship's library.

On June 17, the men from the yacht club arrived again, wearing their bright reefer jackets and white flannels. This time the weather was sunny and mild, and they had brought friends, children, and wives. The workmen gathered around behind them in their rough clothing, hats in their hands. Their wives and children came, too, standing sheepishly behind the rest of the crowd. A table of food and drinks was put out, but, of course, it was reserved for the privileged crowd.

Rowland stood back as well. Even George Steers had not been invited to the lavish victory celebration the New York Yacht Club threw at the Astor Hotel following *America*'s victory (an oversight the club regretted for years following). Ship designers, regardless of their genius, were mere tradesmen, as were the captains who skippered the yachts to victory; the glory went to the gentlemen owners. As the ceremony continued, however, Johnson was kind enough to call out Rowland's name, and, to a ripple of applause, the revered shipmaster stepped forward and briefly tipped his hat.

At a nod from Johnson, Rowland sent an order down to the waterfront. Next the crowd heard the sound of hammers against wood. The chocks that held the *Wanderer* land-bound were knocked away, and then down she came into East Setauket Bay, settling with a whoosh into her new home. The reporters from the New York papers had come out to see her. As the *New York Times* reported:

> *She has long topmasts, on which she carries large gaff topsails; she also sports a long flying jib boom. Her draft of water is 9.5 feet, her bow is concave, after the George Steers model, and her run is so sharp and clean that one would be at a loss to tell where the water would touch it after it passed the midship lines. Her decks, which are of narrow planks, are so scrupulously white that one instinctively looks for a mat on which to wipe his feet on stepping over her rail. The sides of the gangway ladder are ornamented with brass work representing harps. Portions of the steering apparatus are also made of the same material, the whole being kept perfectly bright. No expense has been spared to make the cabin and staterooms all that could be desired for comfort and luxury.*

"The interior," noted *Harper's Weekly,* "is very elegantly appointed. The cabin and the captain's stateroom are even luxurious: Mirrors,

rattan-wood furniture, damask and lace curtains, elegantly framed en-
gravings, Brussels carpets, the library of choice books, expensive nautical instruments—these are the attractive features of the yacht."

To great acclaim, the *Wanderer* settled into a life of privilege. On
August 4 she accompanied the New York Yacht Club's squadron as
it cruised eastward to three days of partying in Newport. Johnson, surrounded on the deck by his family and several friends, was ecstatic. He
beamed as he watched his twenty crewmen, mostly teenage boys in blue
uniforms, with buttons as bright as silver coins (and eyes almost as big
with excitement), scurry up and down the rigging, while he, in the cock-
pit, with the skipper looking on solicitously, took the wheel and held his
new possession close to the wind.

The *America,* Johnson told the party aboard, had nearly lost her gaff
topsail during her sea trials, limping home for repairs. But even as the
weather came up, and the *Wanderer* buried her lee rail and sent the sea
foaming heavily over the decks and back out through the scuppers, she
never trembled or stalled. She was a magnificent ocean racer.

As the party of yachts approached Newport, people lined the shore
and waved flags and their hats. Ladies playing in the surf in their red
flannel bathing dresses screamed with delight as they saw the ships
drawing by. The yacht club's arrival into the harbor was not completely
without incident, however: As they rounded in the harbor, one of the
sloops poked her bowsprit through the kitchen window of the little
steamboat *Water Lilly,* sending the cook and pottery tumbling out the
other side. All this, of course, was good conversation at dinner that
night at the mansion of Mr. Wetmore, where the same ladies reappeared, resplendent in dresses of silk and gammon, the sun still glowing
in their pink faces.

As the *Wanderer* neared Newport, Johnson and his friends went below
deck to the smoking room and returned topside with big Cuban cigars in
their teeth, toasting each other and congratulating Johnson. Pulling
closer, they could see Newport's city hall, bedecked in red, white, and
blue, and the grand Ocean House, the biggest hotel in town, with flags
waving from the top of the copper cupola. The Ocean House, in fact, had
erected an arch made of wire and blue muslin in the center of its portico,
which read, in gilt lettering, "Welcome! New York Yacht Club."

"We have had the Yacht squadron with us for two or three days," the Newport correspondent for the *New York Times* wrote, "and a splendid appearance they made at anchor in the harbor. Of course there was no lack of visitors. Among so many beautiful craft it is almost an impossibility to say which particular vessel bore the palm for beauty of model and finish. The Favorita, Mystery, and the Wanderer were the favorite with the old salts here . . . I understand that 600 ladies and gentlemen visited the Wanderer. Not such a sad and lonely fate for a 'wanderer.'"

At precisely nine in the morning two days later, with a fresh breeze from the northwest, Commodore Edgar fired a shot from his starting pistol and the yachts took off, en masse, retracing their path past Newport, New Haven, and Glen Cove back to Manhattan. As the ships sailed down the East River, past the factories and ramshackle tenements and shanties of the Lower East Side, children in torn and soiled clothing, many of them from the slums of Manhattan's Five-Points and Little Dublin, stood on the piers and ran along the banks, and as the yachts came hissing and snapping by, a few hundred feet away, the image of the sails filled their wide eyes.

Farther on, down at the South Street docks, the merchant brigs and schooners were a forest of masts, and farther still, just below Wall Street, lay the big clippers—the *Flying Cloud,* the *Davy Crockett,* and the *Sovereign of the Seas,* among many others—that had brought treasures from the far ports of the world. Yet as the yachts of the New York Yacht Club swept into the harbor, flags flying, the sun rebounding from their varnished spars and hulls, the owners and their families gazing serenely with their arms crossed on the railings, they drew more attention than any other sailing craft. After all, merchant ships, no matter how sleek and fast, had always been the tool of commerce. But these racing yachts had been built for sheer pleasure—unimaginably expensive toys, fitted out for opulence and comfort.

As much as Johnson had enjoyed the adulation of Yankee society, and the hospitality of his northern guests, his mind soon turned to the South. He thought of the magnolias that flanked the entrance to his plantation in Louisiana, their lacquered leaves, the friends he missed, the swaying Spanish moss that draped the live oak trees. Arriving there would be the real homecoming for the *Wanderer*. And so he ordered the yacht fully provisioned, with all the special delicacies that New York could provide. There were soft clams, crabs, and shrimp from the creeks that ran through the salt marshes of Staten Island; and from the Hudson Bay, baskets of oysters, hard clams, and lobsters. All were placed neatly in the yacht's ice locker. From the tea clippers that lined South Street came ginger, coffee, dates, cheeses, and, of course, tea. He picked out an English croquet set to bring home, a telescope from Germany, and from a toy shop on Maiden Lane, a tin and cast-iron locomotive that had caught his eye.

The *Wanderer* would now embark upon a southern journey that would take her to Charleston, then Savannah, Brunswick, Key West, and New Orleans, and from there, to Havana, and finally back to Manhattan.

A quarter-moon hung over New York City as the crew of the *Wanderer* prepared her for this ambitious journey. A group of Johnson's friends, who would accompany him on his travels, were down below, noisily playing cards. But Johnson had folded his hand, and taking a bottle of French brandy and tumbler in hand, had climbed up to the deck. He spoke quietly to the captain for a few moments, and then watched silently as the crew began to hike the sails. The *Wanderer,* which had slumbered in the summer sun with her sails furled, now stretched and awakened in the cool evening air, her billowing canvas rising with a rustle. A moment later, in the fresh breeze, she heeled slightly and began to slip forward toward the ocean on the ebb tide.

Johnson dropped into a deck chair and looked up at the looming canvas, framed in stars and a few softly drifting clouds. He poured a half glass from the bottle and sipped it slowly. He must have nodded off, for when he looked back at Manhattan, the island had been reduced to a smaller place, the gaslights along the waterfront now but a single arcing glow. He brought the brandy up to his lips and drank again. Very quickly the *Wanderer* was gaining speed. As she passed into the Narrows, between Staten Island and the rounded edge of Brooklyn, he looked back at the city once again. Now the tip of Manhattan was a mere spot of light. He drained the glass, and without checking in with his friends below, slipped down the stairway back to his cabin, and went to sleep.

The following morning, when the people of Manhattan awakened and blinked across the Hudson, the most observant of them noticed that the *Wanderer* was gone. More than a week passed without news. Then, eight days later, the *New York Times* reported that their Charleston correspondent had seen the *Wanderer* come into Charleston. The welcome was tumultuous.

The cannon at the parade grounds in Charleston was fired at the first sign of her foresail on the horizon. Then followed the clatter of hooves and shouts of people as a crowd sped down to the Battery to catch a glimpse of her. For several days thereafter, the dignitaries of the city were rowed out to examine the ship, and in return, Johnson and his friends were received in Charleston's finest homes.

In Savannah, the next stop, the reception was equally warm. The Republican Blues, one of the city's citizen militias, fired the salute. Johnson was invited to the horse races at the Ten Broeck Track, in time to see the four-mile-heat winner receive a $3,600 purse. He attended a performance of *The Barber of Seville*. The *Wanderer* then stopped in Brunswick, near Jekyll Island, where she raced in a local regatta, and beat the fastest schooner in town by an impressive 300 yards. She continued on to New Orleans, where the reception was greater than ever. Among the many guests was William Walker, a soldier of fortune from Tennessee who was gaining fame for having invaded Nicaragua with a ragtag army of "filibusters" and for having installed himself as president.

Once again the *Wanderer* performed in local regattas, and caught the eye of any man who appreciated her speed. Finally, Johnson took the *Wanderer* to Cuba, where she once again entertained dignitaries and demonstrated her agility and finesse. "The admiration for her fine proportions and her fast sailing, which she excited in all these places, were announced from time to time through the press," the *New York Times* noted, "and were the subject of much pride among yachting men."

On April 11, after her four-month sojourn, Johnson and the *Wanderer* returned to New York. Her sails were furled, and Johnson, tanned and somewhat tired by the final leg of the journey, stepped into the yacht's four-man yawl and was rowed ashore. All was well—or at least so it seemed.

7

CORRIE'S WANDERER

WILLIAM EDGAR was at his home in Manhattan, pouring himself a brandy in the library, when the butler appeared and announced the arrival of a Mr. Johnson in the vestibule. Edgar was one of the New York Yacht Club's preeminent members—present at the founding of the club on July 30, 1844, and a frequent competitor in club regattas, generally aboard his 45-ton schooner, *Cygnet*.

With Johnson was another man, a lean, square-shouldered individual with sandy hair and engaging blue eyes. Johnson introduced him as Captain Corrie, William C. Corrie, to be exact. Edgar had heard the name before. Wasn't Corrie that prominent South Carolinian who frequented many of the best dinner parties in Washington and Manhattan, as the papers mentioned in their society columns? The very same, Corrie replied with a handsome smile.

When the butler had taken their coats and hats, Edgar led them into the drawing room. After some small talk, which required cigars and a bit more brandy, Johnson came to the point. He had decided to sell the *Wanderer*, he told Edgar. The yacht was wonderful, of course, but his wife had had enough with the ebb tides and flood tides, squalls and dol-drums. Now she had her eyes on, dare it be said, a *steamer*—you know, steady, stable. Edgar's eyes narrowed with disappointment. Yes, con-ceded Johnson with a rueful laugh, a steam yacht, and very, very boring.

But the good news, Johnson continued, was that Mr. Corrie had ex-pressed an interest in the *Wanderer.* In fact, they had just settled on $25,000 for her. Now Corrie had an interest in keeping the yacht in New York. In fact, if the New York Yacht Club could be persuaded to make Mr. Corrie a member, the *Wanderer* would not even have to move off her present mooring. At the very suggestion, Edgar's teeth tightened around his cigar. The New York Yacht Club was a very exclusive group. They had just denied membership, in fact, to no less a mogul than "Commodore" Cornelius Vanderbilt—rich and powerful, yes, but with-out the manners and pedigree that the club required. Edgar was about to say this when the butler reappeared again, calling the three to dinner.

The china and silver had been set in the formal dining room, in which an oil of the schooner *Cygnet* was dominant. The picture showed the ves-sel with every sail taut, and the New York Yacht Club pennant snapping boldly from mainmast. She was in the process of defeating the *Northern Light,* which lay windward. The *Northern Light* was owned by Colonel William P. Winchester of Boston and was quite a bit bigger than the *Cygnet*—62 feet to the *Cygnet*'s 42—Edgar pointed out, standing at the base of the painting and looking up. She had gotten off to a better start as well, he added, but the *Cygnet* had prevailed.

Corrie listened with great enthusiasm, peppering Edgar with ques-tions and responding himself with a good amount of knowledge about vessels, regattas, and racing. "And so, did you ever race against the *Northern Light* again?" he asked. Edgar laughed. "After that, Colonel Winchester *begged* to join our club," Edgar exclaimed. "We accepted the old boy, and he's been a member ever since!"

As they sat down to dinner, the conversation flowed effortlessly, bounding from international politics to the arts. Edgar found himself quite comfortable around Corrie, drawn, in fact, to the man's spark and intelligence. For his part, Johnson did his best to fan the flames, noting that Corrie came from one of the finest families in the South, had resided for five years in Washington, and was supremely connected there to Congressmen, members of the cabinet, and even President Buchanan himself. Recently, Corrie had succeeded in obtaining a $200,000 grant from Congress, Johnson noted, in recognition of land deeds running back to the Revolutionary War. By the time the meal had been consumed, and the men were back in the library with brandy and cigars, Edgar had been won over.

The following day Edgar contacted Edwin Stevens, the son of the club's founder (and now vice-commodore), as well as Treasurer Robert S. Hone, Fleet Captain Irving Grinnell, and Race Committee members Charles H. Haswell, J. Howard Wainwright, and Robert O. Colt. As they discussed the situation, they all admitted that they wanted the *Wanderer* to remain with the club. The scale model of the ship's hull, carved in pine by Rowland, had been displayed in the club's lounge. It would be nice to continue to see the club's pennant above the *Wanderer,* as she coursed through the waters of New York and New England. And Corrie himself was not without merit. A Southern gentleman with manners, intelligence, and connections could serve the club quite well. The vote was taken, and Corrie was in.

When the New York press caught wind of the club's decision, they were delighted. "A high-toned Southern gentleman, and one of the most liberal patrons of the sports, of any and all kinds, in the South," remarked Porter's *Spirit of the Times,* New York City's leading sports journal. "We congratulate him on his purchase, and the public on the fact that the Wanderer is in the hands of a gentleman who will maintain her name and fame." Added the *New York Times,* "Captain Corrie belongs to one of the finest families of Charleston, South Carolina. His manners are those of a well-bred gentleman . . . He was recently admitted a member of the New York Yacht Club, and was yesterday dressed in the uniform worn by the fraternity."

Now it was time for Johnson to step back into the shadows, and for Corrie, as the new master of the *Wanderer,* to take his position of probity around town. Corrie already was an A-list dinner guest around Manhattan; now the *Wanderer,* and his club membership, lifted his star even higher. One could find Corrie now in the midst of the best parties surrounded by admirers. He might be dismantling to a man the membership of the 35th Congress, or perhaps describing the parties thrown in Washington by the likes of the federal mail contractors, dressed in lavender kid leather shoes and striped silken pants, carrying pearl-headed canes. He might be explaining that Mr. Appleton, the assistant secretary of state, will summer in Portland, Maine; that Postmaster General Brown will make a trip to Tennessee; that Treasury Secretary Howell Cobb will go home to Savannah, or that the president will visit the old soldiers' home in Washington—not that he wants to—it is still in the city and unpleasantly hot—and then make a visit in August to Bedford Springs, the water of which he greatly enjoys.

"Captain Corrie," one admirer blurted, herself a fine package of lace and silk, flounce, and basque, "I understand that you know *every* movement of *every* member of Congress." Corrie stepped back and laughed. Then, moving so close that his lips brushed her cheek, he whispered, in a buttery Southern drawl, "And the *price* of every one of them, my dear!"

In his partygoing, Corrie frequently appeared with another celebrity: J. Egbert Farnum. Farnum was a dark-haired, dashing adventurer who looked out at the world from behind a pair of deeply hooded, penetrating eyes. As he would willingly tell you, Farnum had marched through jungles, rafted rivers, and had had all sorts of adventures, most of them as a commander in the mercenary army of William Walker, the soldier of fortune who had invaded and conquered parts of Mexico, Honduras, and Nicaragua.

Farnum was one of the most famous of the bunch. The *Albany Statesman,* a New York newspaper, described him as "the renowned overland rider, whose brilliant career in Texas, California, and Nicaragua is familiar to so many of his countrymen." On May 23, 1858, *Harper's Weekly* ran a woodcut illustration of Farnum and Walker under the headline: "The Men of Destiny."

To be sure, Farnum often drank to excess. But it was part of his quirky charm. "I appeal to every officer and soldier of the army, who knows me, here in this City and elsewhere," Farnum wrote earnestly in a letter to the editor of the *New York Daily News,* "if it was ever charged— if it was ever shown, that I *ever* was intoxicated while on duty—or more than two or three times at most—while in command of a company." The more brawls Farnum got into, it seemed, the more the public loved him.

In fact, Farnum made the perfect sidekick to the ultrasmooth Corrie. Together they ruled the party lists in New York that summer, and when they boarded the *Wanderer* and cruised New York Harbor, with their many admirers and guests aboard, no one doubted that the glorious *Wanderer* had fallen into the right hands.

One night, however, without even a slice of moon to lighten the harbor, the *Wanderer* slipped her moorings and made her way slowly up the East River, riding the flood tide past Roosevelt Island, through Hell Gate, and out into Long Island Sound. She continued east for 50 miles until she reached Port Jefferson, where she drew toward shore again, and finally dropped anchor just off the shipyard of J. J. Harris. At daybreak, several workmen swarmed aboard, along with the gaunt figure of Thomas Hawkins, who had supervised the construction of the *Wanderer* under Joseph Rowland. Now, with Hawkins barking commands, some of the deck planks of the *Wanderer* were removed, and after that, a few of the pieces of inner framing.

The following day, a series of galvanized iron water tanks were raised above the *Wanderer* with block and tackle, and lowered carefully through the places where the planks had been removed—Hawkins showing the workers where to drop the tanks between the deck beams and lodging knees so that the tanks would settle onto the cabin floor. It was an unusual addition to the *Wanderer,* or any other pleasure yacht.

News of the *Wanderer*'s arrival at Port Jefferson could not be suppressed, of course, and it was not long before the news spread. Among those hearing the rumors was Sydney S. Norton, the surveyor of Port Jefferson. It immediately struck him as odd. Why would the *Wanderer,* or any other pleasure yacht, for that matter, need so much drinking water? Fifteen thousand gallons would give the *Wanderer*'s twelve-man crew and eight passengers enough drinking water—he calculated the number quickly in his head—for more than two years at sea!

Whatever was happening, Norton decided, it required some investigation. Taking a room at an inn near the Harris shipyard, he watched as Hawkins lowered the last of the big tanks into the yacht. As he watched, he became increasingly convinced that the tanks were not being installed for some pleasure cruise, nor even to supply ballast. No, the *Wanderer* was being prepared for an almost unimaginable crime.

———

Considering that the U.S. Congress had outlawed the African slave trade in 1808 and made it a crime punishable by death in 1820, it would seem improbable that American ships would be brazenly fitted out for this piracy in 1858, let alone at the Northern port of New York. But this indeed was the case. Not only was the African slave trade booming in the 1850s, but the epicenter of the activity was New York City.

There, on the wharfs of lower Manhattan, dozens of slave ships were provisioned and sent off to Africa annually, while, in the maze of streets that branched off from Wall Street, slave captains walked boldly, visiting the offices of the agents that managed their sordid affairs. To be sure, these slave captains were not heading to Africa to bring their human cargoes back to *America*. They were sailing to Africa to send their human cargoes on to the thriving slave markets of *Cuba*. Still, by provisioning and equipping the ships for the trade in American waters, the ship owners and captains were violating federal law.

By day one might bump into a slaver on Pearl Street or Front Street, on his way to visit his agent's office. At night, however, one would find them gravitating uptown, frequently to entertain clients at the Astor House, New York's finest hotel. Here, a potential investor—perhaps a failed businessman with some final savings to invest—might stumble up the steps beneath the Greek portico fronting the big hotel, and make his way across the floral carpets into a sequestered dining room. There, in the alcove, he might be introduced to two slave traders sitting at the table. The red velvet curtain would be drawn tight, and, in the hissing gaslight, he would turn to face his new business associates. One of them might be a dark man, dressed in a dark suit. Once engaged in the legitimate palm oil and ivory trade, he would have been drawn into the slave business by the vast profits. He would be familiar with the coasts and rivers of Africa, as well as the human misery that roils in his wake. He is as opaque and emotionless as a lizard.

The other might be an oily, elegantly dressed person, a pleasant Cuban with heavily bejeweled fingers. He is the moneyman, or capitalist, who trolls the city for investors. He is familiar with the notables of this trade, men such as Jose da Costa Lima Viana, who keeps an office at 158

Pearl Street (and trading agents stationed at Punta da Lenha and Banana Point on the Congo River); C. H. S. de la Figaniere, the Portuguese consul general, who runs a firm with his brother at 81 Front Street; and even John Albert Machado, a native of the Azores, who owns several slave ships and operates out of an office at 165 Pearl Street.

As voices and laughter continue outside the alcove, the capitalist would pour wine into each crystal glass, then lean forward to explain the investment. First, he might say, it is a very wise decision. The odds it will turn out magnificently are seven cases out of ten. Men have made thousands of dollars in these investments very quickly, he would say. Of course, men are not alone in seeing the wisdom in this. Two ladies, now attracting adoration at a fashionable watering place, have invested in a little venture of this kind not long ago, and, as a result, have augmented their banking accounts, one by $23,000 and the other by $16,000!

Second, he would explain, the economics are very sound. One must remember that the sugar crop of Cuba is estimated at 600,000 tons, or $60 million. Every Negro imported means an additional ton of sugar. At the current prices of sugar, a planter could spend a thousand dollars on each Negro and still make a 60 percent net profit on his capital outlay. The profit is very good, he would say, as you can buy Negroes on the coast for $50. Consider that margin, and imagine 400 souls brought to the coast of Cuba and traded for a satchel heavy with gold dubloons!

The investor, reflecting on his desperate need for money, might be intrigued. So, how to go about it? he asks. Very easy! is the reply. Good captains are always returning from voyage and their ships are nearly always available. In fact, the Cuban might remark, one of the best slave captains has just returned from a voyage. He and his ship are available.

Of course, one must commission a man to procure the necessary items of trade: puncheons of rum, jerked beef, barrels of bread, tobacco, powder, cheap pistols made in England specifically for the slave trade—whatever it takes to induce an African chieftan to release choice slaves from his inventory. One would also want to procure an apparatus for refining palm oil. Not that one would be refining palm oil! It is only a ruse! The apparatus is tossed overboard. Only the boiler is saved, for cooking the gruel that will be fed to the captives as they cross the ocean.

One also needs a crew. Fortunately, there are gentlemen who keep lists of available seamen and "runners" who will scour waterfront bars, boardinghouses, brothels, and even the Eldridge Street jail for recruits. These salts will sign on for $50, plus $1.50 per Negro landed in Cuba. The most important crewman, though, is the supercargo, a man familiar with the African coast, and the boatswain, who is skilled at herding the captives aboard with his whip, and, frankly, in dispensing a measure of discipline, even brutality, as the voyage proceeds.

Dinner arrives, and the Cuban eats hungrily. After a few moments of reflection, and a careful dabbing of the grease from his face, he continues.

When the ship is ready she must seek clearance from the Custom House. This is not as difficult as it seems! The Cuban tickles his palm with his fingertips, signifying a bribe, and then breaks into a grin. Every corner of the law is framed to protect the trade, he explains with a wink. Slave dealers contribute liberally to the treasuries of political organizations. Very liberally. When the elections are over in New Jersey, Pennsylvania, and Connecticut, he laughs, their bank accounts are largely depleted!

The Cuban then might extract a worn newspaper clipping from his pocket and adjust a monocle to his eye. "This is from the New York Journal of Commerce," he would say solemnly. "Few of our readers are aware of the extent to which this infernal traffic is carried on, by vessels clearing from New York, and in close alliance with our legitimate trade, and that downtown merchants of wealth and respectability are extensively engaged in buying and selling African Negroes, and have been, with comparatively little interruption, for an indefinite number of years." The Cuban glances up, makes eye contact with the investor, and then continues reading. "We are informed by the deputy U.S. marshall that at least fifteen slave vessels sailed from the port within the last twelve months. Last year there were but *five* prosecutions and *one* conviction."

He folds up the clipping and returns it to his pocket. "We have very little trouble," he would add reassuringly, "and even our little worries are always taken care of. Have you ever heard of the firm of Beebe, Dean and Donohue, at 76 Wall Street? They are excellent admiralty attorneys, and very well connected."

In such a manner the failing businessman is coaxed into the scheme. Of course, the capitalist is right—the poor man has a better chance of making money in the slave trade than in any other investment in New York.

But one name has been omitted from the conversation. It is that of U.S. District Judge Samuel Rossiter Betts, who presided over the Southern District of New York, which included all of Manhattan. In later years, Judge Betts would be called the "father of admiralty law in the United States," a sobriquet honoring his accomplishments on the federal bench. But what has been less revealed about Betts is his participation in the slave trade, not through actual slaving, of course, but through the mincing of admiralty law to the point that convictions were virtually impossible to achieve. In Betts's Manhattan courtroom, no amount of evidence seemed enough to convict a slave trader. U.S. marshals could tow a notorious brig back into New York harbor, extract from her hold shackles, chains, neck collars, and huge water tanks for slaking the thirst of 600 Africans, and Judge Betts would nevertheless bounce the case and the prosecutor down the stairs and out into the street. It happened time and again.

One time, for instance, the *Catherine* was stopped in New York Harbor. Aboard, federal agents found a large boiler for cooking food, 1,500 feet of pine planking, casks carrying 7,000 gallons of water, 570 wooden spoons, and 36 tin dishes. Her swarthy crew were well-known slavers. Paperwork aboard advised them to be, "careful, in any cross questions, that you . . . stick to the same story . . ." Betts previewed the case, and, as usual, ruled the evidence circumstantial. All the parties went free. Betts ruled the U.S. District Court in New York from 1823 until he was forced out, forty-four years later.

Betts was not alone: the New York waterfront was rife with corruption. Furthermore, the New York newspapers were remarkably timid in pursuing an investigation. In fact, it was only when the election of a Republican president seemed assured, and the Civil War imminent, that some of the New York papers found their courage. Noted the *New York Daily Tribune*:

> *The traders engaged in this traffic are known; the men who supply their vessels with stores, who fit them with sails, who provide them with sailors, are known also. That knowledge, and much other that is curious and interesting in relation to this subject,*

*awaits the Government, whenever the Government chooses to seek
for it. It does not seek for it. It does not choose to have it. It will not
thank us even for hinting that it can be had, or for providing any
portion of it.*

It was thus that Surveyor Norton of Port Jefferson now suspected
that the *Wanderer* was joining other slavers that had sailed from New
York bound for Africa, and then Cuba.

At dawn, Norton left his room at the inn and crept down the gentle
hill to where the *Wanderer* lay anchored, about 150 yards offshore. She
was a black hulk against the gray water, with only a single riding light
hanging in the fore rigging. Ducking behind a rain barrel, he watched a
group of three men approach, two of them speaking softly in what he
thought was Spanish. As soon as they passed, Norton peered over the
edge. They all had canvas bags thrown over their shoulders. One had a
green kerchief around his head and a long red beard. Minutes later, he
saw them climb into a dinghy and row out to the *Wanderer*.

As the three climbed aboard the *Wanderer,* he saw something else. It
was the squat shape of the *Charter Oak,* a "lighter" that frequently fer-
ried supplies to ships moored around New York Harbor. Now she was
gliding slowly in the morning light up to the *Wanderer*. She was heavily
loaded. Boxes and barrels lay lashed to her deck, and she lay low in water, almost up to her scuppers. As the *Charter Oak* approached, a lean
man with sandy hair came up onto the deck of the *Wanderer,* accompanied by a strongly built man with dark wavy hair. Norton recognized
the dark-haired man as Thomas Hawkins, but he had never seen the
other man before.

As Norton recoiled behind the rain barrel again, he was troubled by
what he felt was transpiring. Slave trading! Port Jefferson and Setauket
had always been freewheeling. During the Revolution the towns had
waged a guerrilla war against the British, and afterward Washington
himself came up to Setauket to express his thanks, staying at Roe's Inn,
and writing in his diary that it was "tolerably decent, with obliging people in it."

But this was different. The slave trade had seeped poison into the
community. Every shipbuilder that offered help, every merchant that

supplied chains, food, or weapons was equally to blame. Norton would have none of it. He stumbled back up the path. Hiring a messenger, Norton ordered him to take the next stagecoach into Manhattan to deliver an urgent message to U.S. Marshal Isaiah Rynders.

At daybreak the following morning, Rynders and Deputy Marshal Maurice O'Keefe steamed into Port Jefferson from Manhattan aboard the revenue cutter *Harriett Lane*. By now, the *Charter Oak* had been warned that the feds were on their way, and had crossed Long Island Sound, nearly to the Connecticut side. The *Harriett Lane* steamed over, and hailed her down. The *Charter Oak* turned into the wind, and with her sails luffing noisily, was thrown a line and towed, squatting and rolling, back across the sound to Long Island.

By now, spies from New York had also informed Corrie and Farnum that the *Harriett Lane* was on her way. At first Farnum proposed flight—a fast exit east, past Montauk Point and out to sea. But with the *Harriett Lane*'s smoke already on the horizon, Corrie preferred subterfuge: Once the anchor had been hauled and the sails hiked, Corrie ordered the *Wanderer* back to Manhattan, as though she had been innocently heading back that way all along. When hailed by the *Harriet Lane,* the *Wanderer* maintained her course, but as the cruiser drew closer, and perhaps with a glance at the vessel's formidable 10-inch Dahlgren guns, Corrie ordered the *Wanderer*'s crew to hove to. Deputy Marshal O'Keefe leaned against the rail and presented a warrant. Corrie barked a few words of protest back, but in the end agreed to lower the *Wanderer*'s sails. As afternoon came, the *Wanderer* and the *Charter Oak* were towed ignominiously back to Manhattan. The New York press, of course, couldn't have asked for a juicier story, and were soon perched on the wharves down by the Battery to get the first glimpse of the unusual procession.

The following morning, U.S. Marshal Rynders, Deputy Marshal Maurice O'Keefe, and Assistant U.S. District Attorney William Dwight boarded the *Wanderer*. By now, Corrie had regained his composure. He greeted them with great courtesy, as though they were his dinner guests. They had his complete cooperation, he averred. First, Corrie showed the entourage the splendid deck of the yacht, complete with her white planking and brass ornamentation. Then they went below.

Directly to the right was the library, he said, pulling a few of the leather-bound volumes from the shelves for inspection. The walls of this masculine enclave were paneled in cherry, the molding crenulated, the armchairs upholstered in Spanish leather. Slightly aft was what Corrie called the "ladies' cabin," a brighter space, with gold textured wallpaper and a comfortable double bunk bed. On both sides of the cabin were matching sofas, upholstered in a bright blue fabric. Farnum, at Corrie's side throughout the inspection, pulled open the drawers and lockers, beckoning Rynders and his staff to peer inside.

Exiting the ladies' cabin and moving forward, Corrie opened the door of the aft pantry, in an exaggerated invitation to investigate its four corners. Rynders smiled and stepped in for a quick glance around. A few feet farther were two small staterooms, each with a sofa and lockers. On the other side and slightly aft was what was called the owners' room. This, larger than the library, had a full-sized bed, a pair of leather armchairs, a small round table, a built-in bureau with glass cabinet doors above, and—voilà—the cabin's own porcelain and brass bathtub. "She's not much of a slaver, is she?" Corrie remarked. Marshal Rynders laughed, and the young U.S. attorney at his elbow blushed deeply. But there was more to see, Corrie insisted. Ahead was the main cabin, about 10 feet by 15 feet, with skylights above, peach-colored Belgian carpeting underfoot, and bright brass lighting fixtures all around; ahead, the kitchen, the pantry, the bread room, the pastry and ice-box room.

As they were peering in the pantry, friends of Corrie's, Captain Murray of the U.S. Steamer *Bibb* and Captain Marriatt, of the U.S. Army, dropped in. When introductions were made all around, Corrie suggested brandy and cigars.

Soon, blue smoke filled the cabin, the brandy glasses were on their third refill, and Corrie had gathered everyone around him, entertaining them with ribald stories about members of Congress. At last, Corrie said that he did not want to belabor the point, but felt required to offer a full explanation. Rynders protested, but Corrie said emphatically that he must clear his name. The water tanks, he began, had been installed merely for ballast. Even the vaunted *America* had put 40 tons of iron in her hull to keep her steady, and when her sea trials demonstrated the need for more, George Steers ordered another eight tons of ballast put into the *America*. Likewise, the *Wanderer* had shown a tendency to bury her lee rail. The tanks would provide water, certainly—but ballast as well.

And why should he have provisioned the *Wanderer* at Port Jefferson, taking her to sea past the tip of Long Island rather than straight from Manhattan? Simply a plan to avoid the vicissitudes of Hell Gate once again, and particularly the risk of crossing the bar at Sandy Hook while the yacht was heavily weighted with provisions. Third, Corrie said brightly, what of the provisions themselves? Merely the extensive menu that a group of gentlemen would require on a long voyage, he laughed, plus those things that would be useful in trade once the yacht began its pleasure cruise along the African coast.

Rynders tried to apologize again, but Corrie graciously declined. The "villagers" of Port Jefferson, he said, had spread such dark and fantastical rumors about the *Wanderer* that he knew he would have to return to Manhattan in any case and submit to an examination, no matter how inconvenient, in order to clear his name. He would have preferred *not* to be towed in at the end of the *Harriet Lane*'s hawser, he joked, but what had to be, had to be!

When Rynders emerged from the yacht and stepped onto the wharf, he was immediately surrounded by reporters. He repeated the story that Corrie had told them. "Boys, that's the whole story in a nutshell," he barked. "In this connection I would state that Captain Corrie never for a moment doubted the ultimate result of an examination, and was rather pleased than otherwise at the turn events had taken; for a growing suspicion, engendered in the minds of villagers, might, unrefuted, grow to large dimensions of an accepted fact." The following day, the New York press spread the word. The *New York Times* put the story in big type:

MYSTERY OF THE YACHT WANDERER

She is seized at Port Jefferson, L.I.—Brought to New York and Overhauled—Curious Outfit—Is it a Pleasure Trip? A Slave Hunt, or a Filibustering Expedition?

An inspection of the yacht by the assistant United States District-Attorney Mr. Dwight and the Marshal, was made yesterday morning, but there was nothing discovered to implicate the vessel in the slave trade. The examination of the lighter's cargo, however, showed that an extraordinary voyage of some kind was contemplated. There was any quantity of barrels, boxes, bags and baskets, consisting of beef and pork, hams, vinegar, potatoes, bread, rice, Champagne, brandy and sundry other kinds of liquors in abundance; olives and olive oil in large quantities, cigars, preserved meats and condiments—in a word, the most curious mélange that was ever seen on board a vessel before; the whole making a year's supplies for an ordinary vessel's crew. There were, it was stated, four large water tanks put aboard, and there were also three or four others found on board the lighter.

The *Times* also said that one of the staterooms below the *Wanderer's* decks had been fitted out as an armory, and contained muskets, pistols, boarding pikes, and heavy cutlasses—enough to arm thirty men.

Why? The best the *Times* could fathom—based on the fact that arms were extensive and that the great "overland rider" Farnum was aboard—was that the *Wanderer* may have been destined for Tampico or perhaps Santo Domingo, as part of a freelance invasion effort. "Though not formidable as a war vessel, she would be an excellent tender to a small squadron, and filled with fighting men, would be more than a match for some larger craft," the newspaper opined. Whatever, that was a voyage of glory, not one of slaving.

The following morning, the *Wanderer* was moved to an anchorage across from the New York Yacht Club's headquarters in Hoboken. The *Charter Oak* was allowed to sidle up and discharge her wares. Partway through the process, the rain began to fall, harder and harder. To Corrie it was an opportunity to invite the entire party—even a *New York Times* reporter who was sitting forlornly on the wharf—back down below, where a sumptuous dinner was soon served. On taking his seat at the head of the table, Corrie laughed that he would now fulfill the scripture injunction that says: "If thine enemy hunger, feed him, and if he thirst, give him drink!" Said the *Times* the following day, "The joke was enjoyed, but the dinner more. The party talked over the arrest. The officers expressed themselves fully satisfied, and took leave of the yacht in the midst of the pouring rain."

On June 18, the *Wanderer* once more sailed from New York harbor, this time passing over the bar at Sandy Hook and out into the Atlantic. Farnum didn't get away from the city, however, without one more incident. The *New York Times* reported that the disturbance grew out of "what was deemed an unwarrantable interference on the part of one gentleman with the exhibition of some card tricks by a third party." Farnum assured the other gentleman that if he were not pleased with the exhibition he might retire. Said the *Times:* "Warm words ensued, blows followed, and, the story goes, Farnum got the head of the man of letters in chancery, and badly punished him. The vanquished man was taken home in a carriage and his physician called. The recovery is considered probable."

After seven hard days of sailing, the *Wanderer* arrived in Charleston. As the yacht passed Sullivan Island, a cannon barked out its welcome, and children ran after her along the beach. Rounding the peninsula, the yacht was met by the revenue cutter *Aiken,* which carried scores of dignitaries, waving hats and handkerchiefs. The reception for Corrie exceeded even that accorded Johnson the previous year. After all, Corrie was not only a Southerner, he was a Charlestonian—and a famous one now at that.

The parties went on late, but by early the following morning the *Wanderer* was being loaded up with more supplies. This time the provisions were not only innocent foodstuffs and trinkets of trade. This time they included thirty 6-quart pans, twenty 5-quart pans, 50 1-pint tin cups—as well as enough rough-cut Georgia pine to construct a second deck beneath the main deck. And the tanks were refilled again, settling the *Wanderer* down with 15,000 gallons of water.

Supervising the loading operations was a red-bearded sailor, his black eyes sunken and flat, his hair wrapped in a green bandana. His name was Nicholas Dennis Brown, or Briggs, or any number of aliases. He had slipped aboard the *Wanderer* as she left New York Harbor, with Farnum giving him a hand up. Brown would captain the *Wanderer* from here on—and he knew the coastline of Africa like the palm of his calloused hand.

Corrie and Farnum didn't remain long in Charleston. On the afternoon of the Fourth of July the *Wanderer* pulled anchor—"amid the cheers of the crowd which lined the shores, and the waving of flags and adieus from fair women, and all that," a reporter on the scene remarked. Eighteen days later the yacht arrived at the rocky island of Trinidad, in the Caribbean Sea, just off the coast of Venezuela. Once again, Corrie was in fine form, throwing a big party for the American consul, the governor of the island, several British officers, and a number of ladies, who, it was rumored, stayed over for dinner and beyond. More supplies were taken aboard—including another 1,200 gallons of water.

Then the *Wanderer* departed again, ostensibly toward St. Helena: Corrie had said he wanted to visit that tiny speck of an island off the African coast, the last home of Napoléon Bonaparte. But neither Corrie nor the *Wanderer* ever stopped there. Instead, the yacht headed straight across the Atlantic for the western coast of Africa, and the Congo River.

On the other side of the Atlantic, by the mouth of the Congo, Lieutenant Hogkinson of the British Royal Navy removed his spyglass from its leather case and scanned the horizon. He was standing on the foredeck of the HMS *Viper,* a 300-ton steamship that was slowly cruising the coast of Africa, searching for slave ships. At his side was a pivot gun, called a "chaser," because in a pursuit it could hurl an 8-pound ball 900 yards into the rigging of another ship. She also boasted four 8-inch-shell guns and eighteen long 32-pounders.

The *Viper* was one of nineteen British warships that, with the inclusion of nine American cruisers, made up what was called the African Squadron. Established in 1842 by a joint agreement between the United States and Britain, the squadron had the job of searching the coastline for possible slavers. According to the American laws, a slave trader, if caught, could hang. The British had a less severe but more expedient solution: If the British found ample evidence that a vessel was a slaver—anything from hatches bolted down to chains and a slave deck below, the British officers had the right to confiscate her on the spot and bring her back to port, or, in the event she was a leaky hulk, merely remove the crew to the shoreline, fire a few incendiary shells into her rigging, and watch her burn to the waterline.

For all this, the African Squadron was less formidable than it appeared. The slave coast ran some 3,000 miles. That was a lot of coastline to cover with some thirty vessels. Moreover, service in the African Squadron was considered a very low rung on the ladder. "Anything more arid, leafless and calcined than this wretched little town and its background of volcanic peaks perhaps does not exist," wrote a newspaper reporter when he visited one of the ports that the African Squadron used to take on supplies. "He who would have recreation here, physical and mental, must, at the risk of a sunstroke, find a coconut grove; or, through streets paved with the debris of yesterday's dinner, seek the worst of billiard tables."

Bad ships and demoralized men. Nevertheless, the African Squadron was out there on the coastline—somewhere—bristling with guns. And it was into this realm of illicit possibility that the *Wanderer* was preparing to sail.

8

INTO AFRICA

ON SEPTEMBER 16, 1858, the *Wanderer* approached the muddy mouth
of the Congo. She flew the triangular pennant of the New York Yacht
Club atop her mainmast—a bright red cross on a field of blue, with a
white star shining in the center. Behind that, from the aft shroud,
snapped the Stars and Stripes. Both emblems represented the power and
prestige of the Western world.

Beneath those emblems, standing at the forward rail, resplendent in
their club uniforms and yachting caps, were Corrie and Farnum. Behind
them was sailing master Nicholas D. Brown, alias "Dennis Brown," alias
"Seth Briggs," his red beard flowing in the wind. And around him was
the crew, a rough assortment of sea-hardened Portuguese and Greeks,
who hung in the rigging and scurried busily down below.

As they had approached the continent, Corrie and Farnum had
watched the gray line of Africa grow green and take shape, revealing its
low mountains and narrow beaches. Now, as they entered the river, an
earthy fragrance washed over them, the perfume of innumerable
brightly colored flowers, hanging thickly from the vines that had scaled

the trees, mixed with the unmistakable odor of rot—the accumulated burden of organic material that was roiled to the surface of the river by crocodile tails and the hooves of the Black Hippos.

As she drifted up the Congo on the flood tide, the *Wanderer* brought the native children running to her, just as she had brought the Irish children to her, running and leaping over the docks along lower Manhattan. These African children, though, were not dirty and torn, but as shiny as drops of tar. Plunging into the river, they ran knee-deep after the yacht in a splashing joyful dance, shrieking with excitement. Their mothers, alerted by the commotion, put down their baskets and watched, while the men, who had been poking around in the gardens behind their huts, dropped their sticks and ran toward the shiny apparition as well.

A Portuguese sailor named Miguel Arguirir was now at the helm of the *Wanderer*. He had traveled to the African coast before, and knew the Congo River as well as any white man could. But now, at his side, stood two muscular black men, each with tattoos that swept across their faces like blue spiderwebs, and teeth that had been filed to fearsome points. They had joined the *Wanderer* as soon as she entered the river, bringing their canoes softly against her side, slipping noiselessly over the rail. Arguirir knew them, and with a smile, handed them the wheel. Now the two Kroomen, as their tribe was named, would take the *Wanderer* the rest of the way up the river.

The first village they passed was soon replaced with another village, with more excited children splashing in the river, more little huts, more smoky fires, more goats and chickens. Then came another village, and another. After several hours, the *Wanderer* reached a point in the river where the banks disappeared, overtaken by mangroves, their branches set with white herons and the roots bent out of the water like knees, with the river eddying and swirling below. It was here, where the river ran raggedly between the shoals, that the *Wanderer* passed a number of wrecked ships—schooners and packet steamers, mostly, that had run aground. All that was left were their blackened ribs, protruding from the yellow mud, or an occasional bowsprit, festooned now with squawking birds.

At last the yacht arrived at a group of buildings set together in a clearing by the river. They had been built on pilings, and over the years the pilings had sunk unevenly into the mud, so that the buildings now leaned haphazardly against one another, as though they were a reflection in wavy water. This was Punta da Lenha, the trading center. It had been built nearly one hundred years earlier, a riverbank crossroads where Europeans could acquire elephant tusks, ivory, beeswax, gold dust, and, of course, the prime export of Africa—slaves. Since the traders were called "factors," the complex itself was called a "factory." As the *Wanderer* approached, Corrie wrote in the yacht's log: "Arrived at Punta da Lenha. Anchoring off the factory."

While they were still a few hundred yards away, Corrie unfolded his brass spyglass and scanned the factory. In the hot afternoon light, not a soul was seen, neither on the wharf nor in the buildings. But as the *Wanderer* drifted closer, a black merchant appeared on the wharf, followed by another, and then, like ants discovering a prize, a dozen more. Soon the wharf was alive with African salesmen. Some held elephant-hair necklaces up for examination; others offered red parrot feathers, antelope horns, and ivory bracelets. Parrots and monkeys, screaming at the end of their tethers, were lifted for examination as well, as were chickens, piglets, and goats.

Corrie and Farnum had barely absorbed this commotion when they saw a band of men heading toward them from the far side of the factory. They were the most desperate-looking knot of outcasts Corrie had ever seen, unwashed, unshaven, and dressed in coarse seamen's clothing. As they stormed onto the wharf, pushing past the merchants, they hailed the *Wanderer* in a swarm of accents—Portuguese, Spanish, Chinese, English, Dutch. Corrie would later learn that these men were sailors that had been put ashore when their slave ships had run aground—or, more likely, had been scuttled through the efforts of the British African Squadron.

Now these captains, pilots, navigators, slave drivers—pirates all of them, and experts in the traffic in slaves—rushed to the end of the pier, offering their services in whatever adventure the *Wanderer* would choose to pursue. With the cries from the merchants, the shouting of the pirates, the barking of dogs, the shrieks of the parrots and piglets, the waving of arms and the grotesque facial expressions of all kinds, what had been a pastoral watercolor moments earlier was transformed into bedlam.

As Corrie watched, a distinguished-looking man in a linen suit could be seen pushing his way through the crowd. Arguirir recognized him, and ordered a skiff put out from the yacht. Once the man was aboard, Arguirir introduced him to Corrie as Mr. Harrington, the chief agent of the factory. With a brief exchange of words, the two descended below deck to the lounge. It was only after an hour of serious negotiations that Harrington emerged again and was rowed back ashore.

At about ten that night, Corrie, Farnum, and Arguirir were rowed to the wharf. The place was not only perfectly quiet again but ghostly in the moonlight, which poured down so profusely that Corrie could see the hands of his silver pocket watch. A few minutes later, Harrington walked out of the shadows and, with a thin smile, shook hands all around. Then he ushered them off the wharf and into the factory. As they walked through the moonlight, Harrington explained that the factory was surrounded by hard clay walls, six feet high. Within those walls were two dozen houses and about the same number of warehouses. The warehouses contained elephant tusks, ebony, and even gold dust, ready for shipment overseas, as well as the merchandise that would be traded for slaves—mirrors, calico, rum, and, most prized of all, muskets and gunpowder.

In the old days, he continued, the slaves were kept within the walls of the factory as well. They were held in barracoons, corrals formed of trunks from the hardest trees, driven five feet into the ground, and clasped together by double ribbons of iron. The roofs were made of hardwood as well, and overlaid with a thick thatch of long and wiry grass. Escape was impossible, and, in any case, the barracoons were guarded by armed men.

The first factories were built one hundred years earlier by the English, the Dutch, the French, the Portuguese, and the Danes, Harrington continued. Every European monarch wanted to be in the business. That's why the factories were so strongly fortified with thick walls: The Europeans continually raided one another's barracoons. In any case, by the time the slave trade had been largely outlawed, in about 1800, some 30 million Africans had been shipped away in chains. But when the Europeans banned the slave trade, the barracoons had to be taken out of the factories and moved upriver. There, on remote islands, the barracoons stood, stocked with slaves. When the call came for a shipment, the appropriate number would be tossed into small boats and brought downriver. Finally, on remote stretches of beach, they would be herded again into temporary barracoons, often mere poles thrust into the sand, and then taken out to the awaiting ships. Meanwhile, the British would be patrolling the shoreline, hoping to snare the ships as they tried to make a break from the coast.

"It's all evolved into quite an elaborate game," Harrington said, stopping at a clearing. He pointed across the river to where a Royal Navy steamer was secured to a wharf, taking on coal. Not 500 yards away, the British kept their coaling station, he explained. Yes, and the Royal Navy very frequently rowed over to the wharf. They knew the names of the slave traders on the other side, and some of the slave traders even boasted openly of their operations. But there were rules to this game, he said. An empty ship—even one with the implements of the trade—was worthless. It would never produce a conviction in a New York courthouse. No, that wouldn't do. If this were a game of cat and mouse, which it was, he assured the men, one had to catch the mouse fully loaded. The ship's belly had to be filled with slaves.

There was another factor at play, as well. The British crews were paid a bounty for every African they retrieved from a slaver's hold. So, for them, there was no reason to hurry after an empty ship. One had to give it time, so that when the ship did break for the open ocean one could be reasonably sure that four hundred bodies or more were locked down beneath the hatches. "So that is why we live in such cordial proximity," he said with a dry laugh. "We are all waiting for the precise moment when the game begins."

With that, Harrington beckoned the group to follow him down a narrow path. Presently they arrived at a house, which looked as charmingly domestic as a cottage in the Cotswolds. Its thatched roof hung jauntily forward, with two window boxes filled with flowers, and a front door painted bright red. Harrington knocked on the door, and a young African woman, clothed in a flowing muslin gown, opened the door and beckoned them in. She escorted them silently into the main room, and, without a word, disappeared.

They were left alone, with the moonlight falling through a skylight in the roof. Upon closer examination, Corrie realized that the skylight was from a ship and had once brought light into the salon. The heavy beam that ran the length of the roofline, meanwhile, was also from a ship, he realized. Adze marks and bolt holes were apparent in the tightly grained oak. The ribs of the ship, meanwhile, had been adapted to run dramatically down the walls to the wainscoting. A figurehead, from some long-lost vessel, meanwhile, had found a place in the corner. In the pale light it revealed itself as a gauzily clothed young lady, with flowing curls and a slight smile on her painted lips, her eyes forever fixed on the horizon.

It was only after a moment that the men saw a figure, sitting at a desk in the corner, writing. A great brass oil lamp, plucked no doubt from some sunken schooner or brig, shed light on his papers. When he sensed, with some satisfaction, that he had been found in the dim room, the man arose stiffly and hobbled around the desk. His coat was of an old-fashioned cut, scarlet, and laced with silver and gold. He also wore a velvet nightcap, from which his hair fell straight down to his shoulders. One eye was blue, and the other, as Corrie noted with a start, was as white and cold as marble. He was Captain Snelgrave, he said, offering his hand, and he represented the great slave-trading firm of Jose da Costa Lima Viana, 158 Pearl Street, Manhattan.

Noting his guest's interest in the house, Snelgrave explained that the timbers had come from a variety of sailing ships, wrecked on the bars or confiscated and then scuttled by the British. Some of the wood was hard pine from Georgia, he said, caressing the figurehead. Then there was hackamatack from Aroostook County, Maine, he said, pointing to the ceiling beam, as well as golden oak from upstate New York. Snelgrave motioned his guests through a door to the patio behind the house. There, he proudly pointed out several brass tubs in which he was growing eucharis lilies. He lifted the heads of several of the flowers, as though he were stroking the chins of kittens, so that his guests could admire them.

"You must live every day fully in the tropics," he said with a hollow laugh, motioning his guests to chairs positioned in a half circle under a flowering tree. "Otherwise, the African fevers will take your pleasures away." When one of the visitors chuckled, Snelgrave snapped his head up unpleasantly. "Aye, it's the truth!" he said harshly. "As soon as they arrive, most white men will fall ill. If they are to die, it will be in eight days. If they survive that, they can live for a few more years." Venereal distemper kills slowly, Snelgrave explained. Cholic, faster. Yellow fever takes ten days. Snelgrave hesitated, and then unbuttoned his shirt. "A hare's belt," he declared, rubbing the dark fur pressing against his flesh. "I wear it against me stomach to improve me digestion." Three spoonfuls of quick lime in the water casks kills the Guinea worms, he said. Sarsaparilla kills the venereal disease. "Of course," he said, with a flash of self-pity, "nothing could save me eye.

"I was aboard a brig, I won't mention her name," he said, his good eye twitching from face to face. "She was two-hundred tons burden, and we came into Bonny Town. That's on the Bonny River on the coast. We had taken on a hundred sixty Negroes and were sailing for Guadeloupe." Snelgrave explained that the captain had ordered the Africans brought up to the forecastle for some air. No sooner had they arrived on deck than some of them began to leap over the gunwale into the sea. The crew struggled to hold additional Africans from the same fate, driving them back with handspikes and cutlasses. To punish them, the captain shot three of them dead and ordered three more hanged. Then he forced all the others into confinement in the lower hold. But this was to create an even larger problem. Stuffed down in the hold, the Negroes began to suffer from a disease called ophthalmia, which can dim the vision, cause temporary, or even complete blindness.

When the disease was recognized, the captain ordered the worst of the sufferers to be brought up to the deck and treated by the surgeon. But the disease only got worse. By the third day, all of the slaves, the captain, the mate, and the surgeon had gone blind. Out of twenty-two crewmen, there was only one man with the eyesight left to man the ship. He gave the orders and the others stumbled to their stations as best they could. Then, just as a storm blew up, swirling the ship and tossing it violently, his vision faded, too. As the sails were blown to tatters and the ship splintered beneath thundering waves, some men were cursing, some praying, and some, having gone mad, were singing, Snelgrave had said.

"We sailed on, and then, one day when the sea was flat, we heard the cry of a human voice in the distance," Snelgrave continued. "It was another ship. She hove to nearby and cried that she was desperately short of provisions. We shouted back that we had plenty of food and water, and dollars as well. But we need men: The entire ship is infected with opthalmia and we are stone-blind. At that, there was silence. Then we cocked our ears and listened. There was nothing." His one eye searched those of his guests. "The other ship had thrown her wheel and sailed off."

The misery that descended on the blinded crew almost killed them, he explained. They spent another week or so floating aimlessly at sea. But eventually some of the men regained their vision, and managed to sail the ship to Guadeloupe. The surgeon and eleven more were irretrievably blind. Five were able to see, but dimly. Snelgrave and four others had lost one eye. Of the Negroes, thirty-nine were completely blind, and the captain ordered them cast into the sea.

By the time Snelgrave had finished his story, the blood had risen in his face, perhaps in response to the painful tale, perhaps driven by a touch of the African fever he so feared. Snelgrave gazed at the floor. When he looked up again, he had regained some of his composure. "In any case, *gentlemen,* you have come on some business that we should well discuss."

By the time the meeting had concluded, Corrie had given Snelgrave an order for five hundred Africans, to be brought down to the beaches from the barracoons higher up on the Congo. After some haggling, the price was placed at $50 each, payable in rum, gunpowder, cutlasses, and muskets. Once those materials were discreetly taken off the *Wanderer,* said Snelgrave, it would do Corrie well to sail away for a week, while the captives were rounded up and sent downriver. One other thing, Snelgrave advised, as he walked his guests to the door. It would be well if his name were not repeated to others. In fact, it would be well if they were never to meet again.

The following day, Corrie ordered the *Wanderer* back to sea. Once she had cleared the mouth of the Congo, she sailed north along the African coast. On the third day she came to Nkomi Lagoon, about 300 miles north of the Congo, and dropped anchor. Soon two long canoes were seen approaching, each with four muscular Kroomen working the paddles. Corrie, Farnum, and Arguirir got into the canoes, settling themselves into the reed mats, and were whisked away.

For the next three days the party went up the Ogowe, a slithering river that runs 160 miles into Africa, ending in rapids and waterfalls. With each exertion against the paddles, the Kroomen sent the canoes forward and the tufted papyrus along the banks waving gently. Leaning into their work, the Kroomen sang songs that were as rich and rhythmic as the muddy river water they crossed.

For the next few days the party visited native villages. In one, the natives were not only naked but painted vermillion. In another, the chief appeared in a white robe, with a headdress of blue cotton and golden silk. He sat on a wooden throne. Velvet umbrellas on long handles provided shade, and silk flags fluttered above. The chief explained that he had sold thousands of slaves to the Europeans, and indeed, just as he said this, a koffle of new slaves, bound in chains, arrived for his inspection. He would take a few for himself, he explained, and would sell the others to slavers down the river.

The most remarkable leader, though, was the chief of the Achango tribe. His throne was made of leopard skins and mirrors. He wore the frock coat of a British naval officer, with some of the buttons missing. Across his bare chest was a necklace strung with sixteen gorilla teeth. His entourage was similarly attired. At the meeting, Corrie wore knee breeches, a cream-colored jacket, and topping it all, a flat-brimmed straw boater. Farnum wore buckskin and fringe. There was a moment's hesitation, on both sides, as each paused to appraise the other's attire.

After a week of exploration, Corrie, Farnum and the others reboarded the *Wanderer* and headed back down the coast. When the yacht was still several miles from the mouth of the Congo, one of the Kroomen in the rigging called down that a ship was visible on the horizon. As they drew nearer, the Krooman added that she flew the ensign of the British Royal Navy. In fact, she was the HMS *Medusa,* the same steam cruiser that had been across the river from the *Wanderer* when she had moored at the factory. Now she was lying at anchor just inside the mouth of the Congo, at a place called Medora Creek, watching for suspicious activity.

As the *Wanderer* drew nearer, Corrie climbed into the rigging and unfolded his spyglass. Drawing nearer he could make out her bristling guns and even the sparkling golden epaulets of the British commander aboard. The British commander had his spyglass deployed as well, and was curiously watching the approach of this elegant yacht, with the New York Yacht Club burgee flying above. As the two ships converged, Corrie put the captain's trumpet to his lips and called out greetings. Then he ordered Brown, who had retaken the wheel, to cut an arc around the *Medusa*. He did so, and, bringing her into the wind, dropped anchor less than a hundred feet away. The anchor chain had not yet finished rattling through the hawse pipe when Corrie issued an invitation to the British commander to come aboard.

After months of tedious Africa duty, the British were more than happy to explore this luxury yacht, and their enthusiasm grew even greater when they climbed aboard and into the hospitality accorded by Corrie and Farnum. After a few introductory drinks on the deck, where basket chairs had been arranged and cocktails served beneath a red-and-white striped awning, Corrie asked the Brits if they would care to return later that evening to dine. That, of course, was gladly accepted.

Just after sunset, when the blistering equatorial sun had finally extinguished itself, the first of two boats filled with the British officers made their way over to *Wanderer*. By then the piglets had been slaughtered, basted, and prepared, the vegetables cooked, and more important, the selection of wines arranged and decanted to breathe. This was all spread in the salon down below, upon the crispest white linens the British officers had seen in years. Later that night, as the delighted guests ascended the stairs, champagne and cigars were offered on the deck.

By now, they were comrades-in-arms, so much so that at one point, Farnum boldly suggested that perhaps they ought to examine the *Wanderer,* to make sure she was not a slaver. For an instant, his words hung in the air—and then the party burst into laughter.

On September 15, 1858, the commander of the *Medusa* sent a terse note to the British Secretary to the Admiralty, which, for obvious reasons, neglected to reveal the amount of entertaining that had gone on:

> *In compliance with Section 6 of the Slave Instructions, I have the honour to report that, on the afternoon of this day, while at anchor off Medora Creek, in the River Congo, I saw a very taut fore-and-aft schooner coming up the river under American colours, and thinking her suspicious I caused her to be boarded by Lieutenant Nott; she proved to be the "Wanderer" yacht, and as her papers were reported to be correct, I did not interfere with her voyage*

up the river. Her papers were freely shown, and there was no com-
plaint made on account of the visit.

After a week of entertaining the British officers, the *Wanderer* sailed
farther into the river for further entertainments. The *Wanderer's* log for
September 18, 1858 noted a bash in which, "all the white inhabitants of
the place" were invited. Indeed, all the expatriates turned out for a little
entertainment and a gourmet meal: British citizens who had received royal
franchises for various commercial endeavors, Portuguese palm oil traders,
American businessmen, Germans, Poles, Russians, French, Dutch, Danes,
Portuguese, and Spanish—a great international community that, in need
of diversion in the sullen tropics, rowed eagerly toward the bright lights of
the *Wanderer.*

And there she lay, a few hundred yards off in the Congo, resting
serenely beneath the evening sky, lit like a lantern, the crew sent into
town to get drunk, house servants brought from town to serve canapés
and champagne, skiffs skimming back and forth from shore, bringing
the ladies, dressed in silk and satin, fanning themselves, enjoying some
break from the dullness and emptiness of their lives. To the party
guests, Farnum was quite the attraction, loud, boastful, and full of stories of guerrilla wars and Wild West adventures. But Corrie was the
most attractive, a celebrity in their midst, the golden orb that they fluttered around like moths.

A few days later, while anchored again by the *Medusa,* Corrie and Farnum were surprised to find a racing yacht, very much like the *Wanderer*
in her hull and sail, approaching them. She was the *Margate,* a 62-foot
pleasure yacht, with clean lines, a sharp bow, and a sternpost that was
raked sharply to reduce her tonnage. The vessel's owner was an acquaintance of the marquis of Anglesey, who, they would later learn, had
founded the Royal Yacht Squadron in 1815. Now, as he wheeled the
Margate into close proximity to the *Wanderer* and put the captain's
trumpet to his lips, the owner archly suggested a race between the two
yachts—a contest that might help clear up the misconception that the
British loss six years earlier to the *America* was anything but bloody bad

luck. With the officers of the *Medusa* offering their assistance in the race, Corrie agreed; the race between the *Wanderer* and the British challenger would begin at 10 A.M.

The following morning ten guests joined the *Wanderer* for the race, while the *Margate* took on two of the *Medusa's* officers. As the breeze freshened from the west, the two yachts swung their bows windward, their big sails luffing noisily. Beneath them, the guests chatted excitedly, while the sailors, positioning themselves to pull anchor and haul sail, prepared for the contest ahead. With a roar from one of the *Medusa's* cannons, the race began. The *Wanderer* quickly sailed up to her anchor. Then Brown, who was at the helm, threw the wheel over. The *Wanderer* came hard off the wind, the jib filled, and like a spring released, she leapt forward. Heeling 15 degrees to leeward, her narrow bow sliced effortlessly through the water, exactly as Rowland had designed her to perform.

The *Margate* had a good start, too, but as the *Wanderer* passed the first 500 yards downwind, her lead against the British yacht widened by 20 feet. Another 300 yards and the *Wanderer* seemed to gain even more speed and more distance. Gazing through his spyglass, the captain of the *Medusa* groaned. He could see why the *Wanderer* had taken the lead: The *Wanderer* stood up to the wind, balanced and strong; the *Margate* heeled nervously at every gust, exposing her shiny copper hull like an embarrassing undergarment.

By the time the two yachts had come about and were heading for the finish line, the cheering of the limeys had stopped, replaced and overwhelmed by the visitors aboard who were cheering the *Wanderer*. That night, Corrie, exuberant at the day's events, scrawled into the logbook: "September 26: Gave the Schooner Margate a trial, and passed her like the wind."

9

OUT OF AFRICA

IN THE late afternoon in the sun-baked Portuguese town of Luanda, 300 miles south of the Congo, Thomas J. Conover reclined on the back veranda of his residence in his underwear, flicking pieces of an orange toward a gray parrot, which, like a pirate, swaggered back and forth across the wooden deck, bending its knees stiffly to retrieve pieces of the fresh fruit. The parrot was an old bird, and much of its plumage had molted away to bare skin.

The same could be said of Conover. His career in the U.S. Navy had begun when he was sixteen. By the following year, 1812, he was aboard the USS *Constitution* as it did battle with the British warship *Garrette*—the two ships blasting each other to pieces with their cannons until they were at such close quarters that the men seized their muskets and began firing point-blank at each other, the smoke burning their eyes and their blood slicking the decks. That was war! That was a battle!

And that was a long time ago. Now an arthritic sixty-one, Conover had refused to retire from the service; and so he was given the kind of sinecure that stubborn men of his rank could expect: He was named commander of America's African Squadron. The position offered no glory and no recognition—and only the surety that once that posting was over, his career was irretrievably done.

The ship that Conover commanded, the *Cumberland,* was similarly on the edge of obsolescence. She was built in 1825, and in her youth had been a handsome square-rigger, serving in the Mediterranean and on the coast of Mexico during the Mexican war. In recognition, she was named the flagship of the Home Squadron in 1846–48, and was commanded by none other than the famous commodore Matthew Perry. But by 1855, aging, leaky, and increasingly outpaced by the new generation of steam-powered warships, she was converted from a relatively fast-sailing frigate to a sloop of war. That meant she was loaded up with fifty heavy cannons, and following that, was sent to the coast of Africa as the flagship of America's African Squadron.

One thing was clear: At 1,700 tons and a draft of 21 feet—a massive mother ship—she was poorly suited for apprehending slavers. She drew too much water to cruise near the shore or up the rivers. She was too slow. Furthermore, there was no reason for her to carry fifty guns other than to fulfill the stipulations of the African Squadron agreement with Britain (for a minimum of eighty guns off the coast per nation) with as little effort and as few cruisers committed as possible. One could imagine a hornets' nest of fast, shallow-keeled cruisers, each with a few stinging cannons aboard to stop the slavers. But that's not what the American government sent to the African coast in the form of the *Cumberland.*

Together, the old ship and the old commander worked the slave coast gingerly. Between August 1858 and mid-August 1859, when the slave trade was booming, Conover ordered the *Cumberland* to take just one leisurely cruise down the African coastline, a 3000-mile trip from Porto Praia (the capital of the Verdes Islands in the North Hemisphere) to Luanda in the South.

Then, after relaxing in his Italianate villa in Luanda for a few weeks (with his gray parrot), Conover ordered a swift return cruise to the Verdes Islands, and from there, a quick trip back home to Portsmouth, New Hampshire. Not only was the journey swift, but Conover ordered the *Cumberland* to stay several miles offshore throughout most of the voyage, in order to avoid any contact with African fevers. The *Cumberland* may have spent a year "patrolling" the African coast in 1858–1859, then, but in truth, she had only been in a position to intercept slave ships for about twenty-six days.

On that late summer afternoon of September 24, 1857, the merchant ship *Sea View* came into Luanda, having sailed nine days earlier from the Congo. As soon as the ship had moored, the captain sprinted into a skiff and made his way to Conover's quarters. Knocking excitedly on the door, which was finally opened by Conover, the captain exclaimed that he had seen two suspicious ships slinking around the mouth of the Congo, one the *Kate Helen,* a suspected slaver, and the other a yacht called the *Wanderer.* Conover listened with feigned interest, thanked the captain, and then returned to his parrot. A full week passed before he finally wrote a note to one of his subordinates, Benjamin J. Totten, commander of the USS *Vincennes,* ordering him to look into the matter.

If any ship were less suited for snagging slavers than the *Cumberland,* it was the venerable *Vincennes.* She had been built at the Brooklyn Navy Yard in 1826 and had notched up quite a career. Sent from New York into the Pacific in 1833, she continued on to circumnavigate the world, the first U.S. Navy ship ever to do so. In 1840, she could be found on a scientific exploration in Antarctica. Next she visited the South Pacific, Hawaii, then Oregon's Columbia River, the coast of California, Wake Island, the Philippines, and South Africa.

By that time she had been around the world three times. She then sailed into Tokyo Bay, attempting to pay a diplomatic call on the reclusive Japanese in 1846—the first U.S. Navy ship to sail into Japanese waters—and ended her travels sailing the South Pacific before returning to New York. By then she leaked, she groaned, and her sails hung so limp that she needed a pasture to be let out into. And so, in 1858, this distinguished old lady, with 150 men and eighteen worn cannons, was sent to the African Squadron.

But a worse fate than that awaited her, for she fell under the command of perhaps one of the weakest commanders in the U.S. Navy of the time, the mercurial and bulbous-nosed Commander Benjamin J. Totten. Commander was a loose term for Totten's abilities, for the officer was a petty tyrant. In one incident, Totten had one of his subordinates court-martialed for a minor offense. When Totten's superiors had the nerve to acquit the man, Totten put him in irons anyway. In another incident he argued with his gunnery officer over the proper way to fire shells. On the same cruise, two more of his officers were suspended for "insubordination." Following that indiscretion, Totten was reprimanded by his superiors for his "oversensitivity," but it made no difference. He distrusted his crew—and they hated him in return.

Totten hated the British as well, especially when commanders of the Royal Navy had the cheek to suggest how he should combat the slave trade. In one incident, Totten was enjoying his shore leave in Luanda when the British commodore urged him to take immediate action against four possible slavers in Ambriz. When Totten refused, the British foreign office lodged a formal protest with the American navy against Totten, the only American naval officer ever formally denounced by the British government for intentional negligence in suppressing the slave trade.

It was to the dubious team of Totten and the *Vincennes,* then, that Conover turned over the cases of the *Kate Helen* and the *Wanderer.* "As soon as your ship is in all respects ready for sea," Conover wrote to Totten, "you will proceed to cruise on this coast, conferring yourself, so far as the service upon which you are employed will permit, to that portion of it embraced between the Equator and to St. Paul de Loando. You will proceed from there to Ambriz, thence up the line of the Coast, touching at every slave mart and commercial place within the limits above mentioned, searching carefully for American vessels engaged in the slave trade, examining closely the Congo River and its immediate neighborhood, and, by cruising backward and forward, striving to deceive the slave dealers and to elude the vigilance of their agents and spies."

Totten responded to the message with no great alacrity. It was a full seven days later—the crew of the *Vincennes* lounging on deck in the meantime, crafting knives out of scrap metal—that the *Vincennes* left port. She sailed north a few miles to the Bay of Ambriz, scanned the coastline for slavers, and then sailed onward a few more miles to the mouth of the Congo. Seeing nothing there of interest, she continued about 25 miles north, arriving at Kabinda on October 14.

But before Totten could find either the *Wanderer* or the *Kate Helen* himself, he received some disturbing news: British sailors from the HMS *Viper* had boarded the *Kate Helen,* even though she was flying an American flag. To be sure, the British merely checked her papers and glanced around;

they didn't order the crew to open the hatches or lead them down below deck for an examination. But at the mere mention of the "visitation" of an American vessel, Totten's face turned scarlet. After all, the War of 1812 was fought to deter the British from high-handedly searching American ships on the high seas. Rather than continue his own pursuit of the *Kate Helen,* or the *Wanderer,* then, Totten decided to pay a little visit to the captain of the *Viper.*

On the morning of October 14, Totten came across the British ship. Boarding the vessel, after his request to do so was granted, Totten exchanged dry greetings with the commander, a Lieutenant Hodgkinson, and asked the Englishman if he had any particular news to share. Hodgkinson replied that he had nothing of significance to communicate. Totten then asked to see the ship's log. Hodgkinson led Totten to the cabin and presented his books. The log confirmed that the *Viper* had indeed "visited" the "*Kate Helen,*" but offered no further details. Satisfied that the British had "visited" the American ship, which was permitted under British-American accords, but had not searched her, which was not, Totten returned to his ship.

As the afternoon wore on, Totten must have felt great satisfaction. He had demanded the proper respect from the British commander, and he had received it. But just as he was gloating over his little victory, the watchman in the top rigging called out that there were some men on the coastline ahead, apparently marooned. Totten picked up his spyglass, and seeing them waving their arms frantically, ordered a boat put out to retrieve them. When the castaways were brought aboard, they told a tale that sent Totten into a rage.

According to the ragged survivors, they were the crew of the American brig *Rufus Soule.* Two days earlier, they said, their ship had been boarded suddenly by British sailors from the *Viper.* The commander, a Mr. Hodgkinson, said that he had received intelligence from his spies ashore that the *Rufus Soule* was awaiting a shipment of slaves held in a barracoon near a promontory called Banda Point. The Americans denied it, but the British commander was unmoved: He gave them a half hour to decide whether to keep the American flag fluttering above, which meant that they would be turned over to the American Squadron and face a possible hanging—or cut the Stars and Stripes loose and submit to British justice, which in this case was the immediate confiscation of their ship.

The captain of the *Rufus Soule* knew he'd been caught. And so he tossed his U.S. paperwork, weighted with iron, over the rail and ordered the American flag drawn down. At that, the British sailors climbed aboard and pulled off the hatches. Down below they found what they had suspected all along: chains, cooking pots, wooden bowls, and big water tanks. Since the *Rufus Soule* was old and unseaworthy, Lieutenant Hodgkinson decided she wasn't worth towing back into port. Instead he ordered her towed a few hundred yards away, and then commanded his gunners to have at her. The crew was dumped onto the beach, left to watch their ship belch flames and black smoke, and then sink, in a cloud of steam, into the sea.

When he heard this, Totten slammed his spyglass across the deck railing, knocking the lens into the ocean, and hurried down to his writing desk. All thoughts of the *Kate Helen* and the *Wanderer* were obscured in a reheated boil of righteous indignation. "Sir," Totten wrote to Conover, his quill scratching angrily across the paper, "I have the honor to forward the accompanying papers in relation to the capture and destruction by fire of an American brig, the Rufus Soule, on the evening of the 11th and the morning of the 12th." Totten explained that the commander of the *Viper* had not only desecrated the American flag in boarding the *Rufus Soule* but had insulted a fellow officer of the African Squadron—himself—through his cursed lying.

He dipped his quill again. "It presents to my mind a case of such gross outrage on the American flag, and irregular conduct on the part of the command of the English cruiser," Totten continued, "that I feel it my duty to return at once towards Luanda, in hope of meeting with you or falling in with the Steamer Viper (her commander having informed me that she was bound directly for that place) to ask a statement of explanation from him."

What right did the British have in burning a ship without condemnation by a proper tribunal? Totten spluttered on. What right did the *Viper* have in tossing the American crew into a "native town, in a destitute condition, with all the horrors of coast fever and starvation before them?" Whatever the answers, Totten concluded, this was an incident of great international ramifications. His first duty, then, was to chase the *Viper* down.

While Totten was dealing with the *Viper,* Corrie and Farnum were still engaged in entertaining the British from the HMS *Medusa.* After several weeks of dinners and drinks, Corrie was beginning to wonder if the British ship would ever leave them, and their liquor cabinet, alone. But then, one night, without notice, the *Medusa* slipped away on business. Relieved, Corrie immediately ordered Brown to raise the sails and point the *Wanderer* down the coast to the town of Benguela. "After eight days beating against the wind and current," the log read on October 4, "we have arrived at Benguela." It was to be the last entry into the logbook.

At Benguela, signals were exchanged with the shore, and a few days later the *Wanderer* dropped another twenty miles south to a place called Mangue Grande. These were treacherous waters, uncharted, and plagued with sandbars. Corrie ordered the anchors dropped at twenty fathoms. Taking a spyglass aloft, Farnum climbed to the foretop and scanned the dense thicket that lay about 200 yards behind the tawny beach. Brown, meanwhile, lit the brass oil lamp, and swung it, three times to port, three times to starboard.

Within seconds a light was seen from the edge of the beach, casting the same signal. The gray light of morning soon revealed activity on the beach. A long canoe was being launched into the breakers. It rose nearly vertically upon the first big wave, but then, through some miracle, climbed over the crest of that roller, and then a second and third, and began to make its way out toward the *Wanderer.* Farnum took a green flag and handed it to the mate, who ran it up the signal halyards. From the shore a green flag waved in reply.

During the time in which the *Wanderer* had been entertaining its guests, and while Corrie and Farnum were visiting the African tribes, Arguirir had been hard at work. Following the meeting with Captain Snelgrave, Arguirir and a physician from the factory took a steamer 30 miles up the Congo, and then continued by canoe up a smaller tributary deep into the jungle. There, on an island, thousands of subdued Africans had been brought together in a marketplace. Some of them were Congo tribesmen from the surrounding areas. Others had been brought 400 miles down the

Congo. Some were even from Bangui, a thousand miles away. Some of the captives were prisoners of war.

Through their internal wars, the Dahomans, Ashantees, Foulahs, Mandignoes, and Bambarras had kept the slave markets well supplied. The Chokwe were also prolific slave traders, using their beeswax and ivory to buy arms, and their arms to obtain slaves in their frequent battles with the Lunda empire. Not all the slaves were war trophies. Many were merely kidnapped by gampsias, slave hunters, as they wandered from their villages or worked in their fields. The Vai, Kissi, Kruy, Bassa, and Glebo tribesmen were particularly renowned for this.

As Arguirir and his party arrived at the island, they were taken into the barracoons. Here bamboo stakes had been driven into the ground, and from these the captives hung from their wrists. Some of the slaves moaned in pain, a few yelled in madness. But mostly, there was stunned silence. Any words spoken were usually in Portuguese. In some parts of Africa, the Arab slave traders ruled. But here, in the Congo basin, where the Portuguese had been slaving since the mid-fifteenth century, they were the masters of the trade.

An hour later, the slave fair began. Other traders had arrived, among them a Dutch trader, a thin Spaniard, and some African chiefs. The slaves were led out, completely naked, their dejected eyes on the ground. At the command of their handler, they were made to jump, squat, and hold their breath. Arguirir's trained eye rejected most of them immediately. But when he saw one of interest he nodded to the physician, who stepped forward and ran a practiced hand over the subject's body, squeezing his joints and muscles, twisting his arms and legs, probing his privates with a wooden tool. The mouth and teeth were most important though, since they not only disclosed health but age.

The Portuguese trader brought out his worst specimens first. Some had scrofula, others had dysentery, and some were insane. He had tried to pretty them up, shaving their bodies to remove the gray hairs, applying palm oil to give their bodies the sheen of good health. Arguirir shook his head as each approached, and with scowling eyes and a clucking tongue rejected dozens of them. Finally, the trader was forced to bring out the others. Now Arguirir saw the youth, the firm muscles, the clear and steady eyes that made him want to buy.

The five hundred that Arguirir chose were taken to a fire, and laid on their backs. A branding iron with the letter *W* was heated and pressed into their flesh just below the shoulder. Their heads were scraped clean and their bodies scrubbed with sand and water. They were transported downriver in a small schooner, some chained to the mast and others piled one upon another below deck. Five days later, the surviving captives reached the sea.

As the canoe from shore closed in on the *Wanderer,* Corrie could see that she was about 25 feet long, with a 6-foot beam. She was built strongly, for ocean travel, with bamboo braces preventing her sides from staving in when her nose plunged deeply into the surf. Six powerfully built blacks—Kroomen like those who had guided the *Wanderer* into the factory—balanced themselves on the gunwales, propelling the canoe forward with powerful thrusts of their paddles. At the bow was a smaller African, who held a piece of red cloth aloft, bringing it down rhythmically so that the Kroomen paddled together. Another African sat in the stern, steering with a long paddle and instructing the paddlers to take a particular wave—or to lie on their paddles and let the roller pass.

The Kroomen were not only pilots and boaters. Both the British and the American navies found them to be superb hands aboard ships of all kinds, especially in the steamy tropics. And the slave traders, likewise, found them adept at handling slaves on the trip to the ship, and even afterward, on the voyage to foreign lands. Now the Kroomen came alongside the *Wanderer* and scampered up the side ladder. First they demanded biscuits and rum. Having consumed that, they ran happily down below deck.

The fine Belgian carpets had already been rolled up and stowed; the fine china and silver and leather-bound books carefully packed away. Now the Kroomen and the Portuguese swiftly secured wooden braces against the ships ribs, and then laid down a second deck beneath the *Wanderer*'s main deck. The slave deck had been expertly prefigured, for the planks fell precisely into place. Corrie went below, and surveying the new configuration, remarked to Farnum that his elegant *Wanderer* was at last a real slaver.

When they went back on deck, Corrie opened his spyglass. From out of the brush, a thin line of Africans was snaking into the heavy surf toward the boats, driven forward by Kroomen brandishing whips and clubs. It took immense strength and skill to keep the canoes facing into the rollers, so that they wouldn't turn sideways, and, full of passengers, suddenly capsize.

When the first canoe full of captives reached the *Wanderer,* they were hauled up by the Portuguese sailors and then hurried down the ladderway to the slave deck below. Here, the first captive in was made to lie on his side on the planking, head to windward facing the bow, with his knees drawn slightly toward his chin. Another was placed in so that his chest touched the other's back, with his knees at the same angle. And so it went, one after another.

Some slavers were "loose packers," who believed in giving the captives more room, so that more would live to be sold profitably at the end of the voyage. Others were "tight packers," who argued that regardless of the increased deaths, more bodies would provide more profits. In the best of the slave ships, each captive was given the amount of space they would have in a coffin—about 16 inches in width, 32 inches in height, and 5 feet 11 inches in length.

But the *Wanderer* conspirators were greedy. They set the 487 as if they were spoons in the available space, allowing 12 inches of width, 18 inches in height and less than 5 feet in length per person. Given the choice, they had chosen to be the cruelest of the cruel.

The last canoe full of captives had not yet reached the *Wanderer* when one of the Kroomen spotted a ship on the horizon, fast approaching. Corrie swung his glass around and saw her topsails. She was a brig of some sort. Corrie was taking no chances. He ordered Brown to push back the last canoe, hove anchor, and sail. As it turned out, the approaching ship was the *Vincennes,* no longer seeking the *Wanderer* or the *Kate Helen,* but in hot pursuit of the *Viper.*

Totten was also surprised. Here was this pleasure yacht, flying the New York Yacht Club pennant, with every bit of canvas crowded on, making her way seaward with haste. Not only that: He had spied a canoe hastily departing her side, making its way back to shore. Collapsing his spyglass with a quick movement, Totten ordered his men to set more canvas. Then he turned to his chief gunner and told him to prepare the 32-pounders to fire.

Aboard the *Wanderer,* Corrie and Farnum watched with increasing horror as the *Vincennes* approached, blocking the *Wanderer*'s path of escape. They began to wonder if they had been tracked by the British all along, who then alerted the Americans. Whatever the case, the taut belly of the *Wanderer* was now full of contraband. Under the terms of the law of 1820, they were pirates. There was no turning back now, and no surrendering.

Despite the general incompetence of the American African Squadron, Corrie knew they had had a few stunning successes. A few years earlier the USS *Porpoise,* a fully rigged brig of 130 tons, carrying eight 24-pound carronades and two long-barreled chaser guns, was cruising off the coast of Liberia when it received information—gained by passing a bottle of rum and some beads to a few natives ashore—that two slavers were anchored up the Little Bonny River and were ready to sail. With this information, the commander of the *Porpoise* positioned the vessel a few miles offshore, so that the slavers would not have the opportunity to turn around and run back for the coast.

The next day, at dawn, a Krooman in the rigging of the American cruiser spotted the approaching topsails of the slave ship. The captain of the *Porpoise* immediately set his course to intersect with the pirates. By now the slavers had seen the *Porpoise* as well, however, and began to take evasive action. Since the slaver was the faster ship she pulled away. But when the winds suddenly died, the *Porpoise* was able to close the gap.

Now the captain ordered his gunners to start firing the ship's long-barreled 14-pounder. Several shots went through the slaver's sails, but no spars or ropes were cut. Then, when all seemed lost, a long shot severed the slaver's peak halyards. The gaff and the gaff-topsail toppled down onto the deck. Finally, the Americans were able to board the ship, and put a pistol to the head of the slave captain. Finally surrendering, the slave captain asked permission to retrieve his papers from below. The request was denied, fortunately: In a locker below the officers found two open kegs of powder, with which, no doubt, the Spaniard would have blown up the vessel and everyone aboard.

Now, as the *Vincennes* gained on the *Wanderer,* Corrie wondered if he would suffer a similar fate. Survival called for a desperate maneuver, he decided—to run as close as possible to the wind and cut either directly before the bow of the intercepting *Vincennes* or, with a last-minute nudge of the wheel, directly to her stern.

The *Wanderer* was flying windward, the sails pulled taut, the rail close to the waterline. In response, Totten ordered the 32-pounders rolled inboard and the gunports shut, so that he could give the *Vincennes* better trim. The two were now on a direct collision course. Totten no longer needed his glass to see Corrie and Farnum gripping the lee rail. The gap between them narrowed to 500 feet.

At 300 feet from impact, Brown, at the wheel, pulled the *Wanderer's* nose even closer to the wind. There, at the point where any other yacht would have fallen into irons, the nautical equivalent of a nervous break-down, with sails luffing madly and the boom shuttering across the deck, the *Wanderer* leaped forward. A collision was moments away. Totten's mouth fell open. Corrie closed his eyes. But in that instant, the *Wanderer* crossed the foaming bow of the *Vincennes,* clearing her by no more than 50 feet.

One of the officers aboard the *Vincennes* later told the *New York Times* that a cannon shot from the *Vincennes* could have "arrested the pursued in her heady flight," but that the men "were too astonished by what they were seeing to react." Indeed, one of the old salts on the *Vincennes* would never stop telling the story: The afternoon the mystery yacht—flying the New York Yacht Club pennant—raced within seconds of a collision with the 703-ton warship. "That cussed fella must ha' laid hisself within two pints of the wind," he told the newspapers later. "Sich sailin' beats old Nick hisself!"

Even if Totten had realized that the passing yacht was a slaver, he wouldn't have chased her: He had a more important mission to pursue—finding the *Viper* and giving Lieutenant Hodgkinson a piece of his mind.

———

By the time the *Wanderer* had escaped the *Vincennes*, the sun was setting. The crew, exhausted, locked down the hatches. That night they
could hear the Africans moaning in their cramped coffin. The next
morning two of the Portuguese crewmen descended into the slave deck
below. The hatch vents had been set with wind sails, which funneled air
to the captives below. But they had not been able to offset the heat of
487 bodies. In the twilight below, they found the captives panting for
air. Six of them were dead, and their bodies had to be brought out and
thrown over the rail.

Following that, the captives were brought up, in groups of fifty, to
eat. The men were sent to the main deck and the forecastle. The women
would eat upon the quarterdeck, and the boys and girls upon the poop
deck. Each received a bowl of hot corn pudding and two sea biscuits.
They remained on deck for about an hour, and then were put below
again. In the afternoon, the procedure was repeated.

On the third day, an awning was spread over the main deck, and the
slaves were permitted to lounge beneath it for several hours. A tambourine and drum were brought out as well, and the captives were encouraged to unbend their limbs and dance. On the morning of the
fourth day, the crew brought the head-pump on deck, and allowed the
Africans to wash themselves from head to foot with cool seawater. This
routine continued, and for several days it seemed that the voyage across
the Atlantic would go unusually well.

But on the tenth day, the steady breezes stopped completely. High
above, cirrus clouds spread, forming a mackerel skin that augured
stormy weather. Brown ordered the crew to furl the topsails and
deep-reef the main and foresails. When the rain arrived, it came
down as hard as musket balls. Lightning exploded from two and three
directions at once, thunder rolled across the sky, and a cold wind
from starboard swept the ship. All night long she pitched and rolled,
the sea foaming over the decks. Brown ordered the hatches shut tight
and even the louvered vents covered with canvas. In his cabin, with
the lantern swinging before his eyes, Corrie could hear the Africans
screaming as they struggled again for air. The next morning, Corrie ordered the hatches opened. The wretchedness and smell were

beyond description. Down below, in a tangled mass, were the bodies. The motion of the ship had rubbed the skin from their limbs. The dead were chained to the living. More bodies went over the rail that day.

From then on, tensions grew aboard the ship. Corrie said he wanted the hatches left open. Arguirir argued it was a dangerous move. One day, one of the crewmen found a piece of iron that had been torn from the forecastle door. When the perpetrator had been singled out, he was brought onto the deck and tied to the ring-bolts, face down.

One of the Portuguese took up the lash and flogged the man until he could whip him no longer. Then the whip was handed to another sailor, who lashed the man until he, too, was spent. The offender never uttered a cry. The Portuguese crewman's face darkened. He took a razor from his pocket, and, with the care of a surgeon, cut long shallow lines in the flesh of the man's back, until the blood ran down in ribbons. Then he ordered the bloody man doused with a bucket of brine. As the saltwater splashed down, the African uttered a searing, awful scream. His back arched like a bow and the ropes on the ringbolts snapped tight. Then silence spread across the ship, with only the winds left to howl.

For forty-two days the *Wanderer* rode across the Atlantic. She made it through the doldrums, where, for several days, the prevailing winds died and the sea became as still as a mirror, and then pressed on toward her destination. Behind her she left a trail of 80 bodies, heaved overboard and into the sea.

As she neared Jekyll Island a rather odd advertisement appeared in the *Savannah Daily Morning News,* placed by Henry and John du Bignon, whose families owned Jekyll. It read:

NOTICE

All persons are warned against landing on the Island of Jekyll, for the purpose of gunning, cutting wood, removing wrecks, or in any way trespassing on said island. Suits will be immediately commenced against anyone found on shore with guns

*in their possession. Captains of coastal vessels will pay particular
attention.*

It was an innocent announcement, the du Bignons' lawyer would later
argue in court—the kind of notice property owners frequently post. But
in this case, the warning was different, for it augured events that would
soon reverberate across the nation.

10

J EKYLL I SLAND

JUST BEFORE dawn on the morning of November 28, 1858, the *Wanderer* appeared off the coast of Georgia, a spectral form with sails hanging limply from her battered spars. Slowly she traversed St. Andrew's Sound, making her way toward the beam of the Cumberland Island lighthouse.

The waters are shallow in St. Andrew's Sound, with sandbars lurking beneath the surface. Rather than risk grounding, Brown had determined that the ship should anchor several hundred yards offshore. Now, as the pale sun passed over them, Corrie and Farnum leaned on the rail, searching the shoreline for movement. Before they had left on their voyage, an arrangement had been made for a pilot—someone who would wait for their return and then guide the *Wanderer* over the sandbars and in toward shore. But as the men scanned the shoreline, no one appeared.

In the meantime, conditions aboard the *Wanderer* were growing worse. Eighty of the Africans had already died. Many of the others were sick. The ship's water was nearly depleted, and so was the food. The cockroaches that had crawled aboard in Africa had multiplied. Now, not a corner of the ship was without them. Besides that, Brown had noticed the sea feathering restlessly from the east, heralding a storm that could possibly drive them ashore.

After waiting all day, Corrie decided to delay no longer. Slightly after sunset, he and Brown climbed into the skiff and rowed through the choppy waters in the direction of the Cumberland light. When they reached the shore, they pulled the boat up on the sand. It was strange to touch land after forty-two days at sea. With each step, they staggered. At one point, Corrie slipped onto his knees; Brown pulled him to his feet again. They continued on, pushing their way through the stiff pampas grass until, at last, they found a faint path. It led to a cedar-shingled house, surrounded by a white picket fence. Nearby, the spiraling lighthouse tower rose sixty feet into the night, spreading its beam across the sea.

When they reached the front door, Corrie ran his fingers through his sun-streaked hair and dusted off his trousers, composing himself for what he believed would be the final leg of this long journey. Then he knocked firmly. They waited. A few moments later the door opened and the head of a young man, with side-whiskers stretching to his chin, emerged. "Say, young man," Corrie said as airily as he could, "are you the lighthouse keeper around here?"

As the yellow wedge of candlelight fell on Corrie and Brown, the young man's eyes widened in surprise. The two men were filthy, sunbeaten, their hair knotted by the wind. One's beard was red and streaked with tobacco; the other's, bristly white. Their shirtsleeves were in tatters. Corrie, responding to the young man's shock, launched into what he hoped would be a restorative monologue: His name was Captain Cook, he said, and this other gentleman was Mr. Brookstone. Their yacht had been seized by a gale. They were subsequently thrown off course and then into the doldrums. Now they needed to bring their yacht in to Jekyll, but, of course, needed a pilot to guide them over the bar.

Regaining some of his composure, the young man, who introduced himself as Horatio Harris, explained that he was not a pilot himself, just the assistant lighthouse keeper. There was a pilot, James Clubb— he was the full-time lighthouse keeper as well—who could certainly help them. But Clubb wasn't on Cumberland at the moment. He was tending the light over at Jekyll Island. Perhaps they could row over in the morning and fetch him? Corrie shook his head. They could not wait, he said. Provisions on the ship were low; a storm was brewing. Harris replied that his rowboat could carry only two. Fine, said Corrie. Brown would return to the *Wanderer,* and he would accompany Harris over to Jekyll Island.

And so, under stars that now spread over St. Andrew's Sound, Harris dipped the oars into the water, making their way over to Jekyll. Harris had asked Corrie a few questions about their ordeal, and in Corrie's evasive replies the young man's imagination had been aroused. Finally, when the rowboat was nearing the shore, Harris could no longer restrain his curiosity. "Well, I certainly hope your vessel is not a slaver," he blurted out. Corrie, sitting in the stern, stared back blankly. "No, I'm sorry," he said dryly. "She's not." The oars pulled again through the water. "But I rather would have liked to have landed forty thousand of them!" Corrie exclaimed. Harris chuckled, and for the moment the matter was put to rest.

Reaching Jekyll, they beached the boat. The moon had risen to the tops of the low oaks and soon lighted their way to a sandy path. For an hour they walked, from the south to the north end of the island, and came at last to an old house, its walls stuccoed with a blend of sand, limestone, and seashells. Harris knocked on the door. It was opened by John du Bignon. Corrie and du Bignon recognized each other immediately, but let Harris make the introductions regardless. Once inside, du Bignon asked Harris to sit by the fire. Then he took Corrie into an adjoining room to talk.

When the two men returned, du Bignon confessed that Captain Cook was actually Colonel Corrie, an old acquaintance. Then Corrie spoke, explaining that the name of the ship was the *Wanderer,* and that she did have slaves . . . make that *apprentices* . . . aboard. When Harris, now wide-eyed again, asked how many, Corrie replied they had started with 487 and now had 407.

By eight that night they found Clubb, sitting in a shack next to the Jekyll Island light. Corrie tried the same story he had used on Harris, but as soon as he mentioned the *Wanderer,* Clubb's eyes lit up. He had heard the rumors. "A damned slaver, don't pull the wool over my eyes," said Clubb gruffly, turning his meaty face away. Corrie grabbed the man's shoulder. She was a slaver all right, he confessed. Now she was out of food and water, and if he didn't get her over the bar to

Jekyll, he'd have to try to sail for Port Royal in South Carolina, and that could prove tragic. The debate went back and forth. Finally Clubb said he'd do it, but for $500, rather than his usual fee of $50. Corrie protested, but du Bignon interceded: He'd pay the fee. Just get it done.

At five the next morning Clubb rowed out to the *Wanderer*. The smell was repulsive and in the shadows he thought he saw people moving slowly about. Rather than look at what he didn't want to see, he tried to keep his eyes forward. The sails and anchor were lifted, and the *Wanderer* rode safely over the bar. As daybreak came, Clubb looked around and for the first time fully realized that he was surrounded by a group of emaciated Africans.

The *Wanderer* was now off the south end of Jekyll, about 100 yards from the beach. The sailors began to shuttle the Africans to the shore, using the *Wanderer*'s two boats and another supplied by the du Bignons. As they reached the beach, many of the Africans fell to their knees, crying. One African, who had survived through the ordeal, died within minutes of reaching land. He found his end at Jekyll in a shallow grave.

The Africans reacted with surprise when they saw du Bignon's slaves. These Africans, they thought, wore cloth shirts and pants, like white men. They spoke the white man's language as well. When a few of the Africans tried to communicate with du Bignon's slaves, they were unable to elicit anything but puzzled stares. But there was one old slave who understood them. His name was Jack. He dropped to his knees by one of the Africans and spoke a few quiet words in the African dialect. The African turned his head slowly and responded. Jack had not heard those words in seventy years. They took him down a long tunnel back to Africa, to a mother, a boy, screams, a dark voyage across the sea. He sat there, stunned. "Jack, what's the matter?" John du Bignon asked him. Jack could only look up at his master, with tears flooding his eyes, and shake his head.

A fire was set by the beach. The *Wanderer*'s iron cooking trough was brought ashore and filled with cornmeal. By now the sun was climbing in the sky, and it sent shafts of warm light through the trees. Following their meal, many of the Africans fell asleep. The *Wanderer*'s crew also found soft places in the beds of pine needles and slept. Crouched by the fire, Harris conversed with the red-bearded Brown. Brown was happy to talk. He told Harris about the voyage to the Congo, of the British officers aboard the *Medusa,* of the race with the English yacht, of the long voyage home. They were savages, said Brown. There were 487 of them at the beginning. Eighty had died, he said, and were fed to the sharks.

That night, when the coastal steamer *St. Johns* came up Jekyll Creek on its regular run to Savannah, two men in a rowboat intersected her path. One was a seaman with a red beard. Climbing aboard, he signed the register as "Mr. Wilson." When the ship reached Savannah the following day, "Mr. Wilson" ran immediately to the house of Charles Lamar on East Broughton Street. As the door opened, Lamar's eyes widened. There before him was the weather-beaten face of Brown, his clothes tattered, his red beard filthy—his eyes ablaze with the news that the scheme had actually worked.

Luke Christie, captain of the iron-hulled steamboat *Lamar,* was browsing at Claghorn and Cunningham's general store on Savannah's Drayton Street that evening when his boss, Captain Stevenson, hurried in with some news. The *Lamar* had been booked for a trip south to Fernandina Beach that night, Stevenson told him, but Christie's presence wasn't required; the clients had decided to hire their own captain. Christie was agreeable, but decided to go down to the wharf anyhow, to make certain the *Lamar* was properly equipped for the trip.

Arriving at the wharf, Christie was surprised to find some of Savannah's best-known personalities gathering on the deck of the vessel. There was Nelson Trowbridge, the domestic slave trader; John F. Tucker, the member of the Savannah City Council; and, of course, Charles Lamar. There was also a red-bearded seaman, a man that Christie had never seen before. The men were anxious to get under way, and indeed, the boilers had been fired and the steam was prepared. But the new captain never appeared. Now, with no alternative, Christie was told to take the helm and head 60 miles south to Jekyll. The big paddle wheel began to turn, and shortly after one o'clock in the morning, the *Lamar* left Savannah, making her way past Tybee Island and then southward down the coast.

At about seven that evening, the *Lamar* reached Jekyll Island. As she drew closer Christie spied a small boat approaching. In the bow was Henry du Bignon, the older brother of John. Henry pointed out the spot on shore where he wanted the *Lamar* to go. Christie brought the steamboat over, and dropped her long gangplank onto the bank. No sooner had he done that than Charles Lamar and his friends hurried off. Christie was told to stay aboard and wait, for what he was not sure.

While the *Lamar* had been making its way down from Savannah, the Portuguese sailors on Jekyll had rounded up the Africans and brought them from the beach over to the island's heavily wooded western edge. Another fire was set, and food was again brought to the Africans. Later that day, a doctor arrived from Brunswick and attended to some of the sick captives. Some of the Africans began to smile for the first time. The food here was plentiful. They had blankets and odd pieces of clothing to wear. Someone had brought out a tambourine and a drum. Some of the African boys stood on their aching limbs, and to the familiar beat of the drum, began to dance.

That evening Christie was left alone on the *Lamar*. He watched the herons fishing at the edge of the channel; he saw several woodpeckers hammering their way through the bark of the pines. The men he had brought down from Savannah returned to the boat from time to time but, as before, said nothing to him. Finally, early the next morning, he heard the sound of men approaching, and with it, the distinct clattering of chains. When he looked up, he saw an astonishing sight: A gang of Africans, bound in groups of six, being led onto the gangplank of his steamer by a group of unshaven and dirty men.

By noon the boat was filled, the big sloshing paddle wheel was turning again, and the *Lamar* was making its way back to Savannah. That afternoon she passed St. Simon's Island, crossed Altamaha Sound and reached Sapelo Island. She anchored for the night there, and then, the next morning, continued past St. Catherine's Island, on to Ossabaw, and finally to Tybee Island.

By the time she entered the Savannah River it was dark again. She slipped unseen past the lights of the city, and continued upriver for another 14 miles. There, she docked on the South Carolina side of the

Savannah River, near the plantation of John Montmollin, and the Africans were unloaded.

Now, the conspirators likewise dispersed. Lamar had left the steamer about seven miles downriver of the Montmollin plantation. Now he was safely back at home in Savannah. Tucker had retreated to his plantation on the Savannah River. Trowbridge helped disperse the last of the Africans from Jekyll and then returned to Savannah as well. Farnum caught the northbound packet steamer to New York. The red-bearded Brown, along with Arguirir and crewman Juan Rajesta, made their way to Savannah, where they holed up temporarily at the City Hotel, awaiting a ship north to New York.

Corrie still had some unfinished business to conduct. Shortly after the Africans had been taken off the *Wanderer,* Corrie had the yacht taken up the Little Satilla River. The slave deck had already been removed and discarded. Now, partly hidden by tall pines, she was scrubbed down with lye and vinegar. Next, a local seaman was paid $100 to sail her into the port of Brunswick, some ten miles away.

On December 5, with the *Wanderer* moored in Brunswick harbor, Corrie strode into the offices of Woodford Mabry, the collector of the Port of Brunswick. With his usual nonchalance, Corrie explained that the yacht had been caught in a gale, and that he would now like clearance to move her back home to Charleston. Corrie handed Mabry the *Wanderer's* papers, and sat back. It didn't take long for Mabry to glance up over his glasses however. The *Wanderer's* papers, he said, didn't show a clearance stamp from St. Helena, which, according to the log, was the ship's most recent port. Corrie responded that the U.S. consul, who should have stamped the papers, was absent the day they arrived, as was the consul's deputy. Corrie, of course, wore his most confident and glowing smile. Mabry was taken in, and without further inquiry, stamped the papers. Now the *Wanderer* was free to sail to Charleston. For Corrie, it was a ticket to freedom.

Had Corrie sailed immediately to Charleston, he no doubt would have made it there safely. But the following day, disturbing rumors began to reach Mabry. Freshly imported Africans had been sighted near

Jekyll Island, he was told. Could the *Wanderer,* as the rumor had it, be the slaver? Mabry didn't think so, but he decided to row out to the *Wanderer* to take a look. A cursory examination showed nothing suspicious. Still, something wasn't right. Mabry pulled out the *Wanderer*'s papers. This time he scanned them with a magnifying glass. Then he saw it. The stamp from Trinidad was a fake!

On December 8, Mabry sent an urgent message to Assistant U.S. Attorney Joseph Ganahl in Savannah, describing the events, the rumors, and the fact that the *Wanderer* was sporting counterfeit clearances. Just as he was posting the letter, Mabry heard the shriek of a steam whistle. It was the *Lamar,* paddling into port to take the *Wanderer* in tow.

Alarmed, Mabry refused to let the yacht go. Corrie, watching from a distance, now realized the jig was up. He took off, fast—so fast that he left behind on the yacht the *Wanderer*'s logs, his notebooks, and even a trunk containing rings, letters, and other personal items.

When Joseph Ganahl received the message from Mabry, he jumped up in excitement. Ganahl had heard the rumors of the landing of the Africans as well, and had, in fact, been busily sending out subpoenas to anyone who might have witnessed the event. Ganahl had also arranged for a hearing before Judge Abraham Henry, in which he planned to lay out the evidence that he had found thus far. Now, the presence of the *Wanderer* in Brunswick harbor was wonderful news, a piece of the puzzle that might prove essential in the case ahead.

Ganahl's father had been a hardworking German immigrant who had done well in the cotton trade. His mother was considered one of the "handsomest women in Georgia." As the Augusta newspaper noted, "She possessed great strength and firmness of character . . . and was known for her kindness, liberality and charity." Ganahl had equally good looks and strength of character. He had studied to be a surgeon. But it was law that captured his interest. It wasn't the money that could be made, but the battles that could be fought, and the justice that could be won, that sent him into the study of law.

Now, at the tender age of twenty-seven, he was Savannah's assistant U.S. attorney. He worked hard, from his office at the U.S. Custom

House at the corner of Bull and Bay streets. Many a night, after he had put his three children to bed and kissed his wife good night, he could be seen walking back to work from his home on the southwest corner of Lincoln and Charlton streets, his thin frame casting a lone shadow beneath the streetlights.

With Mabry's letter in hand, Ganahl sent an immediate reply:

> *Dear Sir, Your communication of the 8th has come to hand. I fear you have done wrongly in granting the Yacht Wanderer a clearance, but if the yacht is still within your reach, seize her immediately on behalf of the United States and inform me officially of your course.*
>
> *From what you have written, and I hear, there is no doubt that the Wanderer is guilty, and if we display the proper energy we can get evidence to prove it. The trouble is to get evidence and here I must call upon you. Certain it is that Wanderer has put a hundred slaves somewhere in your neighborhood and somebody does or ought to know about it. Find out these if possible.*
>
> *I will send down a deputy marshal with blank subpoenas returnable before Judge Henry in this city on Saturday. Fill up these with the name of the parties whom you have reason to suspect know or ought to know about the matter. One of the subpoenas is to be served on you, which will bring you to Savannah, where I can consult with you. So use every exertion in your power in this matter—gather all the information you can in and about Brunswick, along the Satilla and bring up the parties with you.*
> *P.S. The United States will pay the mileage and per diem.*

On the afternoon of December 12, a messenger from Morse's telegraph company ran into the Manhattan offices of the *New York Herald*. He handed a telegram off to a teenage kid who threaded his way to the desk of *Herald* editor and founder James Gordon Bennett.

Bennett took the telegram and adjusted his reading glasses. As the neatly blocked handwriting came into focus, he let out a low whistle. Six months earlier, the *New York Times* had reported that the *Wanderer* was clearly not a slaver, but more likely, with Farnum aboard, bound for some kind of adventure. The *Herald* had been of the same opinion. This telegram didn't indicate that at all, though.

Rising quickly from his desk he went out into the newsroom. There he found one of his star reporters—with his feet on the desk and a toothpick hanging leisurely from his lip. "Hey, O'Sullivan, read this," he said. The reporter took the message, and, after the first sentence, kicked his feet off the desk and onto the floor. "If it's true, Corrie pulled one piece of work over us," he said, looking up in surprise. "Do you think we got bamboozled?"

At the time, the *New York Herald* was the nation's biggest daily-circulation newspaper. Bennett had founded the paper twenty years earlier on a riotous blend of politics, scandal, exposé, crime, and international events. He loved to unearth politicians' dirty laundry; he loved to editorialize against radicals; he loved to make readers shudder with tales from the underbelly of New York; and he loved to scoop his chief journalistic rivals, *New York Tribune* editor Horace Greeley and Henry Raymond, the editor of the *New York Times*. That's what he liked. But he hated a few things, and the thing he hated the most was getting bamboozled.

"I don't know," Bennett said, tugging his chin whiskers. "But you better get down to the waterfront, fast. And get some answers from Rynders—we've got to cover our backs." The reporter did just that. He checked out the waterfront. He went to the federal building. And he found Marshal Rynders, or Captain Rynders, as he was sometimes called, and peppered him with questions.

The following morning New Yorkers picked up the *Herald* to the following scoop:

IS THE SLAVE TRADE REOPENED?

Is the YACHT Wanderer a Slaver?—Curious Conflicting Responses Concerning the Wanderer—Rumored Landing of a CARGO of Slaves Near Brunswick, Ga.— Particulars of Her Arrest at New York in June Last— Prophecy by a Herald Reporter—Marshal Rynders

Outdone—What the Secretary of the Navy Thinks of
the Slave Trade on the Coast.

The yacht Wanderer, whose detention at this port in June last on
suspicion of being a slaver occasioned some excitement at the time,
has turned up somewhere near Brunswick, Georgia. She left here
having on board her owner, Capt. Corrie, who had the sympathy of
a great many sympathetic people, as having been much abused in
having his pleasure party spoiled.

Yesterday, a little more light, and considerably more mystery
about the subject was thrown about the subject by the reception of
the following telegraphic dispatch:

The Savannah Republican of this morning learns, on good au-
thority, that the yacht Wanderer succeeded in evading the vigilance
of the cruisers, and landed a cargo of slaves in the neighborhood of
St. Andrew's Sound, near Brunswick, Georgia, and that part of her
cargo was subsequently sent up the Satilla River on board a steamer.

If this be true, it will hardly reflect much credit on our officials
here, who in June last had possession of the Wanderer on suspicion
of being engaged in the slave trade. It will be recollected that the
complaint was made by the Surveyor of Port Jefferson, Mr. S.S.
Norton, who stated that his suspicions were excited by seeing the
vessel undergoing repairs, new water tanks of unusual size, foreign
sailors, and above all, her clearing for Charleston from Port Jeffer-
son, and paying for the bringing of provisions in a lighter from
New York, when her quickest way would have been to stop at New
York on her way and save the lighterage. All these facts tended to
make Mr. Norton's suspicions very strong and he immediately sent
down to New York and made arrangements for the seizure of the
vessel.

The *Herald* then explained that U.S. Marshals Rynders and
O'Keefe had come aboard and had "expressed themselves as particularly
satisfied with the innocent purpose of the voyage, and quite indignant
that a gentleman just about to start on a pleasure trip should be so wan-
tonly disturbed." The *Herald* continued:

After this very cursory examination by the United States District Attorney, the vessel was allowed to depart, the Surveyor of Port Jefferson having been kept on and off, waiting for some definitive proceedings, until he finally went home in disgust. The affidavit he made at the time was withheld from the reporters, and, we believe, never published. The following conversation between one of the Herald reporters and the Marshal will show how widely two persons might differ on the subject. The reporter met Captain Rynders and Mr. O'Keefe on board the Harriet Lane, on the night of the arrival of the Wanderer at New York, when the following conversation ensued:

Reporter: Captain Rynders, I should like to go on board the Wanderer with you, if there are no objections.

Mr. O'Keefe: Yes, there are decided objections; we don't allow anyone on board.

Reporter: But reporters are exceptions to all general rules.

Mr. O'Keefe: Well, we don't want any reporters on board.

Reporter: Why not?

Mr. O'Keefe: Oh the idea of her being a slaver is ridiculous. She is so costly.

Reporter: Why, my dear sir, don't you know that they could afford to throw away a vessel of that very kind every trip. . . . ?

Mr. O'Keefe: Oh no, she's too small, and her cabins are fitted up beautifully.

Reporter: Well, a carpenter could clean her out below in a few hours, and then she would have a little more room.

The following day, the *Wanderer* story burst onto the front pages of the nation's other big papers. The *New York Times,* the *New York Journal of Commerce,* the *New York Post,* the *New York Courier,* the *Brooklyn Eagle,* the *Washington Union,* the *Washington Post,* the *Boston Advertiser,* and the *Boston Traveller* all carried accounts. Meanwhile, the story was buzzing across the newly laid transatlantic telegraph cable, making the pages of the London *Times* and the European press.

Coverage by the Southern papers, of course, was extensive. The *Savannah Republican* noted, "Mr. Ganahl, assisted by U.S. Marshal D. H.

Stewart, is using every exertion to obtain all the evidence bearing on the case; and for this purpose has sent to Brunswick to elicit information current about the transaction in time for the examination, which will probably be on Thursday next." The paper reported the following day: "We feel assured that Mr. Ganahl will do all in his power to have justice meted out; and if upon a trial they are found guilty, such an example will be made of them as will put a stop to the slave trade, at least in this district . . ."

But just as the story of the *Wanderer* was heating up, a bucket of cold water hit it hard. Had slaves really been brought to the American shores by the *Wanderer*? Or was this just a prank pulled by Corrie and Farnum? Cautioned the New York Times:

> *The Tribune and the Post have treated this matter as one of tremendous political importance, and as establishing the fact that, while the rest of the world is discussing the morality of the slave trade, the South has re-established it, and is supported in its maintenance by the general government.*
>
> *The report has undergone serious modifications since it was first started, it should be noted. The yacht was originally said to have brought 350 or 400 Negroes to the coast of Georgia—but the absurdity of this soon became apparent, and the number has now been reduced to 80. This, however, like the other and larger story, is entirely conjectural—and we should not be in the least surprised to hear that the whole report is a hoax, got up by the sporting characters aboard the yacht for the purpose of furnishing a proper climax to the proceedings they had in this port at the time of her original departure.*

The *Brooklyn Eagle* seemed to agree. "The story . . . has been growing smaller by degrees, and will doubtless disappear altogether as soon as it is brought to close observation. At first the *Wanderer* brought four hundred men and brethren to Georgia, but they have already dwindled that down to eighty . . . One fact, however, is rendered sufficiently plain by this story; and that is that the chimera of a revival of the slave trade is too ridiculous to impose upon any old maiden in the country."

The possibility of a hoax seemed to find its final confirmation in a report published by the *Albany Statesman*. A reporter for the *Statesman*, it turned out, was making his way north from Charleston aboard a steamer when, at the rail, he spied Egbert Farnum, one of the supposed conspirators. Farnum looked a bit weather-beaten and a little uncomfortable in a brand-new suit. But following a few drinks in the salon, the "renowned overland rider" was more than happy to pontificate. As soon as the reporter landed in New York, he pounded out the *real* story:

> *The Wanderer, as everyone knows, is a handsome and very fast sailing yacht. She sailed in July last for the Congo River, and passed some time very pleasantly on the coast, if we may rely upon the history of the expedition given to us by a gallant officer who accompanied Capt. Corrie on the voyage, and whose name is identified with many deeds of daring and adventure. We allude to Capt. Farnum, the renowned "overland rider," whose brilliant career in Texas, California and Nicaragua is familiar to so many of his fellow countrymen.*
>
> *The British frigate Medusa was on the coast at the time of the visit of the Wanderer, and numerous were the friendly visits, and gratifying were the convivialities that passed between the officers of the two nations. The Wanderer's people were entertained and feted by the British and the British in their turn were entertained and feted by those on board the American yacht. So entire was the confidence felt in the latter, and so assured were the gallant John Bulls that their Yankee friends were bent only on a pleasure and information-seeking trip, that the idea of examining the Wanderer, to see if she could possibly be fitted for a slaver, was laughed at when proposed by Capt. Farnum, as "a very good joke" . . .*
>
> *The Wanderer remained some time on the coast. Her people landed at various points of interest and viewed African nature in all its originality and beauty. They visited Native Princes in their palaces. The description given of the habits and appearance of the people by Captain Farnum will one day doubtless excite interest in thousands of readers . . .*
>
> *While there they ran a race with a British yacht, which boasted unusual speed, and beat her as easily as a race horse would beat a common roadster. After remaining on the coast a sufficient time,*

the Americans one night stood out to sea, and turned their eyes homeward. . . .

So that was it, no slave trading at all! Back in his office at the *Herald,* Bennett grimaced. He and the rest of the papers *had* been bamboozled. That fair-haired lobbyist, Corrie, now home in Charleston, feted and celebrated, and most likely laughing wildly, had tricked them into believing that the *Wanderer* had returned from Africa with a shipload of slaves.

Indeed, Corrie may have been laughing. But the truth of the *Wanderer* was still to be told.

11

EARLY EVIDENCE

IN EARLY January a steam locomotive pulled into the Montgomery, Alabama, station and came to a hissing stop. The farmers and merchants who had gathered at the depot with their wagons and produce looked up in astonishment. There, pressed against the coach windows, were the faces of three dozen Africans—tattoos racing across their brows and sharpened teeth showing behind parted lips—their dark eyes as wide and unbelieving as those of the farmers and merchants staring up from below.

The carriage door swung open. Now came the clattering and dragging of chains, as the captives were rustled up in groups of five and six and herded down the steps onto the platform. Two hay wagons pulled up, drawn by mules, and the Africans clamored aboard. The last person out of the railway car was Thack Brodnax, the slave trader. He emerged stretching luxuriously, his pink face beaming. He surveyed his cargo with satisfaction—six men, three women, five girls, and twenty-four boys, all barefoot, all dressed in rough kersey pants and cotton shirts, each of them purchased for $50 in Africa, sold fresh from the *Wanderer* for $500, and now, he was certain, soon to be sold again for about $1,000—and with a nod to the wagons, motioned the drivers to move the cargo ahead.

In the late winter afternoon, with the shadows stretching grotesquely across the street, the wagons made their slow, creaking way through the heart of Montgomery. Some of the Africans buried their heads beneath the blankets. Others, mostly the youngsters, stared out curiously. Some of the Africans, practiced in pantomime, put both hands to their mouths and threw back their heads, indicating that they wanted something to drink.

Old farmers and sober merchants lined the road, watching silently as the procession went by. Although Africans had not been brought directly to America for nearly forty years, slavery had been present in the South for two hundred years. Like a mountain, the peaks and hard corners had worn down. Slavery was familiar. It ran according to set rules. Even the church condoned it. But the introduction of these Africans, still raw and bleeding from their voyage, was a disturbing specter.

Some of the white women turned away, shielding the eyes of their children. The men stared blankly, and they worried. They worried that the African slave trade, which their fathers and grandfathers had banned, would now come flooding back, bringing wild Africans into their villages and towns. They worried that the new slaves might spark a rebellion among the old. They worried that the rest of the nation would react in outrage. They worried that this might be the last straw, the act that would throw the nation into disunion.

Some of Montgomery's domestic slaves were watching the wagons as well. Like the farmers and merchants, they, too, were born into the institution of slavery. It was familiar to them. They knew the rules. The mountain that was slavery had worn down for many of them as well. A black man could get a plug of tobacco for his pipe. A woman could buy a bright-colored bandanna or a fabric for a wedding. One could pull strings to get a pass to meet a friend. A weak master could be manipulated and taken advantage of; a tough road boss could be driven out through a general slowdown. The daughter of the missus, with yellow curls tumbling down to her shoulders, would wait to play every morning with their little girl—with her pigtails sticking straight up, wrapped in red ribbons. But now, the procession was a window into the past, a reminder of the way their parents and grandparents had been brought to this land, naked and chained. It made them think of what they should do, for themselves and those souls on the wagon, and in that bloody image, they were filled with fear. And now, would this spark a rebellion? Would there be reprisals? Would what little they had won be swept away? They didn't know.

The wagons made their way across town to Perry Street, where a slave lodging by the name of Brown's Speculator House was located. By the light of torches the Africans were removed from the wagons, some of them leaning heavily on others, and brought inside. They were fed and freed to find a place on the floor for the night. The farmers and merchants went home, to speak in troubled tones about what they had seen.

Shortly thereafter, though, another crowd, this of rowdy young men, arrived to check out the new visitors. "In a house in the back lot were huddled together 38 Congo Africans!" one observer wrote to a local newspaper. "Don't shudder and say, 'The moral sentiments of Christendom condemn the traffic.' But it is a fact; I have seen the Africans!"

As the men gathered around the Africans, one of them brought out a drum and a tambourine, and now, as a bottle of rum was passed around, the Africans were encouraged to get up and dance. "Most of them were pert and lively, laughing and talking in their native tongue, and pointing at and jabbering about everything that particularly attracted their attention," the observer marveled. "Some of them had very singularly shaped craniums—they almost baffle description. One nearly square, one had a convex face, and another a sort of double concave convex head; but most of them had good heads, large flat noses, big mouths, front teeth knocked out, rather small ears, and quite small hands and feet. Some of them were good looking, but others shockingly ugly; some were what might be vulgarly called puff or hog-jawed. I noticed one, a man, who had very high cheekbones and several scars on his face, and appeared very intelligent. He was 'big chief,' no doubt, in his country."

Mimicry was the biggest crowd-pleaser, however. "I was very much surprised at one thing," the observer continued. "They repeated precisely every word said to them. I asked one, 'Where did you come from?'

and he propounded the same interrogatory to me, but of course without knowing the meaning. . . ."

The next morning, the Africans were fed from a trough set outside, their wooden spoons dipping into the corn mash and bacon. Following that, they were put back on the wagons. Now they were taken down to the banks of the Alabama River, which flowed southward in a serpentine journey to the Gulf of Mexico. At the wharf, the *St. Nicholas,* a side-wheeler, awaited them. A report came back a few days later that "two of the miserable wretches had died . . . many others are reduced to the grave's brink by the sufferings and hardships of the Middle Passage." But after that, they were never heard from again.

While all this was going on, Ganahl was attempting to pull together the evidence to make his case. As soon as he heard the initial rumors, he deputized city constable Matthew Gordon and ordered him down to Jekyll as fast as possible to find John du Bignon and serve him with a subpoena. He also told Gordon to round up as many of the Africans as he could, as they were needed as evidence.

That night Gordon and a friend by the name of Blount took a steamer down to Brunswick. Early the next morning, they hired a sail-boat and a pilot to take them over to Jekyll. Gordon and Blount hunched down in the bow, wrapped in blankets against the chill morning air. A breeze from the northwest brought them over to Jekyll within an hour. Gordon and Blount jumped out and slid the vessel up the muddy bank, and then, leaving the pilot behind with the boat, stumbled into the woods. In the distance, above the tall pine trees, they could see smoke rising. They moved forward, and when they found a faint trail, followed it north.

Before long they heard a steady drumbeat. They followed the sound, finally crawling on their hands and knees until they reached a clump of bushes. A bonfire lay about 200 yards away, and around it were a dozen Africans, slowly dancing. "I'll bet those are African Negroes, now," Gordon whispered to his friend. At the count of three, Gordon and Blount lunged out of the bushes. As they did so, an old Negro, who had been watching the dancers from the side, bellowed out a warning. The dancers scattered into the woods. While Blount pursued them, Gordon grabbed the old Negro, who said his name was Sam and that he belonged to Mr. du Bignon. Just then Gordon heard hoofbeats, and moments later Henry du Bignon broke into the clearing, reining in his horse over Gordon's head. Du Bignon demanded the authority that brought Gordon to the island. Gordon waved his subpoena and said he'd come to serve John du Bignon. Henry replied that his brother wasn't there, and without another word, rode swiftly away.

Just then, Blount reappeared—with a little African boy wriggling in his grasp. Gordon had been ready to pursue du Bignon, but now changed his mind. He decided to get the African boy off the island as fast as possible, and back with him to Savannah. Moments later they were running as fast as they could through the woods, with dogs barking in the distance. Reaching the boat, they pushed her off and jumped in, wrapping the boy in a blanket and tumbling him to the floor. The next day Gordon arrived back in Savannah and locked the boy safely away in the city jail. Now, with the African boy under lock and key, Ganahl had his first piece of solid evidence. But there was more to come.

Price's Clothing, at the corner of Bull and Bay streets in Savannah, was considered the finest haberdashery in town. "Where you will always find an elegant and extensive supply of the best and most fashionable goods for the season," its advertisements read. A mannequin stood in the store window, dressed in a brown tweed topcoat, tan trousers, and a bright yellow shirt, with a display of gloves, ties, collars, and shaving brushes at its feet.

Three days after the *Wanderer* had landed at Jekyll, the window also momentarily reflected the faces of three unsavory characters, two dark-eyed Portuguese seamen, and a man with tousled hair and a flowing red beard. Their reflections lingered in the window for a few seconds, then moved together toward the front door.

William O. Price was working a feather duster over some boxes inside when the bell over the door jingled and the three characters walked in. One of them, the man with the red beard, Price noted, was better dressed than the others: He wore a blue flannel coat. But they all needed new clothes. The three sauntered down the aisle, looking around, and finally arrived at the counter. The red-bearded man did the talking. They were up from New Orleans, he explained, and were planning to take the Saturday steamer up to New York. But, of course, they needed some new clothing. With that, the red-bearded man withdrew a chamois bag and dumped some coins on the counter.

Price sprang into action. An assistant appeared, and, under Price's command, took their measurements and then returned with piles of boxes and a rolling hanger device filled with clothes—double-breasted waistcoats, single-breasted jackets, flared trousers, tweed overcoats, bow ties, and more.

Always curious about his customers, Price attempted to start a conversation with Brown, the red-bearded customer. Nothing seemed to work, until Brown offered up a pair of trousers, which he said needed mending. When Price looked the pants over, he noticed, from the label sewn into the watch pocket, that the garment was tailored in New York. Seizing on that bit of information, Price pontificated for a while on the Empire City, noting, in the course of the conversation, that he was particularly interested in those characters—*those slave traders*—that inhabited the shadows of lower Manhattan. Brown, stepping into a pair of striped trousers, grunted some appreciation for the subject.

Now Price posed a question: Had Brown ever heard of a slaver by the name of Mr. Miller? Adjusting his pants, Brown replied, "Do you mean *Jack* Miller?" Price was astounded. Yes, that indeed was the name. Now Price began to see Brown with different eyes. This was no ordinary seaman, Price figured, as he slipped a silk smoking jacket over Brown's shoulders. He was a slave trader—the genuine article himself!

Following their purchases, Brown, Arguirir, and Rajesta sauntered down to the City Hotel at 157 Bay Street. Waiting for them in the lobby, leaning against the reservations desk behind a copy of the *Savannah Republican,* was U.S. Attorney Ganahl, with Deputy Marshal Stewart sitting in an armchair to the left reading the *Savannah Daily Morning News.*

Ganahl had been tipped off earlier by Michael Cass, the manager of the hotel, that three particularly scruffy-looking individuals had checked in a few days earlier, two of them speaking Spanish, wearing seamen's clothes. One of them had signed the name Briggs into the register, then crossed it out and replaced it with Brown. When Cass asked them where they were from, they seemed momentarily at a loss. Then the man with the red beard spoke up and said New Orleans. That was all that Ganahl needed to hear: He quickly took his suspicions to Judge Nicoll of the U.S. Circuit Court, and got a warrant for the arrests of the three.

By the time Brown, Arguirir, and Rajesta came walking into the lobby, a small crowd had gathered, anticipating, from Ganahl and Stewart's presence, that something of interest might happen on this otherwise unremarkable Saturday afternoon. When Brown reached the desk, Ganahl coolly put down his paper, identified himself and Marshal Stewart, and asked Brown why he was in town. Brown replied that he was just passing through. Ganahl was not convinced. So who were his friends in Savannah? Brown replied that he had no friends— or even acquaintances—in town.

By now one of the spectators had run down to 119 Bay Street, where the offices of attorneys Lloyd & Owens were located. John Owens was not only the most able criminal lawyer at the Savannah bar, he was also a director of the Central Railroad and had been president of the Savannah Jockey Club. With a few quick words, Owens bolted down Bay Street to the City Hotel. Owens had just arrived when Ganahl told Brown and the other two men that they were under arrest and had ordered Stewart to snap on the handcuffs.

Without taking a moment to catch his breath, Owens grabbed Ganahl's hand, shook it once, and then announced that he represented all three men, as their legal counsel, in whatever this was all about. Ganahl stepped back, surveying the richly dressed lawyer. Representing these three common seamen? Yes, replied Owens, regaining his breath. And he would like to post bail immediately. Ganahl laughed. "There is no bail for piracy," he replied. "Piracy, you should know, is a capital of-fense." Owens looked shocked.

As the three men were hustled over to the city jail for arraignment and booking, Owens clung to their side, assuring them that they would shortly be out on bond. When they reached the jail, Owens demanded a private cell for the three, and ordered lunch brought in. Ganahl stood back and smiled. Now he was certain of one thing: This was a big case.

After all, John Owens was not only Savannah's leading criminal lawyer, he was also Charles Lamar's personal attorney. And if Lamar was involved, the rumors about slave trading just might be true.

By now, Ganahl's evidence was mounting. He had the African boy from Jekyll Island sitting in jail. He had the *Wanderer*'s books and logs, including a notation in Corrie's handwriting that read, "On deck, 17th—came to anchor. List of passengers, 487." He had the testimony of Collector Mabry as to the counterfeit clearance stamps. He had Luke Christie, who had piloted the *Lamar* down to Jekyll and back. He had James Clubb, the lighthouse keeper who brought the *Wanderer* over the bar at Jekyll. And now he had three of the conspirators.

With this much evidence in hand, Ganahl had secured December 18 for a hearing before Commissioner Charles J. Henry. Judge Henry would listen to the evidence given by the witnesses, and if he felt there was "probable cause" to believe that a crime had been committed, would order the case to trial in the U.S. District Court. That's what Ganahl was hoping for—a federal trial that would not only nail the first round of lawbreakers but roust the rest of the conspirators as well.

Ganahl would not be alone in the endeavor, however. He would be joined by Henry Rootes Jackson, the renowned philosopher, poet—and attorney. Born in Athens, Georgia, and educated at Yale, Jackson had served as U.S. assistant attorney general and had recently returned stateside following a stint as the American envoy to Austria. Now that he was back, Jackson had caught wind of the *Wanderer* incident, and had asked Treasury Secretary Cobb to get him on the case. Cobb was not only an ardent admirer of Jackson's abilities, he was also his half-brother. After speaking with the U.S. attorney general, Cobb told Jackson to catch the next steamer down to Savannah and begin to help Ganahl assemble the case.

Ganahl was ready. He had the backing of the federal government; several pieces of compelling evidence; and two star witnesses, Clubb and Christie. But Charles Lamar was making preparations of his own.

He had sent a few of his friends over to visit with Clubb and Christie one night—just to explain the risks of testifying against someone like Lamar. Now Lamar was confident again. As he had said many times, in a small place, a man of influence could do as he pleases.

12

THE HEARING

A LITTLE before 9 o'clock, on the morning of December 18, U.S. Commissioner Charles Henry entered the court chambers and climbed up to his high-backed leather chair. The hearing room was similar to any other courtroom: The bench, where the judge sat on high, a jury box, a witness stand, and two tables—one for the defense and one for the prosecution. But since this was a confidential hearing, without the public, or even, in this case, a grand jury, the room was small. It had no gallery or balcony section upstairs. In fact, once the guards closed the oak doors in the back of the room and locked them, the room was sealed—cloaked in secrecy and cut off from the outside world.

It was here that Ganahl would present his evidence, in the hope that Judge Henry would move the *Wanderer* case into the federal courts. Ganahl and Jackson sat at the prosecutor's table; Owens and his defense associate sat at the defense table. The three prisoners were already in the dock. They wore clean clothing and were cleanly shaven, with the exception of Brown, who still sported his flowing red beard.

Henry, a small man with bushy white eyebrows and black eyes that were as honest and direct as he was himself, flipped through the paperwork that had been placed on his desk, and then peered at the group before him. "Mr. Ganahl . . . Mr. Jackson . . . Mr. Owens," he said pleasantly, nodding to the counsels. "Mr. Ganahl," he said, returning his gaze to the young man, "please state the case that you've brought before the court."

Ganahl rose and noted that he was seeking to prosecute the defendants under the law of May 15, 1820, which banned the African slave trade. He named the defendants, Nicholas A. Brown, Juan B. Rajesta, Michel Arguirir, and ran through a list of the witnesses that he would be calling in the coming hours. When Ganahl had finished, Mr. Owens rose to state that he would be defending the three prisoners who were present.

"Mr. Owens, I don't think I need to remind you that this is just a hearing," Judge Henry said when Owens had finished. "No charges are being brought at this time." Owens thanked the judge but noted, somewhat under his breath, that his clients had a right to legal counsel, even at this preliminary stage. Henry made some notes, and when he had finished, asked Ganahl to call his first witness, James Clubb.

Clubb, the lighthouse keeper on Cumberland Island, rose and walked slowly to the witness stand. Clubb was in his sixties, a burly man with deep-set blue eyes and a lock of white hair that fell over his forehead.

"What is your occupation?" Ganahl asked.

Clubb looked up momentarily and then dropped his eyes to his folded hands.

Ganahl was crossing before the witness stand and now stopped and looked at him curiously. "Mr. Clubb. What is your occupation?"

Clubb didn't look up. He just sat there, staring into his lap.

Ganahl glanced up at Judge Henry.

"Mr. Clubb," Judge Henry said softly. "Could you answer the question, please?"

Clubb's face was turning increasingly red, and his watery eyes bulged.

"I cain't . . . on the ground I may *intiminate* myself," he replied.

Ganahl took a step back. "Could you repeat that?" he said.

Clubb raised his head and spoke louder. "I said I cain't—on account I will *intiminate* myself."

Ganahl glanced anxiously at Judge Henry.

Owens jumped to his feet. "You can answer that question, Captain," he said to Clubb. "Go ahead."

"Objection," cried Ganahl.

"To what, for heaven's sake?" said Owens. "For encouraging the witness to answer the government's own question?"

"Mr. Ganahl?" said the judge.

"Counsel for defense has no *right* in these hearings to interfere with the prosecution's witnesses," Ganahl replied, "either by objecting to questions or by telling witness what questions would or would not incriminate him."

"Your Honor," Owens implored. "Counsel for the defense *has a right* to ask the court to charge witnesses that they are not compelled to answer questions which would incriminate them. This is the *universal practice,* Your Honor."

Now Jackson rose. "Your Honor," he said in his usual booming voice, "I protest the interference of the opposing counsel—and I want this protest entered in the minutes of the court. These proceedings are irregular and are directly prejudicial to the administration of criminal justice . . ."

"Now hold on there, Mr. Jackson," cautioned Henry. He turned back to Owens. "Mr. Owens, it is the duty of the *court,* and not the defense, to instruct the witnesses. If you wish to suggest instructions to the court, as a member of this court and counsel in this case, you may do so. But it will be left to the court itself to decide itself whether to act on them."

Owens stood there, his lips drawn tightly. "Do you understand me, Mr. Owens?" the judge inquired. Owens nodded, but not convincingly. "Furthermore, I will not condone any more interference in these proceedings. Is that understood?"

"I do not want to interfere," Owens replied, taking a step back to his table, "any further than is my *privilege.*" Judge Henry's face tightened. Ganahl thought the judge might cite Owens for contempt. But the judge's composure quickly returned.

Judge Henry now leaned over to Clubb. "Mr. Clubb, I expect you to answer the questions. Do you understand me? I *require* it of you. And if you do not answer these questions, I will hold you in contempt of court."

Clubb looked up, still red in the face. He nodded in reply.

"Now, Mr. Ganahl," the judge continued, "please begin your questioning again."

Ganahl finished a glass of water and then approached the witness as before. "Mr. Clubb," he began. "What is your occupation?"

Clubb bowed his head, once again burying his gaze in his lap.

Ganahl waited for a moment, and then glanced up at the judge. The judge leaned as far over the bench toward the witness as he could. "Mr. Clubb," he said, after a moment of observation, "do you have a *problem*?" A laugh burst out from the back of the room, which Judge Henry chose to ignore. "The court has asked you a simple question. What is your occupation?"

Clubb's face flushed again. "Ah cain't . . ." he began.

"Mr. Clubb, I'm giving you five minutes to answer that question," the judge interjected. "I'm *requiring* you to answer that question—and after that I'm holding you in contempt of this court. Do you understand me?"

Owens jumped to his feet again. "Your honor, never in my experience has a witness been as browbeaten as Mr. Clubb here. . . ."

"Your Honor!" Jackson thundered, rising again. "The object of all these interruptions is to create a doubt in the minds of witnesses and induce them to withhold their evidence, thus taking the case out of this court and placing it in the hands of parties who have an interest in defeating it."

"That is patently false," Owens said angrily.

"In my own experience, and long it has been," Jackson continued, "I have *never* known such conduct tolerated in any court. Why, when I had the honor to fill the Superior bench of Chatham County . . ."

Henry picked up his gavel and smacked his desk. The bailiff shouted for order. Jackson and Owens fell mute, and returned to their seats. Silence descended over the room. Judge Henry finished scribbling some notes, and then turned to Clubb. "I am giving you five minutes," he said. "Would you like to reply to the court's question, or would you like to sit in the county jail?" Clubb said nothing. "Fine," said the judge.

Now, as the big courtroom clock advanced with a metallic click, everyone waited. Judge Henry busied himself in paperwork. The attorneys stared vacantly at the walls and ceilings. Clubb sat impassively on the stand, staring at his hands.

When five minutes had passed, Judge Henry muttered, "All right then." Turning to the marshal, he ordered Clubb removed from the courtroom. Once Clubb had been hustled off to jail, the judge ordered the court recessed until later that afternoon.

When the hearings resumed that afternoon, Ganahl called Luke Christie to the stand. Christie, a lanky thirty-year-old, had piloted the steamship *Lamar* down to Jekyll and back. He'd seen plenty, and Ganahl was confident that he would supply the details that Clubb refused to address.

"I understand that you were engaged in running the tow boat *Lamar*," Ganahl began.

"That's right, yep," Christie replied.

"And did you run her to Brunswick about the first or second of this month—that is, December?"

"I did," Christie said.

"Thank you. Now tell me where you went to from Brunswick."

Christie pulled himself up straight in the chair. "Oh I can't do that."

"And why not, sir?"

"Well, I'd be incriminating myself, Mr. Ganahl."

Ganahl hesitated. "Of what crime, sir?"

"Objection!" cried Owens, jumping to his feet. "Leading the witness."

"Where are you going with this, Mr. Ganahl?" asked Henry.

"Your Honor, from the high opinion I have of the character of Mr. Christie, I am certain that he would not be engaged in a disreputable transaction and that he was under a misapprehension," Ganahl replied. "I believe that *he* believes that the transportation of Africans between St.

Andrews Sound and the Savannah River renders the witness liable to prosecution for violation of the slave trading law of 1820."

"And does it?" asked Henry.

"No sir. This law refers to the *coastal* or more accurately the *coastwise* transportation of Negroes. There is no law under which a party can be prosecuted for conveying Negroes from one point in Georgia to another, *inland.*"

Owens stepped forward. "Your honor, the courts of this nation are established to protect witnesses. This lax interpretation of the law threatens the security of this witness, and in no way should be used to mislead the witness into surrendering his Fifth Amendment rights."

"Furthermore, Your Honor," Ganahl continued, ignoring his opponent's remarks, "I believe the witness is laboring under a misconstruction of the law, upon which I believe he has been *previously coached.*"

Owens turned sharply to Ganahl. "That is *absolutely* false," he exclaimed.

"Gentlemen!" Henry commanded, slamming down his gavel. With a wave of his hand he summoned the attorneys to the bench. After a few moments of hot mutterings, the judge raised his head. The court would investigate the legal issues raised, he said, and reconvene in two hours.

When the court returned and Christie had been seated again, Judge Henry turned and spoke to him. "I have read the extracts from the law of the land," he said. "If all you have done in this matter has been the transportation of Negroes from Jekyll Sound up the Savannah River, no offense has been committed."

Christie listened solemnly.

"Whatever other act you may have done that comes under the view of the statutes, you alone can know," Henry added. "I have read the law to you, and you must now decide for yourself."

Christie sat there with a troubled look on his face. He glanced over at Owens, as though looking for instruction. Ganahl realized he hadn't a moment to lose. Striding briskly to the witness stand, he leaned over Christie like an egret towering over its prey. "Mr. Christie, I have my eye on you," Ganahl snapped, "and upon the steamship *Lamar,* and upon others as well, and wherever the Almighty has given me the power to direct it."

Christie looked up. Ganahl met his gaze firmly and continued. "I will keep my eye on everyone connected with this violation of the law of the land, and as prosecuting officer of the Government I will prosecute everyone connected with it, directly and indirectly, from the highest to the lowest," Ganahl said. "Witnesses might not be made to answer; juries might not give their verdict, even the *courts* might not come up to the mark, but for me, *thank God,* I have taken an oath to perform my duty, and so help me God, so long as I have an arm to raise, or a voice to speak, I will perform it to the full extent of my ability!"

Owens began to rise, but Henry motioned him to sit back down.

"The government has no interest in prosecuting any witnesses. The witness so far has committed no crime," Ganahl warned. "But if witness withholds his testimony, if he refused to testify, he will perfect a crime, and the government must then prosecute."

By the time Ganahl had finished, Christie's face was pale. Even Owens had remained glued to his seat. The room fell silent.

"Now, Mr. Christie," Ganahl began. "Let me ask you a few questions."

Christie straightened up in his chair.

"From Brunswick, you went *where* with the 'Lamar'?" asked Ganahl.

"I went opposite Jekyll Island, to Jekyll Creek," Christie said softly.

"Can you tell us what you saw there?"

"Well, I saw a lot of Negroes."

"American Negroes?"

"I don't think so."

"How many?"

"I reckon there was about three hundred of them I seen, but I didn't try to count 'em."

"Tell us what else you saw on the island."

"I saw some white men with 'em. I reckoned they were in charge. They helped put 'em aboard."

"Anything else?"

"I saw a vessel lying three or four miles off."

"The *Wanderer*?"

"She might have been the *Wanderer* or not, I could only see her topmasts. A fore-and-aft schooner, she was."

"When was this?"

"December the second."

"Then what happened?"

"There were six or eight white men engaged in putting the Negroes on board. Then I carried them up the Savannah River fourteen miles, and landed 'em on the Carolina side."

"Where?"

"I don't know the name of the place. I'm not well acquainted with the river above Mr. Potter's place. Several white men went up with me, like I told you, some of the same men who put the Negroes aboard at Jekyll."

"Who did you deliver the Negroes to?"

"I didn't deliver the Negroes to anyone. The white men pointed out the place where they wanted 'em landed. I ran along the shore and put them there."

Ganahl took a step closer to the witness.

"Who were the white men who put the Negroes on board at Jekyll?"

Christie pursed his lips. "I don't know the names of any of 'em," Christie stammered.

"State the names of the men who were present and saw it done," Ganahl repeated.

Christie hesitated, then sighed in resignation. "A Mr. Trowbridge was one," he said. "Captain John F. Tucker was another; Mr. Henry du Bignon; and Mr. C. A. L. Lamar."

"Those are the men you carried from Savannah to Jekyll?"

"Yes. Lamar, Tucker, Trowbridge . . . and one more, I don't know his name."

Ganahl pointed to the red-bearded Brown, sitting in the dock. "Is that the man? Was he one of them?" Ganahl asked, his voice rising.

Christie glanced over. "Yes," he said.

Ganahl looked up at Judge Henry. "No further questions."

Ganahl called additional witnesses before the hearing closed—a Dr. Hazelhurst, the physician who attended to the Africans on Jekyll; Collector Mabry, who testified that the *Wanderer*'s papers had been faked; and Constable Gordon, who brought the African boy back from Jekyll.

Ganahl also presented the charts and logs from the *Wanderer*, which demonstrated her course to Africa and back. In the end, even Clubb came through: He explained that Lamar's men had threatened him. During the hearings, he confessed, he had even carried a pistol in the pocket of his baggy trousers, with his finger on the trigger. But after a night in jail, and more pressure from Ganahl, the lighthouse keeper signed an affidavit that described what he had seen.

By the end of the next day, Judge Henry had heard enough. "From the evidence already produced, I feel authorized to commit the prisoners for the action of the grand jury of the U.S. District Court," he said. "Furthermore, as the district attorney has requested that the witnesses should be required to enter into recognizance for their appearance when wanted at the District Court, I therefore order them to appear before me at 12 o'clock today, prepared with sufficient securities to give bond for their appearance."

Judge Henry looked over at Ganahl and Jackson. "Gentlemen," he said somberly, "this case can go to trial." Ganahl burst into a grin. Jackson leaned over and shook the young man's hand.

Charles Lamar was sweating it now. "I returned this morning from Augusta," he wrote Nelson Trowbridge. "I distributed the Negroes as best I could, but I tell you, things are in a hell of a fix; no certainty about anything. The Government has employed H.R. Jackson to assist in the prosecution, and they are determined to press matters to the utmost extremity. . . . The yacht has been seized. . . . They have all the pilots and men who took the yacht to Brunswick here to testify. Dr. Hazelhurst testified that he attended to the Negroes and swore they were Africans, and of recent importation. I tell you, hell is to pay . . ."

But once the initial shock had worn off, Lamar's feisty confidence returned. He ordered the best foods to be served to Brown, Rajesta, and Arguirir in jail, and had jailer Van Horn running out at their bequests for the best cigars and claret wines. The entire cell was refurbished as well, with a new wood floor laid atop the damp stone. That wasn't all. On January 28, 1859, Lamar had a note slipped to Brown. "If a true bill be found against you by the grand jury, it will be done upon the evidence of Clubb and Harris, and, of course, they will testify to the same thing," Lamar assured him. "In that case I think you all ought to leave, and I will make arrangements for you to do so, if you agree with me. I have offered Clubb and Harris $5,000 not to testify; but the Government is also trying to buy them . . ."

Lamar also wrote to his father. "Mr. Ganahl has made a great ass of himself," he said. "So far as the trial is concerned, I have no fears for myself . . ."

In the first weeks following the landing of the Africans, some of the Southern newspapers had cheered the affair. The *Natchez Free Trade* said: "Cotton, corn, sugar, tobacco, etc. need and must have the labor of these Africans. We'll take a few ourselves—on the market terms!" The *Macon State Press* said: "The South needs more slaves, and the general Government might as well attempt to bridge the Atlantic as to try to prevent her from getting them . . ." The *Charleston Mercury* dismissed the voyage as a "naughty" adventure.

But most of the Southern press condemned the landing of the Africans as severely as the papers in the North. "It is with much regret that we are compelled to believe that this act has been perpetrated on Georgia soil," said the *Savannah Republican*. The *Augusta Chronicle* wrote: "The people of Georgia should not hesitate to resort to any and all legitimate means, to arrest at once and forever cease a traffic so disastrous to the public weal of the South." And said the *Edgefield Advertiser*: "We feel it to be our duty as a gazetteer to advise our citizens to think well before they commit themselves to the support or countenance of the African slave trade in any shape, and however tempting."

The comments of the *Montgomery Advertiser* of Alabama were particularly pointed, considering that the procession of Africans had passed through its town:

> *There are few of our readers that have not had occasion to view with a pitying eye the inevitable separation of the slave mother and son, nay, even the husband and wife. Happily, such events are of rare occurrence, but are still occasionally to be bewailed. It is one of the glories and the blessings of our system of labor that these sunder-*

ings of the bonds of natural affection are less frequent in the South than perhaps in any other nation of the globe. For one slave family that is thus rudely dismembered, hundreds of the poorer classes of the North are forced by bitter necessities to separate, and go forth singly to combat the demons of hunger and nakedness.

But what would our readers think of the destruction of a whole town by its neighbors in order to sell a remnant of its inhabitants? What would they think of the alliance of three counties of our state for the purpose of warring upon and conquering a fourth county for the sake of gain? And yet it is by bloodshed and fire and rapine that the slave ships of Africa are to be filled . . .

We are not willing to encourage bloodshed, even among brutish savages, for the aggrandizement of a few ship owners. We are not willing that those cruelties that we have enumerated should be carried on in the name of the South, and for the ostensible benefit of Southern interests. In the name of Southern civilization and enlightenment, we protest against the slave trade and its concomitant horrors.

For a moment, then, the *Wanderer* affair seemed to have drawn the nation together in equal indignation, and in that, had helped bind some of the nation's wounds. "The Southern press is practically a unit in denouncing the business, and invoking the execution of the laws," enthused the *New York Times*. "The Savannah papers are eloquent in condemnation, and even the local journals in South Carolina, in the vicinity where the Negroes are quartered, clamor for the penalties."

But within a few weeks, the Northern press began to demand more of the South than mere passive consternation. The perpetrators must be tracked down, tried, and if convicted, hanged, the Northern press roared. Never mind that no Northern slave trader, sailing with the blessings of Judge Betts from the Port of New York, had ever been hanged, or even imprisoned for any significant period of time. Now, for the South to separate itself from the *Wanderer's* shame, it must convict the conspirators and send them to swing from the gallows.

"It will be quite useless to urge what we have no doubt is true—that the people of the Southern states are opposed to the traffic, and lend no countenance to its restoration," the *New York Times* explained. "For if they fail to hang the men who engaged in it—if their officials are so lax, or their juries so perjured, as to permit this trade to be carried on with impunity, in face of all our laws against it—they will suffer all the consequences of an actual complicity in the proceeding itself . . ."

And what were the consequences? The *Times* stated them unequivocally. "The whole sentiment of the country will be aroused and arrayed against them," the newspaper warned. "While it will be utterly impossible for the conservative people of the Southern States themselves to vindicate such a policy, the entire population of the North will wage upon it a relentless war of extermination."

When Ganahl returned home, he sat with his family on the back porch and recounted the exciting events of the day. But later that night, with his family asleep, he awoke, his worries driving him from his bed. He moved to the bentwood rocker by the window, where he could see the moon flowing white over the honeysuckle below. In the trial ahead, he mused, he must win a clear conviction. Without that, the South would seem impotent. "If they fail to hang the men who engaged in it," the *New York Times* had warned, "the entire population of the North will wage upon it a . . . war of extermination . . ." That dark message kept running through his head.

He heard a rustling, and turning his head saw his wife, Harriet, standing silently in the doorway. In the previous days, both he and Henry Jackson had received death threats. Now he could see that her thin frame was trembling. He rose and took her by the hands, but there was nothing he could say.

13

THE PRESIDENT

PRESIDENT JAMES Buchanan stood at the window of the Oval Office and gazed out over the White House lawn. There was much unfinished business in Washington. The Washington Monument was partway through construction, just 140 feet tall. The Capitol building was unfinished, its classic cast-iron dome yet to be completed.

His term in office was finished, at least it would be in another two years. But what worried him was the unfinished business of the Democratic Party. Once so strong as to sweep him into office, the party now lay seriously divided. Stephen A. Douglas, the "Little Giant," who was the Democratic party's best shot for the presidency, had straddled the fence on the slavery issues, and, as a result, had alienated both Southern and Northern voters. Meanwhile, the Republican Party was gaining strength, and its dark horse candidate, Abraham Lincoln, was becoming increasingly popular.

The whole situation struck Buchanan as strange. Just a few years earlier Lincoln was a nobody, a leather-skinned circuit court rider from Illinois. Now he seemed to be everywhere. Well, Lincoln *was* a formidable debater. He was a good stump speaker, too. He could tell some funny stories. In fact, Lincoln's sense of humor was so odd that it was hard to imagine that he would be taken seriously. Sometimes the man would be sitting in a meeting, with the speaker at the front table droning on, and Lincoln would suddenly snort aloud with laughter: Something funny had flashed through his oddly shaped head. Some people said that if Lincoln ever won the election he'd be the nation's first Laughing President. That was incomprehensible to Buchanan, who was rather proud of having no sense of humor at all.

Buchanan gazed down at the report on his desk. On December 16, 1858, the United States Senate had passed a resolution demanding that Buchanan communicate to the Senate "any information in his possession in relation to the landing of the barque *Wanderer* on the coast of Georgia with a cargo of slaves." The House issued a similar declaration the following day. Buchanan knew he needed a response. He needed to reassure Congress that the administration had this thing under control.

Buchanan had always favored the South. He'd been a champion of most Southern issues—and especially the right of Southerners to the institution of slavery. Lincoln, of course, had also said that the South could have their slavery. But Lincoln was adamant that slavery could not spread outside the South. Lincoln refused to make America a slave nation. Buchanan disagreed. He'd leave that up to the individual states and the Supreme Court to decide.

But there was one thing upon which both Buchanan and Lincoln agreed: The African slave trade was inhuman and had no place in the South or anywhere else in the nation. Most Southerners agreed wholeheartedly with this. But now, the *Wanderer* was making the South look like it was seething with defiance on the issue. It was making Buchanan and the Democratic Party look particularly bad. If Buchanan's administration did nothing about the *Wanderer,* and if, as the *New York Times* had suggested, the South didn't prosecute the conspirators and *hang them,* his party would have a hard time holding on to its Northern voters. In fact, many of them were already drifting to the Republican side.

What if the *Wanderer* pushed more voters into the Republican camp—and the Laughing President was elected? It would be no laughing matter, Buchanan mused. South Carolina would secede from the Union, for sure. Georgia might also. In fact, the South might go down like a row of dominos. Would the Laughing President let the South walk out of the union? Or would their secession spark a civil war?

There was knock on the door and in walked Treasury Secretary Howell Cobb.

"That cousin of yours . . ." Buchanan began.

"Mr. President," Cobb interrupted, "when I married Caroline Lamar I didn't know I was adopting her lunatic nephew."

Buchanan shook his head and motioned Cobb to the couch. "Have you read Wednesday's *New York Times*?" he asked.

Buchanan picked up the paper and started reading. " 'With every day's mail that reaches us from the Southern States, our suspicions about the *Wanderer* are fast resolving themselves into the most deplorable certainty. We are now called upon to believe that the State of Georgia—the state of Oglethorpe, the State of Whitfields, and of Wesley's special labor—the one state of all the South which has heretofore claimed and held the proudest position in the vanguard of law-abiding, orderly, loyal adherence to the principles which have made, and which alone can maintain us a nation—has assumed the damning responsibility of endorsing afresh the most accursed system of organized inhumanity which has ever afflicted the earth.' "

The president glanced up at Cobb and continued. " 'Meanwhile, some Washington correspondents blandly assure us that the case of the *Wanderer* has not excited that much attention in the national Capital— and this although the State of Georgia is represented in the national councils and in one of the highest offices of the Cabinet, by one of her most conspicuous sons!' " The president glanced over at Cobb. "That's you, my friend."

Just then Jeremiah Sullivan Black, Buchanan's attorney general, walked in. Black was a tall, loose-jointed, former farm boy who, not unlike Lincoln, had risen to a higher station through his brilliance and irrepressibility. Black was the perfect complement, in fact, to the buttoned-down president. He was a proslavery man, like Buchanan, and abhorred the slave trade, but above all he believed in the law.

A few steps behind Black came Henry Jackson, talking volumes, as usual, and dressed in the sartorial splendor he had used to dazzle the foreign courts.

"Gentlemen, we have a serious problem," Buchanan began. "I've been reading Wednesday's *Times* to Mr. Cobb here. The responsibility for this has not been placed on this administration. But what happens next will." The president picked up the paper again. "Let me explain, in the words of our friends at the *Times,* what's at stake here," he said, and began to read: "'There is a small but vigorous party in the Southern States determined to elect an Anti-Slavery President. It devotes itself to the creation of political issues sure to arouse the most intense indignation of the North, and to put the South obstinately and immovably in the wrong.'"

The president pursed his lips and continued: "'If these men have their way, the revival of the Slave trade is the practical issue for the elections of 1860. They propose to open the trade itself, to import Negroes from Africa and land them upon Southern soil, not openly, of course, for the power of the Federal government would speedily suppress any such endeavor, but secretly. . . . The immense profits of the traffic will reward them if this scheme succeeds, while the fact that the slave trade is stealthily restored to the Southern States will be quite sufficient to arouse and unite the people of the North, and thus pave the way for that sectional contest and victory which these men trust will lead to the dissolution of the Union.'"

Buchanan lifted eyes to the others and then continued: "'Whether they accomplish that result will be doubtful. But they have every prospect of success in their preliminary undertaking, and if they succeed in the practical nullification of the laws against the slave trade, they will be very likely to elect a Republican President in 1860.'"

Buchanan put down the paper. "We have to stop this from going further," he said. "We have to stop it now." For the rest of the hour, the three men huddled together to determine just how. Jackson told them about the hearing before Judge Henry, how Lamar's people had tried to intimidate the witnesses, but how he and Ganahl had put the testimony back on track. The president nodded his approval. How much influence could Lamar wield in the upcoming trial? Both Jackson and Cobb replied that it could be considerable. Lamar could buy off the jury, and he would certainly intimidate them, said Cobb. The president asked Black what legal maneuvers they could employ. Black described some of the possible strategies.

And what about Ganahl? He was just a kid. Was he too green for this case? Black said he felt that Ganahl could handle it. "Well, by God, you need to impress upon him the stakes at risk here," Buchanan said. Black nodded.

The president ended the meeting with another reading of the *Times*. " 'We all look to the Federal Administration, which is charged with the execution of Federal laws, to put a stop to this movement. If it fails, it will be because it *chooses* to fail—because it is the servile tool of the most unprincipled section of the Pro-Slavery ultralists, who seek disunion as the consummation of their hopes. The Administration and the Democratic Party, then, will be held responsible for any failure to put an end, instantly and permanently, to these attempts at renewing the slave trade. They have the power—they acknowledge their duty, and they are assured of the cooperation and sympathy of the great mass of the people of the Southern states. If with all these advantages they cannot enforce the laws, and protect the nation, then they must make way for those who can.' "

Buchanan looked up. "I can't say it more clearly than that," he said.

By the gaslight that night in his office, Black worked his quill rapidly in an urgent letter to Ganahl. "When Mr. Jackson was here, he had several conversations with the President, with the Secretary of the Treasury and with me, in which our views were fully expressed. He is, therefore, entirely aware of what we expect from him and yourself, as well as from other officers of the United States in your district," Black wrote.

"The President relies confidently on you to prove by your success in these prosecutions, that the acts of Congress, passed in pursuance of the Constitution, are too strong and too much respected to be set aside by a mere local opposition. This is no question of town-meeting politics, but a great judicial cause involving principles of obedience, loyalty, and good order, in which the whole nation is interested.

"If you produce sufficient evidence to show the guilt of the accused parties (as I doubt not you will), their escape from justice would be a public calamity; for their acquittal could then scarcely be ascribed to any cause except some indirect and outside pressure upon the jury. If possible, you must save us from this. You are, of course, not required to go a step beyond your convictions of right or to use any means except such as are perfectly fair. But the President relies on you to leave nothing undone, which will promote the ends of Justice, and by Justice he means the execution of the law upon all who have incurred its penalties."

To that end, Black noted: "I sent you some days ago a written paper authorizing you and Mr. Jackson jointly to promise the President's pardon to any person confederated with these offenders, whom you may deem it desirable to put at his ease. Such a power is very seldom delegated to a local officer or counsel of the government, but after a conference with Mr. Jackson, the President thought it might be necessary, and he relies confidently on you to use it discreetly."

Black also addressed Ganahl's concerns, confided in an earlier letter, that the flamboyant Jackson was stealing the spotlight, and had already tried to take the case away from him. "The government has the most entire confidence in both of you," Black wrote consolingly, "but it has determined to double the guards, in the hope that the dignity of the laws may be indicated and their strength be made known. It is confidently believed that we could not have given you an associate more agreeable to yourself personally, nor any one abler to give you the assistance which the magnitude of this case seems to demand."

The president seemed to have everything under control. He had a brilliant attorney general directing the case, the famed orator Henry Jackson in the courtroom as associate counsel, and a young firebrand, Ganahl, to hammer home the government's interests.

It was with some sense of confidence, then, that Buchanan replied to Congress that "effective measures have been taken to see the laws faithfully executed," including, he said, the appointment of Henry Jackson as special counsel to aid the district attorney in the prosecution. The president also attached a statement from Attorney General Black, which noted, "To find the Negroes who were clandestinely landed, to identify the parties engaged in the crime, and to ascertain other important facts connected with the transaction—all this had been attended with many difficulties, but there is good reason to hope that they will be overcome, and justice, according to the law of the land, will be executed upon the offenders."

That may have been so in Washington, D.C. But farther down South the case against the *Wanderer*'s conspirators was beginning to go haywire. Ganahl's evidence, in fact, was literally disappearing into the woods.

It was Christmas Eve in Savannah, the holly and wreaths hung, the trees decorated with candles upon their branches. A cold front had swept through the city, and the fires glowed as people gathered for their last celebrations before Christmas Day.

Toward the end of the day, one could hear the muted sound of horse hooves as a carriage came down Bay Street. Driving it was Deputy Gordon, who had been sent down to Jekyll Island by Ganahl, and by his side, wrapped in a blanket, sat an African boy, his eyes wide at the sight of the grand buildings and glowing homes before him. That evening, while Christmas Eve stole across the city and citizens were tucking their children into bed, Gordon brought the boy to the Savannah police barracks and checked him into a cell. He motioned the boy to a bunk, and, covering him with a rough blanket, gently bade him good night.

On Christmas morning, at about 10 o'clock, U.S. Marshal Stewart strode over to the cell. The boy had arisen and had been given his breakfast. He seemed to be in no particular distress. But Stewart surveyed the facility and felt otherwise. The lad's health was too frail for him to remain in that cell, he told the jailer. Rather, Stewart announced, he would personally escort the boy over to the lodging facility of George W. Wylly, a local slave auctioneer. Wylly, whose business at the corner of Drayton and Bay streets in Savannah sold "real estate, bank stock, Negroes, etc." and had "constantly on hand, carpenters, blacksmiths, cooks, seamstresses and field hands," took the boy in.

Once again, the prospects of an African in their midst was a novelty in town, and soon the boy had attracted a crowd of spectators. "We visited him and found a boy, apparently about 13 or 14 years of age, of a rather pleasing and intelligent countenance," a reporter for the *Savannah News* wrote. "He repeated, almost perfectly, everything we said to him, whether in English, French or Spanish and seemed to 'bear his honors' with commendable modesty and good humor."

Christmas must have not had much of a hold on many of the

drifters and vagabonds around Savannah, for by the afternoon several hundred people had gathered to catch a glimpse of the boy—so many, in fact, that Wylly was compelled to put another Negro boy in the cell from time to time while the African took a break. The ruse worked so well, said the *Savannah Republican,* that "many persons visited the room and came away thoroughly convinced that they had seen a real bona fide African . . ."

That night, after the crowd had disappeared, and after the boy had gone to sleep, curled beneath his blankets, and after Wylly himself had gone home, two white men and a Negro crept toward the hotel and rapped softly on the front door. Wylly's caretaker, Simon, who slept above the office, raised the window and stuck his head sleepily out. Lodging was needed for the Negro, one of the white men hissed.

With some muttering, Simon threw on his robe and lumbered downstairs. Reaching the first floor, he set the candle down on a table. Then he unlatched the door and opened it. As he did so, the glint of gunmetal flashed in the candlelight, and the barrel of a revolver impressed itself against the side of his head. If he made a sound or any resistance, the intruders promised, they would blow his brains out. Stumbling back upstairs, Simon led the men to the sleeping boy. He was awakened and dressed, and, with the revolver still lingering on Simon, smuggled out the back door. He was never seen again. The first piece of evidence had vanished into the Christmas night.

A short time later, John F. McRae, a deputy U.S. marshal in Worth County, Georgia, was sitting down to lunch when a friend burst in: Thirty-six Africans from the *Wanderer* had been spotted on mule-drawn wagons—heading toward the Alabama line. McRae jumped up: This was an opportunity for some excitement, and besides, there was a bounty attached to each one of those captives. McRae deputized ten local citizens and within an hour the posse was off, spurring their horses on toward Alabama.

By the time the posse overtook the two wagons, with thirty-six Africans, five domestic slaves, and one white man aboard, the Alabama line was just a few miles ahead. McRae reined in his horse just ahead, and, waving his revolver, told the white man sitting by the driver to stop the wagons and step down. The white man, as it turned out, was Richard F. Aiken, a prominent Savannah citizen. Aiken, in fact, was an officer of the Savannah Jockey Club, a member of the Savannah regatta club, and, not surprisingly, a friend of Charles Lamar's.

Aiken demanded McRae's authority for stopping them. McRae showed Aiken his badge. Aiken smirked and told the marshal to move aside. McRae, spitting a wad of wet tobacco on the ground, pulled back the hammer of his .44-caliber percussion revolver and told Aiken that if he didn't step down immediately, he was going to have to shoot him.

Aiken got the message. The wagons were turned around. The group traveled some 75 miles southeast, crossed back into Telfair County, and finally arrived at the county jail in the town of Jacksonville, Georgia. There, McRae placed the Africans and the five domestic slaves under guard in the courtyard, and then sent an exultant telegram to Marshal Stewart in Savannah: The Africans are here, he said; now what should I do with them? For several days, McRae waited for a reply. In the meantime, the Africans drew the usual spectators, and performed their usual crowd-pleasing pantomimes.

McRae waited for a week. He dipped into his own savings to keep the captives fed. He drummed his fingers. He wanted to get his reward money and go home. No reply came from Stewart. Finally, on the tenth day, a telegram arrived: Stewart wrote that he couldn't choose a course of action without instructions from Attorney General Black, and, unfortunately, the attorney general, despite repeated telegrams and letters, could not be reached. For that reason, therefore, McRae had permission to let the captives go.

McRae was shocked, but with the expenses for the Africans being paid out of his own pocket, he had no choice but to let them go. The last time he saw the *Wanderer*'s thirty-six Africans was as the wagons rose over a hill, disappearing into the woods on their slow trek west. They were never seen in Georgia again, and a second chunk of evidence was gone.

Still later, U.S. Marshal Thomas L. Ross was standing on the platform at the Macon train station, enjoying a cigar, when a passerby mentioned that there were some strange things going on in the smoking car ahead. Climbing aboard, Ross saw two exultant Africans at the far end, entertaining a crowd by imitating whatever dialect was thrown their way. "You must be a couple of damned fools!" Ross heard one white man exclaim. The Negroes threw the sentiment right back at him, with such gusto and perfect fidelity that the car erupted in laughter.

The Negroes had pointed teeth and tattoos and spoke no English (other than what they mimicked). Ross asked to whom the two belonged, and when no one spoke up, he arrested them. Ross took the two Africans into custody and brought them to the city jail. The jailer, however, was attending the circus; so Ross put the two in the guardhouse, and immediately telegraphed Marshal Stewart in Savannah.

As the morning train came steaming into Savannah station from Macon the next day, Ross and the two Africans were sitting in the first coach car. Awaiting them at the station were no less than ten armed federal officers—nine federal officers from the U.S. Revenue Service, sent by Mr. Boston, the collector of Savannah's port, as well as an officer sent by Marshal Stewart. It seemed that the government had finally netted the evidence it needed.

The Africans were placed in the Chatham County jail. Several weeks went by. The two Africans were given jobs—sweeping up and tending to jailer Charlie Van Horn's horse. They also performed the pantomimes that were requested by the frequent crowds. Then, one morning, a federal officer arrived at the jail and handed Van Horn a warrant, which directed him to bring the two Negroes to the office of Magistrate John Staley.

When Van Horn and the two Negroes entered Staley's office, there, waiting for them, were none other than Charles Lamar, his friend John Tucker, and U.S. Marshal Stewart. Staley explained to Van Horn that Lamar had laid claim to the Negroes, on the grounds that they were his. John Tucker, in fact, had already sworn that he had seen Lamar with the two of them back in December. Van Horn was astonished. He protested that the Negroes were federal property. Then, thinking as fast as he could, Van Horn said he needed to find Ganahl—for permission to release the two Africans. Staley considered this, and said he'd give him twenty-five minutes. Van Horn ran out the door after Ganahl, but

Ganahl was in the midst of a proceeding at the Court of Admiralty, and was unreachable. Twenty-five minutes later Staley asked Marshal Stewart if the federal government had any interest in the Africans. Stewart said no. The two Africans now belonged to Lamar.

By now, Lamar was feeling pretty confident. He had swindled the government out of its evidence without much work at all. Now he decided to have some fun. The next day, he seated one of the African boys next to him in his buggy and gleefully cruised around downtown Savannah. Lamar made sure to contact the newspapers on the way. Reported the *Savannah Daily Morning News*:

> *Some of our citizens were taken aback on Saturday by the appearance on our streets of a* bona fide *live African, who occupied a seat in the buggy of its owners, Mr. C. A. L. Lamar, and seemed equally delighted by the ride and the attention which he attracted. Our citizens were prepared by an article in the* Republican *to see a savage creature, but little raised in intelligence beyond a brute, and without a solitary feeling of personal attachment or sense of duty. Judge, then, of their surprise when they saw in the person of this distinguished stranger, a bright, intelligent boy, somewhat abashed in the presence of so many people, but courteous and respectful, taking off his hat with true African politeness, when replying to anything said to him, and repeating many things with wonderful accuracy when bidden to do so. He seemed much attached to "Mass Charley," as he called his owner.*

On his circuit around town, Lamar made a point of looking up Mr. Boston, the federal collector for the port of Savannah. As a crowd gathered around, Lamar introduced the little boy to Boston. As the boy dutifully doffed his cap, Lamar confided—in a voice loud enough to be heard by the crowd—that he had decided on a name for the boy: It was to be "Corrie." The crowd burst into laughter. Boston, red with embarrassment, scurried away. Following that demonstration, neither "Corrie" nor the other African boy were ever seen in Georgia again.

As these events unfolded in the national press—and many of the major Northern papers were covering them by now—the Buchanan administration was left looking increasingly foolish. Black ordered Ganahl and Jackson to redouble their efforts. Meanwhile, Black personally fired U.S. Marshal Stewart—whose complicity in the loss of witnesses was obvious—and replaced him with a federal officer who would do the job.

But there still was one more piece of collusion between Lamar and federal marshal Stewart to come. And it was undoubtedly the most outrageous of them all.

On January 26, 1859, U.S. District Court Judge John C. Nicoll had convened a Court of Admiralty to determine the fate of the *Wanderer*. Since its impoundment by the government, the yacht had sat on the Savannah River, padlocked and forlorn. In the case, the government argued that the *Wanderer* had clearly been outfitted for the slave trade. Supporting that allegation were signed affidavits from Clubb, Christie, and several other witnesses. The ship's log and charts were entered. As for her ownership, the name "William C. Corrie" appeared in florid script on her Charleston registry, dated June 8, 1858.

Judge Nicoll, a former mayor of Savannah, was known for his impartiality, and on February 25 ruled that the *Wanderer* should be condemned and sold at public auction. The advertisement read:

> *By order of a decree in the Court of Admiralty, the yacht Wanderer is now advertised to be sold here on Saturday, the 12 day of March. She is a staunch and trim little craft, of about 210 tons, in first rate order, of unexceptionable model, and, as shown by her recent and early performance, a remarkably fast sailer. She was built somewhere near New York, a few years since, and originally cost $30,000. To those of the yachting fraternity, or to speculators, the Wanderer offers an excellent opportunity for a good investment. She would likewise be a valuable acquisition to the Revenue service.*

On March 12, a crowd gathered before the massive columns of Savannah's Custom House for the sale. When Charles Lamar arrived, a crowd of his friends eagerly surrounded his buggy. Lamar was dressed nattily that morning, and was as cocky as a bantam rooster.

As the crowd surged forward toward the steps of the custom house, who should climb a few steps above the crowd to officiate but the notorious Marshal Stewart, waving and smiling to his admirers. It was to be his last official function before his removal from office. Stewart began by describing the attributes of the *Wanderer,* ranging from her lavishly appointed cabins to her dashingly designed lines.

No sooner had he finished his description of the yacht than Lamar pushed through the crowd. "Gentlemen, this vessel belongs to me—in every sense of the word," he bellowed, thrusting his arm above him like a Roman gladiator. "She has been taken from me by the high hand of the law."

The crowd roared its approval. Lamar continued. "The United States claims her; but I say she is mine. And I shall not expect any one to bid against me."

When the cheering subsided, Lamar turned his face up to Stewart. "I bid one dollar," he shouted.

Once again the crowd cheered.

Stewart smiled broadly. "Are there any other bids?" he asked.

The plaza fell silent.

Then, from the center of the crowd, a single voice cried out, "I bid four thousand dollars."

A cry of surprise swept through the crowd. With a shuffling of feet, the throng parted. There, dressed in an ill-fitting suit, was the county jailer, Charles Van Horn. He ran his fingers nervously through his thinning hair.

Lamar glanced hastily at Van Horn and then swiveled back to Stewart. "I bid four thousand and one," Lamar said.

"SOLD—to Mr. Lamar," Stewart hollered without hesitation. "The yacht *Wanderer.* Four thousand and one dollars."

The crowd surged toward Lamar to offer its congratulations, but Lamar would have none of it. Instead he ran through the crowd toward Van Horn, faster and then faster. His face was twisted with rage. Van Horn backpedaled, but not fast enough. Lamar threw a punch at Van Horn's face. The big man went down backward, blood splashing against the cobblestones. The crowd caught up and formed a circle. "Kill him, Charley!" one man urged Lamar. Van Horn, stunned, staggered to his feet, and then fell immediately over onto his face.

Lamar leaned over the jailer with his fists clenched, waiting for his opponent to rise. But Van Horn was out cold, his hair askew and his white shirt wet with blood. Cheered again, Lamar walked defiantly away.

As soon as a report of the incident hit the press, it caused a sensation. To some Northern editors, it proved that defiance and rebellion had swept the South—as though the federal government had been punched to the ground, rather than Mr. Van Horn. "Mr. Lamar said that, it being 'his property,' as a matter of course no *gentleman* would bid against him for his vessel," the *New York Times* remarked. "The appeal was so far successful that no one in the crowd took any part in the bidding, except a Mr. Van Horn, who ran up to four thousand dollars this splendid yacht (worth, perhaps, twenty or thirty thousand at the least) and received immediately afterwards a sound pummeling for his pains at the hands of the valiant Lamar and some half-dozen friends, and in the presence of the law officers of the Federal Government.

"Now if the yacht and the Negroes landed from her were in reality Mr. Lamar's property," the paper continued, "as he insolently claimed them to be, then Mr. Lamar is a slave-dealer, a kidnapper of Negroes, a felon guilty of an act equivalent in the meaning of the statute to piracy, and he should have been arrested on the spot. Instead of which, he was suffered to stand there—after his public and defiant avowal of a crime punishable by imprisonment and fine—and dictate terms at the auction of the vessel . . ."

Henry J. Raymond, thirty-eight, the cofounder and editor of the *New York Times,* had little use for Lamar, and nothing in common with him. Slight of build, with dark hair and bright blue eyes, Raymond was born on a farm in Western New York, a precocious kid, who was reading fluently by the time he was three. In 1851, at the age of thirty-one, he decided to start his own paper, one that emphasized city news, one that had two correspondents in Washington, and others that spread up and down the East Coast—and even a correspondent in Paris as well. Moving into a half-completed building at 113 Nassau Street, with a Hoe steam press installed in the basement, the *New York Times* began. As the conflict between North and South grew in the 1850s, Raymond consistently held the view that slavery was evil and wrong. But above all, he felt the Union must be preserved, and he feared that radicalism on either side—by fire-eaters or abolitionists—could soak the nation in blood.

But now Raymond was finding himself not only editorializing against the *Wanderer*'s conspirators but being drawn into a personal and increasingly precarious verbal battle with Charles Lamar himself.

It began with an odd, anonymous letter critical of the *Times*'s coverage of the auction, and particularly of its description of Charles Lamar as a "slave-trader, Negro stealer and felon." "You may search the country in its whole length and breadth," the anonymous writer advised, "but you will not find one who stands higher in estimation of those who know him as a high minded, honorable, frank and fearless gentleman. His opinions on the slave trade may be wrong, but he honestly entertains them. They are the same that were generally entertained in Great Britain and America half a century ago. The fact that he does not conform to your views on that question, furnishes no justifiable cause for the language you have applied to him. It is not my desire to get into any newspaper controversy on the subject. I merely request you will withdraw what you have hastily done—if you can do so with a sense of propriety. Yours, &c."

Who was the anonymous writer? Most likely that prominent New Yorker Gazaway Lamar, for Raymond treated his remarks with complete deference: "The above comes to us from a source which entitles it to entire respect and we yield prompt evidence to all its statements and concerning the character of Mr. Lamar and the general estimation in which he is held in the community where he lives," Raymond wrote in the following issue of the *Times*. "We are equally ready to add that the epithets employed in our article upon the subject in the Times of yesterday were not designed to have any application to Mr. Lamar's general character, or to be used towards him in any way outside of his connection with this specific transaction; and even in that respect perhaps they were stronger and more sweeping than the occasion required."

That said, though, Raymond stuck to his guns: "His conduct at the sale of the Wanderer was simply insolent. Every man present at that sale has a perfect right, at law, in morals, and in honor to bid upon that vessel, and Mr. Lamar's assault upon the only man who seems to have had the spirit to disregard his dictation, was as gross a breach of chivalry as of decency and law . . . We shall not do the people of Savannah the injustice of supposing that they were fairly represented, in sentiment, in temper, or in demeanor, either by Mr. Lamar or 'the crowd' in this transaction."

That may have salved the wounds between Gazaway Lamar and Editor Raymond, but it was not enough for the prickly Charles Lamar. In his own letter to Raymond, Lamar said the editorial was "personal and offensive to me." These were important words, for they set up the groundwork for a duel.

"Sir," wrote Lamar, "I have been informed by friends that I have been mistaken in my estimation of your character (and they derived their information from personal friends of yours), and that you would respond to any call made upon you. The object of this is to inquire if you have been properly represented by your friends. It is my purpose to go to Cuba next week, unless circumstances should arise to prevent, and a telegram, which will be paid for here, announcing your decision will be much obliged. Respectfully yours, C. A. L. Lamar."

Raymond parried brilliantly: A duel, Raymond explained, must be fought between equals. And since Lamar had "avowed his connection with a traffic which the laws of his country denounced as piracy, and the civilized nations of the world looked upon as odious," wrote Raymond, no such engagement between the two of them could be possible.

Replied Lamar: "Sir: I received yours of the 4th this morning. You have taken the usual refuge of a coward, who, afraid to fight, undervalues his adversary. Common as is this course in your meridian, the boast of your friends induced me to believe that you would hold yourself responsible to those whom you had offended. But for this, and the previous impression I had formed of your character, I would have had no correspondence with you."

Lamar had failed to exchange gunshots with the editor of the *New York Times,* but he was not giving up quite yet. "I'll put an indignity upon him in a public manner—such as slapping his face," Lamar bragged to a friend, "and then, if he doesn't resent it, why, I shall take no further notice of him."

This never came to pass, but Lamar was finally able to reach out and touch *someone*. A few days later, Lamar accused a visitor from Rhode Island of penning an article for a Northern newspaper about the auction that was critical of Lamar's conduct. Before the visitor could fully explain that the account was a private letter that had fallen into the hands of a reporter, who had embellished it, Lamar slapped the man in the face, demanded a duel, and, short of that, told him to get out of Savannah on the next train.

When the news reached Raymond at the *Times,* he was compelled to write another acidic editorial against Lamar. "It will, no doubt, be news to the public to learn that the power of banishment from the City of Savannah, if not from the state of Georgia, is vested in Mr. C. A. L. Lamar, who, we believe, has never been elected to such an office," said Raymond. "It will be still greater news to those gentlemen who uphold the 'Code of Honor,' that it is chivalrous to follow up an offer of satisfaction for a slap on the face by ordering the aggrieved party to quit the scene of the insult and the place where the 'satisfaction' would be obtainable. To the minds of most people, however, the slapping of a man's face for having written 'an account of the recent sale of the Wanderer to a Rhode Island paper,' will suggest more of the rowdyism of the bully than the chivalry of wounded honor."

That Lamar had become a bully was something that the citizens of Georgia were reluctantly beginning to realize. When one citizen called for a meeting to criticize Lamar, he was compelled to write a hand-wringing apology. "In my notice for the meeting, I meant nothing disrespectful to those gentlemen who may have been in possession of Africans," the transgressor confessed. "I regret that I should have said anything in that notice to give offense to any of my friends in the district."

When other citizens issued a bill of indictment against Lamar for stealing away the two Africans from jailer Van Horn, they, too, found themselves begging for mercy. In an advertisement in the Savannah papers, they said that the court had *compelled* them to move against Lamar—and, in fact, they were all for the slave trade. "We unhesitatingly advocate the repeal of all laws which, directly or indirectly, condemn this institution (African slave trade), and those who have inherited or maintain it . . ." they declared.

Even when Deputy Marshal McRae and the members of his posse traveled to Savannah to testify about the release of the thirty-six Africans, they found themselves personally engaged with Lamar. Gathering before the judge at the Chatham County courthouse, "To our great astonishment and mortification, we were *arrested,*" wrote one of the posse members. Their confusion turned to shock when Charles Lamar emerged from the back of the courtroom with his attorney, John Owens, and accused them all of "stealing" the five domestic slaves that had accompanied the Africans on the wagons. The defendants were bound over in the sum of $1,000 each, to appear at the October 1859 term of Worth Superior Court, to answer the charge of larceny.

By now Lamar had critics apologizing, grand juries shaking, and the citizens of Savannah cowed. "Lamar is a dangerous man, and with all the apparent recklessness and lawlessness—but a cautious one, too, for he never ventures in the presence of any save those whom he may regard as followers, or whom he may readily intimidate," confided Charles C. Jones, a Savannah native who would become mayor two years later. "Such men . . . now run riot without let or hindrance . . ."

Indeed, Lamar was feeling confident—so confident that he decided to take a little vacation aboard his newly reacquired yacht: He would take the *Wanderer* to Cuba with his good friend Trowbridge and a few others, and maybe even find a buyer for her there.

But as the *Wanderer* filled her sails and headed out to sea, an item appeared in the local press that served as a reminder to anyone who might try to take advantage of Lamar while he was gone:

> *SUCCESSFUL SURGERY—Mr. Henry du Bignon of Georgia, who was shot about twelve months since on the Savannah Race Course by C.A.L. Lamar, of the Wanderer notoriety, recently came on to this city for the purpose of having the ball extracted. We are pleased to learn that the bullet, which was found imbedded in the bones of the face three inches from the surface, has been safely extracted, after a severe surgical operation by Professor Carnochan.*

A year earlier, it seemed, Lamar had gotten into an argument at the racetrack with his friend, Henry du Bignon. Tempers flared. Du Bignon drew a knife, then picked up a heavy glass inkwell and hurled it at Lamar. Lamar drew his pistol and fired. Now, it seemed, they were friends again. But the newspaper clipping served as a timely reminder: Bad things could happen to people who opposed the iron will of Charles Lamar.

14

THE BRITISH

"I MUST acquaint your Lordship that the yacht Wanderer was condemned, at the present term of the Admiralty Court, for being engaged in the slave trade," the British consul in Savannah wrote to the British foreign secretary on March 1, 1859, "and is advertised by the United States Marshal for sale at public auction on the 12th of March."

From the moment that British authorities identified the *Wanderer* as a slaver, they kept a steady watch on her. Their interest was not so much in the yacht itself, however, nor even on the issue of slave trading, but on the much greater issues looming over British-American relations.

In the 1850s, an American war with Great Britain was not inconceivable. Britain had taxed the colonies, and then bloodied them during the War of Independence. She had burned the White House and cut a swath of destruction during the War of 1812. She had ruled the seas for two hundred years, and despite two defeats by Americans on land, was still ruling them. Now she was challenging U.S. domination in the Western Hemisphere with her incursions into Central America, and with her boarding of American ships for the purpose, she argued, of stopping the trade in slaves. In the 1850s, in the eyes of many Americans, Britain was the evil empire.

The coasts of Africa and Cuba were frequent collision points between the two naval powers. It was here that the two nations, supposedly united in an effort to eradicate the slave trade, were still acting out old aggressions, still smarting from old wounds. This was why the American commander Totten, when he had discovered that the *Rufus Soule* had been boarded, searched, and sunk by the British, wrote to his commander, "Whether the Rufus Soule is engaged in the slave trade or not is not the question. *She wore the American flag. . . .*"

It was why President Buchanan, in his annual message to Congress in 1858, stated that slavers flying the American flag were preferable to British ships that stopped American vessels and boarded them. Said he: "The occasional abuse of the flag of any nation is even less to be deprecated than would be the establishment of any regulations which might be incompatible with the freedom of the seas."

It was why U.S. Secretary of State Lewis Cass wrote:

> *Who can doubt but that English cruisers, stationed upon that distant coast, with an unlimited right of search and discretionary authority to take possession of all vessels frequenting those seas, will seriously interrupt the trade of other nations? . . .*

And it was why the naval correspondent for the *New York Herald* complained,

> *What a farce is the English suppression of the slave trade! Every English officer that comes here is after money, and they leave nothing underdone to get it. Boarding vessels with American colors and correct papers is a common thing. By threats and bargains they get possession of the vessel, landing its crews on this sickly coast without any provision; they resort to threats which they dare not carry out, and act toward our legal traders in a way to intimidate any honest man . . . In my opinion, the boarding, search, detention and seizure of the Rufus Soule is the greatest outrage ever committed upon our nationality—an insult to our flag and to our nation which calls for immediate action.*

The conflict between America and Britain was bad enough in the early 1850s, but in 1858, Britain, having finished its work in the Crimean War, decided to make an all-out assault on the slave trade. Now vessels that had once blocked Napoleon III in the Mediterranean were redeployed to Africa and Cuba. Extra seamen and artillery were brought over. The British set up a virtual blockade around Cuba. On the African coast, British seamen poured over the gunwales of suspected slavers in unprecedented numbers, regardless of the flag they flew; they fired on fleeing ships as well, blasting away the spars and sails of suspects, only later looking under the decks for signs of the crime.

In 1853, James Buchanan, then minister to London, had written: "We shall probably have war with England before the close to the present administration." That comment was evoked by British aggressiveness in Central America. But now it was equally true. America was ready to fight. Republican senator William H. Seward, who would be Lincoln's secretary of state, threatened war. So did his political enemy, Democrat Stephen A. Douglas. Across the nation, in fact, newspapers demanded blood—from the abolitionist *New Era* (which declared that the U.S. must "resist to the death the insolent assumption of any foreign power to subject our ships to detention and examination") to the fire-eating *Charleston Mercury*. It seemed to be an unavoidable showdown: Two navies steaming toward each other, in a confrontation that only one could win. But this time it was different. For generations Britain had held the upper hand on the high seas. Now America was ascendant, and the British, on the verge of a relative decline. The British knew it, or at least they could feel it in the American resolve on the African slave coast.

Just six months earlier, the British were still trying to stop the atrocities that were being committed under the Stars and Stripes. Earlier in 1859, Commodore Wise of the British African Squadron had written to the British secretary of the admiralty:

> *In my letter of the 26th of August last I had the honour of bringing before their Lordship's notice two most glaring instances of the prostitution of the American flag, particularly in the case of the (Kate) Ellen of New York, boarded and searched by Commander*

Truscott . . . when a slave deck and other fittings for the slave trade were found on board, and released, as her papers clearly showed her right to the flag of the United States.

It is now my duty to report that the Ellen a few days later, ascended the Congo, and was boarded by Commodore Bowden of the Medusa, who pronounced her papers correct. She subsequently descended the river, and, with her cargo of slaves on board, cooped up and dying under close-locked hatches, the Ellen of New York, under the American flag, boldly passed Her Majesty's ship Medusa.

When the Ellen was boarded, on passing, the stench sufficiently indicated that numerous human wretches were stowed below, and the reports from Punta da Lenha confirmed the opinion, but further examination was strictly forbidden; and, as the right of the Ellen to the flag of America had been proved on two occasions, she was permitted to sail, without molestation, with her rich cargo of death, disease and misery . . .

But as the spring of 1858 unfolded, and the British faced the wrath of American public opinion—and the formidable mustering of American naval power, which was now on high alert and sent out of port—the British became increasingly pragmatic. Why must Britain be America's moral instructor? Why should Britain, which required Southern cotton and Northern trade, step into the fray against its best trading partners? The Conservative government of Lord Derby, which had inherited the slave trade issue (when it had replaced Palmerston's government in February), also questioned the fight, since it was not of its own making.

Even moderates admitted that plantation masters in Cuba could get all the slaves they needed, regardless of the efforts of the African Squadron: Higher demand meant higher prices for slaves, which only encouraged the slave traders to redouble their efforts. As it stood now, a slave trader could sell his cargoes in Cuba for thirty times what he paid for them in Africa.

After days of heated debate, the British Parliament came to a historic decision. They capitulated completely to the American demands. Following the vote, the British sent orders to their cruisers to cease all inspections of American vessels. The "right of visitation" was finished.

Said British foreign secretary Lord Malmesbury, "I have put it as strongly as possible to the American Government, that if it is known that the American flag covers every iniquity, then every pirate or slaver on earth will carry it, and no other." But the message did not sink in, he said. The London *Times,* after demanding U.S. cooperation on the African coast for years, finally said it was giving up on the Americans. "It is no business of ours to drill them into virtue," it remarked bitterly. "It may be our duty to try persuasion and remonstrance; but if they smile at our persuasion and reject our remonstrance, we must needs stop short."

In the United States, however, the news was received with celebration. The Yanks had fought the British on the high seas since the Revolution. The last remaining vestige of that bondage was the "right of visitation"— the right that Britain had imposed, even after the War of 1812—to search suspicious American vessels. Now that final link had been broken. Now America was truly free.

At the Fourth of July party thrown in London that year by the American minister to Britain, George M. Dallas, the tables were set with American flags; red, white, and blue carnations filled the room; bunting and banners decorated the floor-to-ceiling windows. At the appointed hour, one hundred and fifty guests excitedly took their seats. Dallas, who had fought the British in heated telegrams for several years on the issue of visitation and the search of American ships, glowed with anticipation.

As the faces of the Americans at the party looked up at him expectantly, he raised his glass. He spoke of the bond that America had with Britain, but also of the struggle America had fought, not only in the early days of independence, but more recently, for equity and respect on the high seas. Now, he said, that victory had been won. He lifted his glass higher. "The termination of that for which we have struggled—for nearly half a century—has been achieved!" he exclaimed. Every person in the room rose to his feet and cheered.

Equal enthusiasm was shared by President Buchanan. "It must be a source of sincere satisfaction to all classes of our fellow citizens—and especially to those engaged in foreign commerce—that the claim on the part of Great Britain forcibly to visit and search American merchant vessels on the high seas in time of peace has been abandoned," he said a few months later, in his final address to Congress, adding, "This was, by far, the most dangerous question to the peace of the two countries which has existed since the war of 1812."

Indeed, America had demonstrated its new place in the world. No longer would Americans face the indignities of random search. No longer would American commerce be subordinate to that of Britain on the high seas. From British rule, America had finally achieved emancipation! Little did they realize, in this liberation, that America had achieved victory over the issues of the past, at the expense of those that would haunt the nation for generations to come.

While the superpowers were locked in this conflict, the slave trade was booming. Demand for slaves was already high: Cholera had swept through Cuba in 1853, killing thousands of slaves and requiring replacements. Sugar prices climbed to an all-time high. Shipbuilders, meanwhile, had built too many vessels in the 1840s and 1850s—and this was followed by the depression of 1857. Now vessels were cheap and plentiful. Slavers could pick up 250-ton brigs at bargain prices, load them with a thousand slaves each, and create a business that boasted a monstrous economy of scale. Or they could buy the speediest of clipper ships, and easily outsail and outfox the Americans and Brits. It had become a sport.

Either way, as the 1850s wore on, slaving became a bigger and bigger business. In 1857, a group of well-heeled investors started the "Spanish Company," a well-run slaving operation with offices at, no surprise, 158 Pearl Street in New York. "The Spanish company was like an octopus," wrote maritime author Warren S. Howard, "thrusting its tentacles into several ports simultaneously. Where officials were not vigilant, or where they were hampered in performance of their duties, the tentacle took hold firmly; if seizures were made in those ports, the tentacles recoiled or even withdrew entirely for a time until quiet was restored. As one tentacle recoiled others increased their pressure so that the desired three or four slavers left for Africa every month."

Bigger enterprises were under way, though. One start-up, capitalized at $1.2 million, was said to have thirty-seven American-made vessels ready for business. Its prospectus promised much more: eighty ships, with a regular scheduled departure for Africa every two weeks. Even with heavy losses, the enterprise boasted it could eventually be landing 150,000 to 200,000 Africans in Cuba every year. The entrepreneurs may have been overstating their capacity, but not the possible demand for slaves. If the fire-eaters succeeded in spreading slavery to the western states, and should slavery enlarge into a formal Republic that would include Mexico, Central America, and Cuba, as the fire-eaters hoped, millions of new slaves would be required. And so, on the very eve of the Civil War, few businesses had healthier prospects in America than that of the trading in slaves.

While the British were keeping their eyes on the *Wanderer,* they were also paying particular attention to William Corrie. Robert Bunch, the British consul in Charleston, had met Corrie several times, and didn't like him at all. In a letter to British foreign secretary Lord Malmesbury, Bunch pulled no punches in his description of the man the New York press had described as a "high-toned Southern gentleman":

> *Mr.—or as he styles himself—"Captain" Corrie is a South Carolinian by birth; his father was a Scotchman, who earned a precarious livelihood in Charleston by mending the wheels of the rough plantation carts of the country. The son followed the army of the United States, during the Florida wars, in the capacity of a sutler.*
>
> *He has, for some years past, fixed his residence in Washington, where his occupation has been what is called here "lobbying," that is, bribing members of Congress to vote for the payment of pecuniary claims upon the Government of the United States. His business appears to have prospered; indeed, there are several notorious instances of his success. His influence at the capital is very great; I was assured not long ago by one of the Members from this State that he had more power than all of the South Carolina Delegation.*
>
> *Personally, he is a vulgar, swaggering fellow, addicted to drink, habitually boasting of his power in Congress, and fond of specifying the exact sum for which each Member is to be purchased. Such being his antecedents, I need hardly add that he is capable of slave trading, or any other villany.*

In the wake of the *Wanderer* incident, the British were not alone in reexamining Corrie. On February 3, 1859, the New York Yacht Club resolved "That the name of the yacht Wanderer be erased from the list, and that William C. Corrie, proprietor of said yacht, and a member of this club, primarily for his deliberate violation of the laws of the United States, but more especially from his being engaged in a traffic repugnant to humanity and to the moral sense of the members of this association, be, and he hereby is, expelled from the New York Yacht Club." Simultaneously, the wooden half-model of the *Wanderer,* which had been displayed in the library, was sent in disgrace down into the basement.

Years later, in its official history, the club noted of the *Wanderer,* "She could have been called the Wicked Sister of the virtuous America, as for many years her name could not be mentioned in the presence of a New York Yacht Club member."

Corrie may have been reviled by the British consul, and shown the door by the New York yachting society, but he was deeply beloved in Charleston. When he arrived, in fact, there was an impromptu parade in his honor, with the subsequent popping of many champagne corks. "The Washington correspondent of the Boston Advertiser states that a gay and happy festival of the friends of Captain Corrie in that city celebrated the news of his arrival in the Savannah River with his cargo of slaves from Africa," the *New York World Telegram* reported on Christmas Day, 1858. "Success to all such enterprises was drunk in flowing bumpers of champagne by the elated company."

But of all of Corrie's friends in Charleston, the most valuable was a U.S. district court judge by the name of Andrew G. Magrath. Magrath had been born in Charleston and had received his law degree at Harvard. But he hated Cambridge, especially the abolitionist fervor of the place. In 1850, at the age of thirty-seven, he wrote a fiery pamphlet advocating disunion. And when Lincoln was elected president ten years later, Magrath dramatically threw off his robes, quitting the federal bench. He later became the Confederate governor of South Carolina.

As a federal judge, Magrath may have sworn to uphold the Constitution and the laws of the land, but by the time that Corrie had made it back to Charleston, Magrath was a fierce disunionist, and eager to challenge the authority of the federal government. Magrath was well aware that Ganahl, Jackson, and Attorney General Black wanted Corrie back in Savannah, to stand trial with Brown, Arguirir, and Rajesta. Corrie's signature, after all, was on the *Wanderer*'s ownership papers, as big as the words John Hancock on the Declaration of Independence. But Magrath was equally determined not to give Corrie back.

Thus, when Ganahl filed an affidavit, based on the piracy statute of 1820, demanding Corrie's arrest and repatriation to Georgia, Magrath refused. Since Corrie had been arrested (reluctantly) in South Carolina, Magrath ruled, Corrie would be tried there. Thwarted in his initial attempt, Ganahl shifted gears and charged Corrie on a new indictment, under the Act of 1818, for the lower offence of aiding in the fitting out of a vessel for the slave trade. Magrath again declined to surrender the prisoner, alleging that Corrie would be held to the 1820 statute, a higher charge, which kept him in South Carolina. Ganahl once again had to sit and wait.

When Corrie finally appeared before a grand jury in Charleston in May, and the case was argued, the legal standoff got even stranger: The grand jury at first found no reason for Corrie to stand trial. But then, as the court was breaking up, Magrath realized that with no offense to hold Corrie in Charleston, Ganahl could demand him back in Georgia. Scrambling at the last minute, the grand jury was reconvened. Now they reversed their decision, charging Corrie with piracy, which put him back under Magrath's control. Although piracy was a capital offense, without bail, Corrie was offered bail immediately. Corrie was the toast of the town once again, attending dinners, sailing, and resting easy at his South Carolina plantation.

In fact, the word was out that Corrie was writing a book. The *Charleston Mercury*, a big Corrie fan, was all over it. "Look out! The forthcoming book, on the cruise of the yacht Wanderer, will make a sensation," the newspaper exclaimed. "It is brought out by a person who took part in her adventures, and will give a minute account thereof, and will disclose facts hitherto unknown and unsuspected, involving the reputations of many public men, from United States Senators down to the government small fry."

Perhaps. But the *New York Times* had a different take on the project: "Expelled by the New York Yacht Club, cast off by the President, repudiated even by a Georgia Secretary of the Treasury—a martyr to his faith in the white man and his fondness for the black," the *Times* said. "If Captain Corrie can give us any authentic information on this subject, his book will have a value and a bearing of which the author himself can hardly be conscious."

It never happened, however. Corrie's tell-all book, for better or for worse, never saw the light of day.

Gazaway Lamar

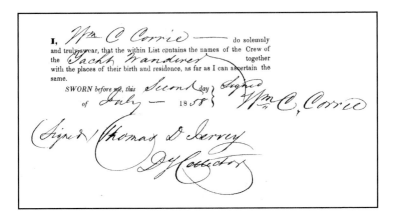

I, *Wm C Corrie* ——— do solemnly and truly swear, that the within List contains the names of the Crew of the *Yacht Wanderer* together with the places of their birth and residence, as far as I can ascertain the same.

SWORN before me, this *Second* day of *July* —— 18*58* Signed *Wm C, Corrie*

(Signed) *Thomas D Ierrey*

Dy Collector

Half model of schooner *Wanderer*
Copyright © Mystic Seaport Collection, Mystic, CT, #97.129.15

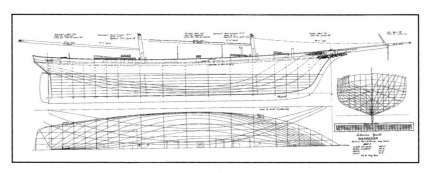

Schematic plans for the *Wanderer*
Courtesy of the Smithsonian Institution, NMAH/Transportation

The *Wanderer*
The Rudder Magazine. *Vol XV, February 1904, page 52.*
Copyright © Mystic Seaport, G. W. Blunt Library
Collection, Mystic, CT

Charles Lamar
*Courtesy of the Georgia
Historical Society*

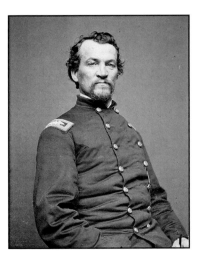

J. Egbert Farnum

Illustration from the *New York American and Journal,* April 19, 1905, depicting the *Wanderer*'s crossing of the Atlantic

John C. Calhoun, twice vice
president of the United States,
and chief architect of the
Southern Rights movement

The Fire-Eaters

James DeBow

Edmund Ruffin

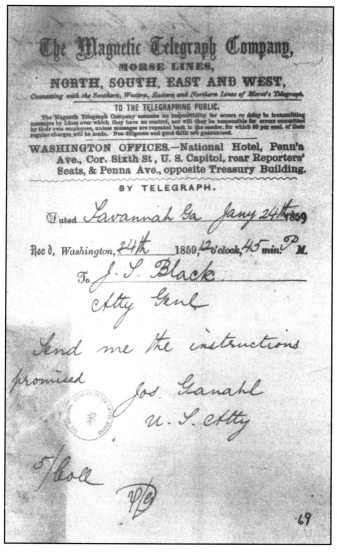

Message from U.S. Attorney Joseph Ganahl in Savannah to U.S. Attorney General Jeremiah Black, requesting assistance in the *Wanderer* case

Raising the first Flag of Independence in Savannah, November 8, 1860

15

Vicksburg

LEONIDAS SPRATT mopped the humidity from his steel-rimmed spectacles and, dodging fat raindrops that began to fall again as he stepped from his carriage, strode through the mud to the meeting hall in which the Southern Commercial Convention would be held for the year of 1859.

However refreshing the ocean breezes were on Corrie in Charleston in late May, in Vicksburg, Mississippi, the first wave of summer heat had descended, sending the cicadas into stunned silence during the day and whirring madly in the trees at night. In the cotton fields, which spread as far as the eye could see, the white tufts of cotton had yet to emerge. But the green bolls, no bigger than a pinhead, were drawing strength from the sun and rain. They would bloom for a day, a red flower, then build slowly into a greasy ball of cotton. The moment the cotton bolls ripened (and you could smell their rich aroma), thousands of sweaty black bodies would lean into the fields, picking the crop, with the overseers riding up and down among them, wiping the sweat off their faces with handkerchiefs, and pulling their straw hats down low over their eyes.

The previous year, the Commercial Convention had been held on the dirt floor of a cotton warehouse in Montgomery—and it had been as muddy and as miserable as pig slop by the end of their sweaty confabulation. This was better, thought Spratt, looking around the new convention hall. There was a plank floor beneath his feet. He stomped his feet appreciatively on it. Brass gaslights ringed the room. Ionic columns graced the entranceway. At the front of the hall, the stage rose two feet above the floor, as he had instructed, and was big enough for Spratt to strut and pace upon.

Later that afternoon, General Charles Clarke of Mississippi met with Spratt. Clarke was a corpulent aristocrat whose plantation worked more than two hundred slaves in its cotton fields. They sat at a table at Spratt's hotel and plotted out the next day's events. The meeting would start with a few economic issues, they decided, just to give the convention an aura of respectability. One man would speak on direct trade with Europe; another would tackle taxation issues. But very quickly the discourse would turn to political matters. The next delegate would offer a resolution requiring the South to separate from the Union—should a Republican win the election in 1860. That resolution would probably not pass, they agreed. Following that, another delegate would deliver a resolution making the Gulf of Mexico, Cuba, and Central America part of a vast, Southern-dominated, slave-owning empire. That one would be wildly accepted.

By then, the sun would have dipped beneath the trees. Inside the convention hall, the gas fixtures would have been lit. Outside, torches would have been casting orange light through the windows. And at that point—when all the delegates had arrived, when the sweat was already shining on their faces, when the cigar smoke had filled the hall and the anticipation was running high—that's when Spratt would make his presence known, climbing to the stage.

By 9 o'clock that night, the hall was thick with cigar smoke, the gaslights hissed, the torches flickered outside. Heat lightning flashed in the humid sky above. The conventioneers pressed toward the stage, eagerly awaiting the arrival of Spratt. For his part, Spratt leaned against a pillar in the shadows, and waited. His thick black hair, parted severely in the middle, hid his angular face. General Clarke had climbed onto the stage to scattered applause. Now he held up his hands. The room began to quiet. He announced that the next speaker would be a writer, a philosopher, a great orator, and most important, a soldier in the great Southern rights movement.

Even before he had finished, the crowd had jumped to its feet, cheering. Spratt emerged from the shadows and strode toward the stage. The crowd enveloped him, their hands extended for his to touch. He leapt onto the platform and, rising to his full height, threw his head back and ran his fingers through his hair. Two girls presented him with flowers and then took turns throwing their arms around his neck. Spratt hugged them, and then, disentangling, grasped the edges of the podium.

"I have awaited you—and you have come," he thundered.

The crowd roared in reply.

"I will not disappoint you," he said.

"No."

"I will supply that which you need."

"Yes," the group replied. Spratt smiled and swept back his hair again.

"When the census was taken in 1808," he began, "the Northern and the Southern states were equal in number—and nearly equal in population. Since that time, *five million foreigners* have come to the North. And no new slaves have come to the South."

"That's the truth, Leonidas," a man called out.

"At present, therefore, the South has ten million people. The North has sixteen million people." Spratt gazed across the room. "As the equality was lost to the South by the suppression of the slave trade," he cried, "so the slave trade would of necessity restore it . . ." The delegates rose from their seats in applause.

"There is *honor* in the African slave trade," Spratt said. Casting his eyes across the hall, he saw Charles Lamar below him, looking up with shining eyes. "My friend, Lamar, already hoists the slave-trade flag," Spratt cried, "and floats it from his masthead!"

Lamar, glowing in his mentor's recognition, thrust his clenched fist in the air.

Spratt took a sip of water, and pushed back his hair again.

"The foreign slave trade, gentlemen, would give political power to the South. It would also give prosperity and progress to us."

"Amen," said a man in a stovepipe hat.

"This is not a visionary speculation. When foreign slaves were first introduced, the rural parishes of the Charleston district were the brightest spots in all America. Taken from the slave marts of Charleston, to the lands adjacent, they gave to everything they touched the spring of progress. They gave drainage to the land, cultivation to the soil and provision and abundance to the artisans and operatives of the city. These in turn, with labor and provisions cheap, struck boldly out on the field of competition. Leather was tanned, cloth was manufactured, shoes, hats, clothes and implements were made for consumption and for export. The town advanced, the country prospered. Swamps were reclaimed, mansions arose, avenues were planned, pleasure grounds laid out, commerce started, ships sailed to every corner of the world, parish churches in imposing styles of architecture were erected, and spots more progressive, and more true to the principles of religion, and more warmed by hospitality were never seen than in the town and parishes of Charleston district."

"I'm a witness to that," one man cried, and the crowd cheered.

"But upon the suppression of the trade, and the rising price of slaves, their splendors waned. Their glories departed. Progress left them for the North. Cultivation ceased. The swamps returned. Mansions became tenantless and roofless. Values fell. Land that sold for fifty dollars per acre now sells for less than five dollars. Churches are abandoned. Trade no longer prosecuted. Of twenty tan yards, not one remains. Of shoes, hats and implements of industry, once put upon the trade of foreign towns, none now are put upon our own. And Charleston, which was once upon the road from Europe to the North, now stands aside, and while once the metropolis of America, is now the unconsidered seaport of a tributary province. Such are the effects of the foreign slave trade. The experience of that district, to a greater or lesser extent, has been the experience of other sections of the Southern seaboard.

"Prosperity," he said, looking into the faces of the crowd. "And does this argue then for the return of the African slave trade?" he asked.

"Yes, it does!" the crowd replied. Spratt smiled.

"With cheap slaves and cheap subsistence, our enterprising tradesmen could compete with tradesmen at other sections of the world. A larger amount of products and fabrics would encourage transportation. Hotels, railroads and steamboats would begin to pay; wealth would flow in upon us; importance would come to us. And instead of standing as we now stand, in provincial admiration of the Vanderbilts of the North, resplendent with the prosperity that has come upon them with five million slaving foreign laborers, we ourselves could stand up still more resplendent in the prosperity to be poured upon us by turning thousands our way from the plains of Africa."

The delegates again rose from their seats, cheering and applauding.

"Is it of injury to the Negro?"

"No!" cried the crowd.

"I venture to affirm that no Negroes that were ever born have been so blessed in themselves and their posterity as the 400,000 Africans imported to this country," Spratt said.

"Is it of injury to the white man?" he continued.

"No!" cried the crowd.

"I would venture to affirm that there are no men at any point upon the surface of this earth so favored in their lot, so elevated in their natures, so just to their duties, so up to the emergencies and so ready for the trials of their lives as are the six million masters in the Southern states."

"Is it of injury to society?"

"No," they repeated, their bodies pressing forward toward the stage.

"Throughout history, social revolutions have disturbed the constitutions of almost every nation. In France, the props of social order have been stricken down. Right now democracy advances upon the conservatisms of every European constitution. They, like France, may sink at length to a sea incarnadine. But from this evil the slave society is free! There can be no march of slaves upon the ranks of masters. They have no reaching to a higher sphere. There is no contest of classes for the same position. Each in its order balanced!"

Spratt poured himself a glass of water and drank thirstily. "I can see what will happen," he began quietly. "I can see where these societies are bound to go." He swept back his hair again. "Can you see it?" Outside, heat lightning was arcing in the sky. The rumbling of thunder was growing more distinct. "Well, then," he said with a smile, "let me tell you.

"I have perfect confidence that when France shall fall again into the delirium of liberty, when the peerage of England shall have yielded to the masses, when democracy in the North shall hold its carnival—when all that is *pure and noble* will have been dragged down, when all that is low and vile shall have mounted to the surface . . ."

"Amen!" someone shouted.

Spratt's voice grew stronger. "When women shall have taken the places and habiliments of men; and when men have taken the places and habiliments of women . . ."

"Amen!"

"When free love unions and phallicists shall pervade the land. When the sexes shall cavort without the restraints of marriage. When youths and maidens, drunk at noonday, and half naked, shall reel about the marketplaces—when these come to pass, the South will stand serene and erect, as she stands now. The slave will be restrained by power. The master by the trusts of a superior position . . ."

Spratt grabbed the podium. "And if there *ever* is to be a hope for the North—a hope that she will ever ride the waves of bottomless perdition that roll up around her—it is in the fact that *the South* will stand by her, and lend a helping hand to rescue and to save her."

Again the crowd roared. Flowers, thrown by the children, rained down onto the stage. Spratt held up his arm to quiet the crowd.

"The North," he uttered with flat disgust. The floor erupted with hisses. Spratt shook his head sadly. "Her every interest is parasitic; her cities are dependent on the South for customers; her factories dependent on the South for markets. They would have our customer and trades upon their own terms, but they must have them. Without them their factories would fail. New York would be shriveled to the dimensions of a common town. If the South were independent, New York could not have it. The South would trade direct to foreign countries. The factories of the North can barely stand now, are protected by an impost duty of twenty-five percent; they could not then stand under such competition. The stake, therefore, is one of existence, which the North can never risk on such a venture."

He shook his head again. "No. It is time to speak out like men. If we practice slavery—let us avow it!"

The delegates began to pound the floor with their boots and canes.

"Let us own it *as a right!*"

The crowd cheered. Spratt, smiling with pleasure, came to the edge of the platform and touched the hands that reached up for him. He paraded across the stage, redoubling the cheers. Then he went back to the podium, and looked down reflectively. His hair fell down across his face like a curtain. After a few moments—after the cheers and applause and shuffling of feet had ceased—he looked up again.

"Let me ask of you a question," he said calmly. "Can the South accomplish this without the rupture of existing ties? Without the rupture of relations that are still fondly cherished?" He paused. "Without imbruing her hands in blood?"

Spratt looked around the room. He allowed time for his words to sink in. "I don't know," he said sadly. "I don't know.

"I will tell you this, though," he continued. "There may never be a peaceful solution between North and South. We won the equality of man from Great Britain only through *revolution*. The principle that equality is the right only among *equals,* however, may need another revolution to deliver us.

"Yes, my friends," Spratt continued, "we are not *only* in contest with the North, which bears the banners of democracy, but with democracy itself."

A troubled murmur crossed the room. Spratt held up his hand. "Let me explain. The social principle that triumphed in our American Revolution was that of the equality of *man*. That principle entered the constitution of our government. It declared that suffrage shall be universal, that all offices shall be elective, that all restrictions on individual liberty shall be removed. It was at the dictate of that principle that the word *slave* was not admitted to the constitution; that in 1794 we prohibited the transportation of slaves from one foreign country to another; that in 1808 we prohibited the introduction of slaves to this country; that in 1819 we sent armed ships to cruise against the slave trade; that in 1820 we made it piracy. It was for this principle that in 1842 we joined England in a maritime crusade against it. We see nothing more horrible in this union, in fact, than any evidence of man's dominion over man."

Spratt took off his coat and handed it to an aide. He unbuttoned his shirt cuffs and rolled them. The crowd had begun to grow uneasy. Spratt waited. He let the restlessness die down.

"But while this Union is a democracy," he said, very gravely now, "the South is *not* . . . a democracy." The hall was completely quiet—quiet against the low rumbling of approaching thunder. "Yes, the South is so in its external character, and so in sentiment, perhaps," he continued, "for there are very many of us who yet sympathize with the feeling that equality is the right of man. But in its social condition the South is not . . . a democracy. On the contrary, it is perhaps the purest form of aristocracy the world has ever seen."

He looked around the hall. "Shall we affirm it? Is it not a higher order?" Then he suddenly shouted: "If you do not think so, let the enquirer look at the rivers of blood that flow from free and equal France; let him look at the brigandage that rules in Mexico. Let him look at the fearful portents of the North; let him look at the prostration of all that is elevated, at the rise of all that is low . . ." Spratt's eyes rolled wildly, his hair swinging across his face. "Let him look at the reptiles that crawl from the sinks of vice to brandish their forked tongues about the pillars of the Capitol; at the bands of thousands of workers that march the streets of New York with banners inscribed with 'Liberty' on one side and 'We Will Have Bread' on the other . . . and then say whether equality be indeed the right of man. Or whether inequities of some sort, no matter how objectionable in theory, are not of necessity in social practice.

"No, we cannot have this," he cried. His body was shaking now. "The Thracian horse, returning from the field of victory, still bears a master on his back. And so, we must wage a deadly contest with our enemies in the North. And then, when that is won, prepare for an even deadlier contest with our enemies at home."

A fight had broken out in the back of the hall. Fists were flying, canes were working the air, and, like a rolling wave, it slowly moved forward. Bodies collided with grunts and groans; chairs were upset; ladies screamed. Spratt watched, detached, sweat pouring down his face. The bolts of lightning now struck nearer. The thunder crashed overhead. A gust of wind blew against the side of the building, slamming the shutters and doors. Spratt continued. His words rose and fell in the pandemonium, lost occasionally, as though in a storm.

"Having achieved one revolution to escape democracy in the North, we must still achieve another to escape it in the South . . ." he cried.

"Any attempt by the President of the United States to stop the reopening of the trade will cause the sun to rise upon the reeking plans of another Lexington or Concord. . . .

"Rights, liberties and institutions are more worthy than the Union. . . . They must be free to expand, if necessary, by armed resistance to the Federal Government!"

At that, Henry S. Foote, the former governor of Mississippi, climbed onto the stage. A quick man with a ponderous, twitching mustache, the governor was one of the South's most ardent Unionists—a man who refused to let the issue of slavery split the nation. "Treason!" Foote screamed, thrusting an accusing finger at Spratt. "Treason! To say that the Constitution of the United States is no longer a valid and binding instrument, that the sacred laws of the Union—enacted by wiser men than now live, and wiser men, I fear, than will ever live in the country again—amount to absolutely nothing . . ."

Some of the men in the room cheered—others hissed and booed. ". . . that they may be set aside," Foote continued, "that the Government functionaries defied, and that reliance may be confidently placed on the juries of the country by perjury to acquit felons—*That* is one of the most monstrous and vile propositions that could be made in the hearing of an intelligent and high-minded people."

Foote pointed his finger again at Spratt, who was standing on the side of the stage with a bemused look on his face. "I had hoped this monster of treason would unfold himself to public view," he thundered, "that he might be attacked, and, in all his monstrous deformity, put to death by the voice of free men!"

Spratt laughed.

General Clarke and a few others grabbed Foote by his arms and tried to force him off the stage. But the little man broke free, ripping his sleeves. His face was red with anger. "I speak for my country and I take all the responsibility for what I say," he cried out. "And I will meet the whole band of Southern chivalry at the sword's point, or pistol's mouth, or anywhere!"

Other men pushed to the stage in support of Foote. There was Walter Brooke, of Mississippi, and Colonel I. M. Patridge, of Vicksburg, among others. "All we have had from Mr. Spratt today, this counseling of the South to armed and bloody opposition to the American government, all this will lead to greater hostility to Southern institutions," Patridge shouted. "It will strengthen the Republicans. It will supply the enemies of the Union with a plausible pretext to hasten Southern secession!"

In the end, Foote and his supporters stormed out of the building. Spratt had already slipped away into the rainy night. Now it was up to General Clarke to finish the convention's business. Restoring order, he called on the convention to vote on a resolution, one that would endorse the reopening of the African slave trade. The delegates passed it by a large margin.

When this was done, and the hall brought to order, Clarke addressed the delegates standing before him. "In the great contest that may arise hereafter, I trust you will be found on the same side as myself," he said. "And I hope that my hand, and my heart will be with yours, and that I will march with you shoulder to shoulder." He slammed the gavel down. "I now hold this assembly of the Commercial Convention officially closed."

For years the Northern press had belittled the Southern Commercial Conventions. Said the *New York Herald*: "The ultra pro-slavery men— those fire-eaters, restless salamanders, desperate politicians, commercial regulators and vagabond filibusters of the sunny, swampy South—have been holding their annual pow-wow." The *New York Times* called the conventions "loathsome from the beginning . . . an exhibition of low, contemptible demagoguery and political cant."

But the Southern press was critical as well. The *New Orleans Picayune* called the convention of 1859 "an escape valve for gassy bodies that would otherwise burst." Said the *Memphis Enquirer,* "We dismiss it from further consideration by borrowing the epitaph upon Billy Pringle's pig: "When it lived, it lived in clover / And when it died, it died all over."

The *Savannah Republican* questioned who the "delegates" were at the convention—and who elected them to "represent" the South:

> *We perceive, from the minutes, that the State of Georgia was represented by two individuals by the names of Jones and Morton. The first named we take to be a venerable old disunionist who resides somewhere in the Cherokee region, and has long been considered crazy on all matters political. Of the other Georgia member, we must plead entire ignorance. Whoever he (Mr. Morton) may be, we would be pleased to have him unite with his colleague, Mr. Jones, and tell the world by what authority they went to Vicksburg as the representatives of the people of Georgia, and when there, in their behalf, cast 10 votes in favor of a revival of the African slave trade.*

But Spratt cared little for the opinions of the Southern press. What was important was the impression in the North that the "South" had not only endorsed slavery, but slave trading and revolution as well. Sure enough, the Northern papers took the bait. Shortly after the convention, for instance, the *New York Times* offered this slice of commentary on the implications of the slave-trade resolution:

> *There is one little trade . . . which has recently opened up to Southern gentleman, and which seems so much a favorite with them that we should think it might ease the strain upon law, physic and politics. We allude to the profession of piracy.*
>
> *Pirates, we believe, are now beginning to take as high a stand in certain sections of Southern society as any. Carpentry, machine-making, clock-peddling, patent medicine and other low Yankee trades need not be resorted to, it seems to us, until this new field has been more thoroughly explored. . . .*

This was a gift to the radicals—a way to anger Southern moderates, and force them into the fire-eaters' camp.

16

TRIAL, PART I

AT ONE o'clock in the afternoon on November 13, 1859, a crowd began to gather around the U.S. Custom House on the corner of Bay and Bull streets. Politicians, farmers, bankers, seamen, merchants, cotton planters, and church leaders moved in the same direction in the gray afternoon light. Slaves hurried by, some with bundles wrapped in colorful cloth atop their heads, craning their necks to see what was happening. Children, black and white, raced around the steps. Some people arrived from the countryside by carriage and wagon. Some came by train, and several others from the morning steamers arriving from Augusta, Brunswick, and Charleston.

The U.S. Custom building was modeled after the Temple of Nike in Greece—and served as a powerful statement about federal authority. Four columns of gray New England granite, weighing 15 tons each, supported the portico, and steep steps led to the top. When the people reached the summit, many took a moment to look back over the crowd, which had spread itself across the cobblestone street and grassy squares below. Others hurried through the big iron doors, up the marble staircase that wound itself in a circular fashion to the second floor. Here, a federal courtroom stood. The judge's bench, the prisoner's dock, the defense and prosecution tables, the jury section, and several rows for the public were awaiting the spectacle that was to come. The room itself had regularly spaced floor-to-ceiling windows, which promised to let the pale autumn light wash across the proceedings, and gave spectators an opportunity to scribble notes and drop them to friends below.

As the crowd pushed into its seats, the newspapermen took their places as well—some looking professorial in tweeds, others dressed gaudily, as though they'd just tumbled out of the Ten Broeck Race Track—representing the *Savannah Daily Morning News,* the *Savannah Republican,* the Augusta papers, the Brunswick papers, and the Charleston newspapers. The Northern press hadn't sent reporters, but they had made arrangements for the Southern newspapermen to telegraph them the headlines and a few paragraphs, and dispatch the rest as quickly as possible on that evening's coastal steamer.

Looking around, the reporters noted the presence of Nelson Trowbridge, the sallow slave trader, who had partnered in Lamar's exploits since the *Rawlins*. Richard Aiken, the bank director who had smuggled thirty-six of the Africans into Alabama, was sitting nearby. None of the other *Wanderer* conspirators were present, however: Corrie was safely ensconced in Charleston, Farnum had disappeared up North, and Lamar, though still in town, had been tucked under the protective wing of his attorney, John Owens. Lamar had received a subpoena to appear as a witness—to which Owens submitted an affidavit, stating that Lamar had nothing to say.

At about 1:15 P.M., Ganahl strode into the courtroom, carrying his customary briefcase, and laid it carefully on the prosecution's table. He wore a wool jacket with a green tie, and kept his eyes straight ahead as he made his way through the crowd. Henry Jackson arrived next, in sartorial splendor as usual, with a double-breasted waistcoat and a red silk scarf. As he arrived, he pulled off his kid gloves and stopped to shake hands with the throng of people who'd pushed up to greet him. At the defense table, John Owens had not noticed Ganahl's arrival. But at the hubbub surrounding Jackson, he glanced up and nodded courteously, then continued to converse with his legal team—a group of three or four younger men who gathered around him like players in a football huddle.

Now Brown, Rajesta, and Arguirir were led in. The crowd craned their necks, eager to get their first look at what had been billed as the notorious slave traders of the yacht *Wanderer*. A murmur arose. The three, staring blankly, hardly looked like pirates. They were neatly dressed, cleanly barbered, and remarkably fit after nearly a year in jail. Brown was tall and bald, with a neatly trimmed black beard. He carried a monocle on a red ribbon, which, by necessity or simply for effect, he placed occasionally over his left eye. The other two could have been twins: They both were short, with deep-set eyes under heavy brows. Their hair had been cut almost to the scalp, and they wore white cotton shirts. As a group, the defendants were as unremarkable as bank clerks. Once seated, the guards removed the chains that had wrapped around their waists and had secured their hands.

By two o'clock in the afternoon, most of the players were in place. But there was one significant exception. Ever since Lamar had returned from his cruise to Havana, the *Wanderer* had remained firmly locked down and tied to the wharf that extended out from the Lamar Cotton Press. But then, a week before the trial was to begin, the *Wanderer* had abruptly disappeared.

As it turned out, Lamar had agreed to sell the *Wanderer* a week earlier. The buyer was a well-dressed stranger by the name of Captain Martin. In the days preceding the trial, Captain Martin prepared to take possession of the yacht: He ordered $2,000 worth of supplies brought aboard; retrieved the *Wanderer*'s spare sails from the rafters of Lamar's cotton press; and filled the notorious water tanks. Lamar even threw a dinner party for Martin aboard the yacht. The next day, Lamar went away on business, anticipating full payment from Martin on his return.

The following evening Martin sent word out along the waterfront that the *Wanderer* was hiring. The yacht would be sailing in eight days. Liberal wages would be paid, in advance. That night, more than a dozen young sailors were drawn aboard. With the gaslights of Savannah twinkling from the bluff overhead, and plenty of rum, champagne, and whiskey passed around in the main cabin below, the party was roaring.

It was all quite convivial, in fact, until Captain Martin suddenly stepped into the doorway, a pistol in each hand, a cutlass at his side, and two of his henchmen nearby. "Not a damn man goes over that rail tonight," he said. "I'll shoot the first mother's son that tries."

With that, Martin's thugs herded the sailors together. Martin placed the barrel of his revolver against each of their heads, and asked, in turn, if they wanted to go ashore. None did. "Good," growled Martin. "Then we'll make sail." The waterfront was being swept by sheets of rain, but nevertheless, in the darkness, the *Wanderer* slipped from the wharf, foundered on a bank midriver, and then, with the rising tide, was under way. "Now mind what you're about, or I'll blow the damned heart out of you," Martin warned the helmsman.

By the following morning, word had reached Lamar that the *Wanderer* had been stolen away. Bounding up the steps of the Exchange Building, the highest vantage point in the city, Lamar could see his yacht, seventeen miles downriver. Her masts were angled sharply; it was clear that she had run onto the bar near Tybee Island. Lamar bolted down the stairs, hired the steamboat *Columbus,* and, with a few of his friends, all heavily armed, gave chase. The pursuit was futile, however. As the spectators back in the tower of the Exchange Building witnessed, the tide rose, the *Wanderer* righted, and the yacht disappeared beyond the horizon.

Some people thought that Lamar was a co-conspirator—that the theft of the yacht been staged. But for once, the tables had been turned. Martin had outfoxed Lamar. He had stolen the yacht out from under Lamar's nose. The trial would go on, of course. The witnesses were all there. But the *Wanderer,* like an apparition, was gone.

At about 2 o'clock the big doors in the back of the courtroom closed. The bailiff called out, "All rise . . . this court will come to order!" As the assemblage noisily rose, Justice James Wayne appeared from a side door and climbed to the bench. "Please take your seats," he said, settling himself into his big chair. As Wayne took his place, the courtroom seemed electrified by his mere presence.

Nearly seventy now, Wayne was still a striking, aristocratic figure, with glowing eyes and a full head of white hair that framed his long, handsome face. "The ladies used to be enamored of his flowing locks and general beauty of appearance," the *New York Herald* had remarked in a biography a year earlier, "to which he was not wholly insensible." Dressed in a flowing silk robe, Wayne sent a murmur racing around the room.

Born in 1790, and educated by a private tutor in the family home at West Broad and Indian Streets overlooking the Savannah River, Wayne was something of a prodigy. As a child he quickly absorbed the literature in his father's library, and at fourteen was accepted into the freshman class at Princeton. Returning home, Wayne became the mayor of Savannah in 1823, a member of the U.S. Congress a few years later, and in 1835 was appointed to the U.S. Supreme Court by President Andrew Jackson. He was just forty-four years old.

Now, as he looked down upon the audience in the courtroom, he couldn't help but be struck by a certain irony: Twenty years earlier, as a young Supreme Court justice, Wayne had presided over the memorial service at Christ Church for the survivors of the *Pulaski* disaster. His eyes had swept sympathetically over the remaining members of the Lamar family, as they huddled, bent in grief, in the front pews. Now he was back in Savannah, once again dealing with the Lamars, but this time with orders from the president of the United States to convict the conspirators, and if possible, sentence them to hang.

But this was not the only reason for foreboding in the courtroom. On October 16, 1858, a group of white men, accompanied by several Negroes, and led by the feared abolitionist John Brown, had attacked the federal armory at Harpers Ferry. The purpose of the raid was to secure arms that would be used in an insurrection—a slave revolt—that Brown imagined would spread like a wildfire from Harpers Ferry throughout the South, eclipsing in its ferocity even Nat Turner's uprising of 1831, in which sixty whites were murdered by a group of slaves. "Terrible Insurrection at Harper's Ferry," ran the first headline from the *Savannah Daily Morning News* on October 18. "Rumors received in the city this forenoon of a serious insurrection at Harpers Ferry. The railroad trains were stopped, the telegraph wires cut, and the town and all public works were in possession of the insurgents."

Following Brown's capture and imprisonment, the South was still tense. But there was general relief that the Northern press and politicians had generally condemned Brown's bloody deed. "It was an attempt by white men to get up a revolt among the slaves in which the slaves refused to participate," wrote Abraham Lincoln. And yet, as Brown went to trial, a second wave of Northern opinion began to break, this far more sympathetic to the condemned man. The Tremont Temple in Boston held a "sympathy meeting" for Brown, which raised more than $400 for Brown's family. Massachusetts governor John A. Andrew referred to Brown's trial as a "judicial outrage." Rumors began to fly of a secret army, an abolitionist force that would descend on Virginia and free Brown from jail. And many Northern papers began to adjust their point of view, noting that while they disapproved of Brown's methods, they couldn't help but admire his message.

As these reports from the North tumbled into the Southern press, they sparked anger and anxiety. To the South, John Brown's offense was not a theoretical argument opposing slavery, nor a constitutional musing upon the rights of slave owners and slaves. It was a physical attack on Southern families, who were the targets of Brown's bullets and blades. For the first time, a war between the states seemed not only possible, but even likely. "The South Must Prepare," ran a headline in the *Charleston News,* a normally moderate newspaper:

> It was hoped that the Harper's Ferry outrage would have produced some political reasoning at the North, and that all the peaceful, right-minded and Union-loving of that section would have combined to rebuke and reprove the tendency to Abolition Jacobism. But a reckless fury seems to possess it, and that spirit has given triumph to the Republican Party in the late elections. . . . In view of these facts, is it not time for the South to prepare? To prepare to defend her soil, to prepare for a severance from her enemies and for her self-government, and to prepare all which may be necessary to secure and defend her independence and nationality?

Had anyone at the courtroom been able to step back far enough, they would have seen the symmetry in play. In May of 1858, in the town of Chatham, in Upper Canada, John Brown had walked into a meeting of his financial backers. "I have formed a plan of action," he said, describing a raid somewhere along the Appalachian Mountains that he was certain would ignite a slave rebellion. In the same month of the same year, Charles Lamar was readying the *Richard Cobden* for its voyage, warning Howell Cobb, "I will re-open the trade in slaves to foreign countries—let your cruisers catch me if they can."

Now, as John Brown was sitting stiffly in his jail cell in Virginia, receiving his final visitors and reluctantly coming to terms with the martyrdom that the North was preparing to bestow upon him, the defendants in the *Wanderer* case were assembled in the Savannah courtroom, awaiting their fates as well. Their stars were starting to align. John Brown's presence hung over the courtroom—and nothing would escape it in the days ahead.

"All rise for the jury," the bailiff exclaimed. From a side door came the jurors in a single file. A few had the sun-reddened skin and the homespun clothing of farmers. But most of them were town people, in Sunday clothing. As they took their seats toward the big floor-to-ceiling windows, their faces looked flat and expressionless in the late autumn light. "Gentlemen, are we ready to begin?" said Wayne, looking over to Ganahl and Owens. "The Government is ready, Your Honor," said Ganahl, rising. "The defendants are present and ready, Your Honor," echoed Owens. Justice Wayne nodded. A deep silence fell over the courtroom.

"Mr. Foreman and gentlemen," Wayne began, shifting in his chair to address the jury, "we have met to perform those duties which are assigned to us by the Constitution of the United States and the legislation of Congress, for the judicial administration of both." There was complete silence in the courtroom now. "Such a delegation of trust imposes upon yourselves as Grand Jurors, and upon this court, conscientious responsibilities and large functions. Let us proceed, gentlemen, to discharge them, in conformity with the confidence with which they have been conferred."

Following a few more minutes of explanation, Wayne said he wanted to review the history of the slave trade. "The first act was passed on the 22nd of March 1794," Wayne began, "when George Washington was president. It was intended to prevent any citizen or residents of the United States from equipping vessels within the United States, to carry on trade or traffic in slaves to any foreign country. That is, though slaves might be brought into the United States until the year 1808, in vessels fitted out in our ports for the purpose, they could not be carried by our citizens or residents in the United States in such vessels into any foreign country."

The justice then explained that the penalty for that offense was the forfeiture of the vessel, and that that penalty was still in force. The law also imposed a $2,000 fine on any person fitting out such a vessel. The law was tightened and expanded in 1800, Wayne continued, noting that it was a *South Carolinian,* in fact, a Judge Bee, who raised the fine to ten thousand dollars, pushed the imprisonment to a maximum four years, and made the president of the United States and the U.S. Navy responsible for enforcing it.

Justice Wayne stopped and studied the jurors momentarily, as if he were assessing whether all this was sinking in. Their faces stared back without expression. Wayne adjusted his glasses and, leaning forward with even greater intensity, continued. "The next act of Congress was passed on the second of March 1807, when Mr. Jefferson was president," he said. He next described that statute in detail—and then elaborated on the further improvements made to it in 1818.

"That brings us to the last act upon the subject—that of the 15th of May, 1820," he said. "It denounces any citizen of the United States as a pirate, and states that he shall suffer death who shall become one of the crew of a ship's company of any foreign ship; and that any person whatever becomes a pirate, and shall suffer death, who shall become one of the crew or ship's company of any vessel, owned in the whole or in parts—or which shall be navigated for or in behalf of any citizen of the United States, or who shall land from such vessel on any foreign shore and shall seize any Negro or mulatto not held to service or labor by the laws of either of the states or territories of the United States, with intent to make such Negro or mulatto a slave, or who shall decoy or forcibly bring or carry, or who shall receive on board of such ship any Negro or mulatto with intent to make him a slave." That was the law, he explained, upon which the jurors would have to base their deliberations.

Wayne emphasized the part Southerners had played in ending the trade. "From the very beginning of our nationality," he said, applying all of his considerable authority upon the jurors, "the distinguished men of both sections took an active part, none of them more decisively than *Southern statesmen,* in every act that has been passed, including the last. There has never been *any* manifestation of popular or sectional discontent against them on account of their opinions concerning the African slave trade, or their legislation to repress it . . . no serious attempt has ever been made to repeal any one of those acts. . . ."

Now Wayne shifted his discourse to a description of the African slave trade itself. "From remote antiquity," he explained, "the seizure and abduction of men and women, with the intent to dispose of them as slaves, by the crew or ship's company of vessels roaming at large for the purpose of plunder and traffic, have been deemed and always called acts of piracy," he told the jurors. "It was a capital offence by the Jewish law, and to steal a human being, man, woman or child, or to seize and forcibly carry away any person whatever from his own country into another, has always been considered to be piracy, and is now so considered by all nations enjoying Jewish and Christian instruction, punishable by death . . . Nor was it ever recognized in Europe to be allowable trade upon any other principle," he added, "until the emperor Charles V authorized in 1516, the introduction of Africans into the island of St. Domingo from the establishments of the Portuguese on the coast of Guinea, to work the mines in that island."

Once again, Wayne described the role of Southerners in ending all of this. Thomas Jefferson of Virginia, Judge Berrien of Georgia, Calhoun of South Carolina, Johnson of Louisiana—he called out their names in a clear, ringing voice. "There is no question of public morality which has been more clearly and solemnly maintained than that on which this legislation reposes," he said earnestly. "It would be a retrograde movement of more than a century to consent to abate one line of the condemnation of this trade, or to relax any effort for its extirpation."

When Wayne had finished, there was a general rustling throughout the courtroom as the assemblage decompressed from what had been an eloquent but daunting lesson in civics and history. Wayne poured himself a glass of water. He drank it slowly and then turned again to the jury. "History, morality and the Constitution aside, however," he said, "the prosecution has three pragmatic obstacles standing between freedom and conviction. First, they have to show conclusively that the owner of the vessel was an American citizen. Second, that the defendants were of the crew or ship's company. Third, that the defendants had sided and abetted in the importation of the Africans, with a purpose to enslave them. These are the three measures, gentlemen, that you must now use to reach your verdict."

Wayne peered over his half glasses to see if these instructions had sunk in. Then he leaned back in his chair and rubbed his forehead, apparently drained from his exhortations.

Throughout his career, Justice Wayne had made clear his unwavering support for the institution of slavery. "War, want, crime, climate, peace and mistaken views of religion have been the pretexts for reducing men into slavery," he told the American Colonization Society in Washington a few years before the *Wanderer* trial. "But pretexts as they are, when slavery has become habitual, and has been for a long time a part of the policy of any community, its safety may not permit the dissolution of the evil all at once."

In Washington, where he kept a home and entertained frequently, Wayne's four servants, including his coachman, were Irish—a gesture to the sensitivities of some of his Northern guests and, no doubt, a dodge to avoid criticism himself. But back home in Savannah he had nine slaves, and a few years earlier, when he still owned "Red Knoll," a rice plantation, he owned about thirty slaves. Wayne's father, an industrious entrepreneur, not only owned slaves but sold them as well. One of the first advertisements for his general store in Savannah noted the availability of "Very Prime Slaves Just arrived from the river Gambia."

But Wayne's fame—or, in many quarters in the North, notoriety—came from his coauthorship, in 1852, of the Supreme Court's Dred Scott decision. Here the high court of the United States had decided that Negroes had no civil right. Rather, they were mere property, just as cattle and hogs were property. Wayne had urged the high court to take the case in the hopes that the court's decision would close the issue of slavery in the United States forever, particularly in terms of slavery's expansion into the West. Instead, Dred Scott went down in history as the court's most morally reprehensible decision, one that irreconcilably split the nation and made disunion almost inevitable.

A racist and a blatant supporter of slavery. And yet, Wayne was a vehement and sincere opponent of the African slave trade. Slavery was right, in his cultured mind, but the African slave trade was wrong. Chains at the auction house in Savannah were right, but those along the Congo were wrong. This was the unspoken dissonance that plagued the psyche of more than one Southerner. Now, in the *Wanderer* trial, it was out on the table. Wayne knew it. His aristocratic face, framed between muttonchops, was gaunt and gray. He gazed out over the courtroom now, his hand to his lips, and wondered what the next few days would bring.

Justice Wayne turned to the clerk. "Please call the first witness," he said.

"Horatio Harris," the clerk called out. Harris emerged from the witness room and strode to the stand. Harris, twenty years old, had lived on or near Cumberland Island most of his life, and was, in fact, as thin as an island egret. Now, as he stood there wide-eyed, with his hand on the Bible and his Adam's apple working itself nervously over his bow tie, he seemed to have fallen out of his nest and into a bigger and more dangerous world.

After welcoming Harris to the stand and extracting from him his full name and occupation, Ganahl strolled over to the dock, to where the three prisoners sat stiffly in their new clothes.

"Have you ever seen these men before?" Ganahl asked, waving his hand at the three. Harris looked over. "I have. I seen them all on the beach that night on Jekyll Island."

"Where?" Ganahl asked.

"The south end of Jekyll Island. They was dirty, though, probably from the journey, and I think they was wearing some kind of disguises. But that's them. I'm sure of it. That one there," he said, pointing to Brown, "he was better dressed than the other two, but he was with them. So was that fella there," he added, pointing to Rajesta.

"I see," said Ganahl, walking over to the prisoners. "This gentleman right here?"

"Yes, sir."

"Would the court please note that Mr. Harris is indicating prisoner Rajesta," Ganahl said.

"And what else did you see?"

"There was quite a number of Negroes."

"Mr. Harris, how many were there?"

"I'd say between one hundred and five hundred."

"What did they look like?"

"Some was naked. Some had blankets, strips of clothing . . ."

"I see," said Ganahl. "Now tell me how you came to get on the beach."

"A man calling himself Captain Cook said he wanted to go to Jekyll Island to take on some gentlemen for a pleasure excursion. I did *not* want to go on in the boat, but finally did consent, and remarked, I hope it is not a slaver, to which Captain Cook replied, no, but he wished it was."

"Interesting," said Ganahl, making a wide circle that stopped in front of the witness.

"And then what happened?"

"We went to Jekyll Island and stopped at John du Bignon's house where there was some talk that I did not hear. Captain Cook then told me that the ship was the *Wanderer,* full of Negroes. He called them indentured apprentices."

"And then?"

"We got Mr. Clubb at the lighthouse and then proceeded to the *Wanderer.* And then the Africans were brought ashore."

"Tell the court what you saw there."

"I seen boats passing between the vessel and the beach which belonged to the vessel. I seen three boats carrying people from the ship to the shore. One was Mr. John du Bignon's boat."

"How many trips?"

"Each made five or six trips and would carry six or eight Negroes each trip."

"Now, Mr. Harris, it was Mr. Corrie who was calling himself Mr. Cook. Is that right?"

"Yes, sir."

"What did Mr. Corrie tell you?"

"Captain Corrie said the vessel was his, and had been out after cargo, that's what he called the Negroes—and had got them from the coast of Africa, where he saw many vessels . . . and gave dinner parties and had been to Trinidad."

"Dinner parties?" said Ganahl, turning to the jury with a smile.

"Yes, sir. Mr. Corrie said he passed these compliments with a British ship."

"Very good. What else did Mr. Corrie tell you?"

"Let's see now. He said his ship was a fast sailer. It was four months on the voyage. That he got the Negroes out of the Congo River. He started with 490 and had 400 aboard."

"Interesting," Ganahl said again, drumming his fingers on the prosecution desk as he circled by. "Now you rowed out to the *Wanderer,* is that correct?"

"Yes, sir."

"And what did you see?"

"I seen three or four staterooms for officers and crew, and a large space about midship. It seemed that the Negroes had free access to all part of the ship, from all appearances. She was very dirty. She smelt badly."

"And the Negroes?"

"Some were fine-looking. Others small. Maybe they looked smaller because they was naked. Some was lying on the beach looking sick but most were cheerful and lively."

"Very interesting. Thank you, Mr. Harris."

Ganahl walked back to his seat.

As Ganahl sat down, Henry Jackson stood and approached Harris.

"Mr. Harris, did you have any conversation with any of the white men while on the island? And if so, would you repeat the substance," Jackson asked.

"Objection, Your Honor," shouted Owens. "The general declarations of a person cannot be admitted with the view of incriminating the prisoners."

"Objection overruled," Wayne replied flatly. "Go ahead, Mr. Harris."

"Well, sir, I had a general conversation with Brown going over to Jekyll," Harris continued.

"What did he tell you?"

"He said the Negroes were *savages* brought from the Congo River. He said they left with about 490. Now later, when I came ashore, I seen Mr. Rajesta and Mr. Arguirir with the Negroes. But by then Mr. Brown was gone."

Jackson walked over to Rajesta and Arguirir. "Mr. Harris, take a look at the prisoners. Do they look familiar?"

Harris looked over at the men. "I think they was the same men I saw on the beach with the Negroes," he said. "But I can't swear to it. Their faces sure are familiar. But their clothes ain't."

Jackson walked back to the witness stand.

"Mr. Harris, how long did you stay on Jekyll?"

"Tuesday, Wednesday and Thursday. I left Jekyll on Thursday, at which time the Negroes had been taken away."

"And could you tell the court what you saw there?"

"On Thursday?"

"Yes."

"There were a good many white men there."

"Tell us who they were."

"John du Bignon, Henry du Bignon, John Tucker, and Captain Denny Brown," Harris said without hesitation. "And some of the crew, including, I think, some of the prisoners at the bar."

"At that time did you see Brown on the beach?"

"Yes, I did."

Jackson walked back to the dock and pointed to Brown.

"Was he the same man that is here now?"

Harris looked Brown over, and a bit of puzzlement crossed his face. "When I seen him on the beach he wore a hat—so I couldn't tell you whether he was bald or not," Harris said. "His whiskers was red on the beach. I thought he had red whiskers," Harris stuttered.

"Thank you, Mr. Harris," said Jackson, and returned to his seat.

Now Owens rose for the defense. Jackson and Ganahl had laid out the evidence for the jury, like a trail of bread crumbs. Now Owens—the trim and efficient blue jay—would swoop down and peck them away.

"Mr. Harris, the prosecution wants us to believe that more than 400 people were aboard the *Wanderer*," Owens began. "When you went aboard, did you see provisions for so many men as that?"

"No, I didn't," replied Harris.

"Did you see provisions landing?"

"No."

Owens went back to his table and studied his notes for a moment. Then he returned to Harris.

"Mr. Harris, you said earlier that you felt that you could identify the men sitting here today as those on the beach."

"Their faces are familiar to me."

"But, sir, these men are in this courtroom—with guards on either side of them." Owens walked over to the prisoners. "If you ran across them in the street would you have identified them as the men you saw on the beach?"

Harris looked over at the men sitting in the dock. "I'm not positive of that, sir. If there was no circumstances to draw my attention to them, then maybe not."

"I see," said Owens. "Maybe not." Owens stroked his jaw thoughtfully. "Now you said the Negroes on the beach were Africans. Are you sure of that?"

"They was different from Negroes here."

"How is that?"

"Well, I couldn't understand anything they said."

"But does that mean they were from Africa?"

Harris thought that over. "I can't say that for sure, sir."

"Mr. Harris, would it be correct to say that you *believed* that they were from Africa?"

"I think so."

"Because that's what others had told you?"

Harris hesitated. "I suppose that's right. Yes."

"Thank you, Mr. Harris. No other questions."

Harris unwrapped his long legs and strode out of the courtroom. Justice Wayne glanced at his pocket watch and called the attorneys to the bench. They whispered together for a moment and then returned to their seats. "This court is now adjourned until tomorrow morning," Wayne said. "I need now to remind the jury not to hold any conversations with any persons whatsoever. You are not to allow anyone to approach you in reference to the case before you and I'm ordering five bailiffs here present to see that the court's instructions are enforced."

With that, Wayne brought his gavel down and the court adjourned. Ganahl, Jackson, and Owens gathered up their papers. The prisoners were taken back to their cells. And almost as quickly as they had convened, the crowd dispersed into the late autumn afternoon.

17

TRIAL, PART II

THE FOLLOWING day, the courtroom was again packed to overflowing. With the closing of the doors and the falling of Justice Wayne's gavel, the proceedings continued.

"Captain L. N. Coste," the clerk called out. The director of the Port of Charleston, a heavyset man with a full beard, strode forward and took the stand.

As the jury listened, Coste stated his name and briefly described his duties as collector for the port.

"Mr. Coste," Ganahl asked, pointing toward the prisoners in the dock, "have you ever seen these men before?"

Coste looked over at the three defendants. "Yes, sir, I have."

"And where was that?"

"In Charleston harbor."

"And when was that?"

"It was the summer of 1858."

"I see. And what was the situation in which you saw them?"

"They were rowing to and from the *Wanderer*."

"Very good. Thank you," said Ganahl. "No further questions."

Owens rose. "Inspector Coste, you say that you saw the defendants *rowing* to and from the *Wanderer*."

"Yes, sir."

"Rowing, to and from. But do you know whether any of these men *went to sea* with the *Wanderer* when she left port on July 4?"

Coste hesitated. "No," he said. "I don't."

"I see," said Owens. "Just rowing back and forth to the *Wanderer*. Is that correct?"

"Yes," replied Coste.

"Now, Captain Coste, was it unusual for people to come and go from the *Wanderer*?"

"When she was moored off Charleston?"

"Yes."

"Well," Coste said, "Captain Corrie had many acquaintances."

Owens turned to the jury, and continued to address Coste.

"Captain Coste, isn't it true that while the *Wanderer* was lying in Charleston many, many people—people, in fact, from many parts of the South and even from foreign countries—were passing to and fro from her."

"Yes.

"In fact, she was visited by more than one hundred people, of all kinds."

"Yes. I believe so. Yes."

"Now they didn't *all* go to sea with her, did they?" Laughter rippled through the courtroom.

"No, sir."

"In fact, you don't know for a fact if *any* of them did, do you?"

"No, I don't."

"Thank you. No other questions."

Next the court called Nicholas King, the captain of the steamship *St. Johns*. King testified that during his regular trip from Florida to Savannah the previous December, he picked up a passenger who looked like the present prisoner, Brown. When the clerk of the court produced his boat register, King showed the court where the passenger had been listed, under the name Wilson. The date was November 30, 1858. "No other questions, thank you," said Ganahl.

"Captain King," Owens asked on cross-examination, "many coasters moor in Jekyll Creek, don't they?"

"Yes."

"And don't sailors and crew from vessels lying there frequently board your steamer there, for transport, north or south?"

"Yes, they do," replied King.

"Captain, please direct your attention to Mr. Brown." King looked over at Brown, who returned his gaze from the dock. "Can you swear that this man is the same person you took aboard your ship on the evening of November 30?"

King studied Brown for a moment and then turned back to Owens. "No. I cannot swear to it."

"Thank you, Captain. No other questions."

Joseph Haywood, a barber, was called next. Haywood testified that he often dyed beards in the course of his business.

"Mr. Haywood," asked Ganahl. "Does the prisoner Brown's beard appear dyed?"

Haywood studied Brown for a moment. "Yes," he replied. Brown's beard appeared to have been colored black.

"Mr. Haywood," Owens said, rising for the cross-examination, "is it unusual for a man to have his beard dyed?"

"No," the barber replied. "Many men darken their beards."

"Why would they do that?" asked Owens. "For appearance sake?"

"Yes," replied the barber.

"Not, though, as some sort of *disguise*?"

"No."

Now Luke Christie took the stand. At the hearing before Judge Henry a year earlier, Christie had described how he had taken the steamer *Lamar* down to Jekyll Island and had returned with a cargo of Africans. Now he repeated that testimony, and said that he believed that Charles Lamar, Nelson Trowbridge, John Tucker, and Brown were among the passengers.

When Christie had finished testifying, Owens rose and strode to the witness stand. In his hand was a deposition. "Is this your signature?"

Owens asked, holding the affidavit before the witness. Christie bent forward to examine the document. "Yes," he said. At that, Owens turned to the jury, with the piece of paper waving before him like a banner. "Captain Christie was unwilling a year ago, when the thing was fresh in his mind, to swear to the identity of the prisoners," he declared. "Nor is he willing to imperil innocent lives by swearing to their positive identity today."

He turned to Christie. "Thank you. No other questions."

Judge Wayne glanced at the clock in the back of the courtroom, and noted that the court would have time for one more witness. William O. Price, the proprietor of Price's Men's Clothing, was called. Price, as might have been expected, was fashionably dressed, with a mauve bow tie crowning his apparel.

It was toward dusk on December 7, Price testified, that the prisoners entered his store. Brown "had on a nice blue navy flannel coat," recalled Price, and the others were dressed in plain dark clothing—the kind that would normally be worn by seamen.

"What happened next?" asked Ganahl.

"Well, I have this nagging curiosity about my customers," said Price. "I love to know where they are from and where they are going. So I asked Mr. Brown where they were from and he told me they were from New Orleans, and I said, 'Oh, I presume then that you are traveling North.' People traveling North frequently purchase clothing in Savannah."

"And what did Mr. Brown say?"

"Well, he didn't reply, but he did give me a pair of pants to mend. The name on the watch pocket was in Spanish or Portuguese, but the label said, 'Cornell, New York.' From this I presumed that Brown may have been a resident of New York. So I asked Mr. Brown if he knew a Mr. Miller, a celebrated slaver of New York who frequently goes to Cuba with a cargo of Negroes. 'Who, Jack Miller?' Brown replied. 'Yes, Jack Miller!' I replied."

"And from that you inferred that Mr. Brown had been engaged in the slave trade?" asked Ganahl.

"Yes, sir, I most certainly did!"

"Thank you."

Owens strolled over to the witness. "Mr. Price," asked Owens, "are you acquainted with anyone in New York who is engaged in the grocery business?"

"Oh, yes, sir, a good many," Price replied.

"Then may we infer, sir, that you are in the grocery business?"

Price blushed. "No," he replied, "I'm in the clothing business."

"I inferred differently, sir," replied Owens, "as you seem to suppose that because the prisoner at the bar knew Jack Miller, who was engaged in the slave trade, that he was therefore engaged in that trade himself."

The courtroom burst into laughter. "Thank you, Mr. Price," said Owens.

With that Judge Wayne called the court to recess for the day, with proceedings to resume the next morning at 11 A.M.

By the time the first day of the trial had ended, the *Wanderer* itself was a thousand miles away. Having gained his freedom, and now on the high seas, Captain Martin ordered the crew to assemble on the deck. The captain's gaze was still cloudy from a night of heavy drinking, but his intentions, it was soon learned, were perfectly clear. "Now, boys," he exclaimed hoarsely, "we're off for the west coast of Africa, and we're going for a cargo of blackbirds." The captain eyed them suspiciously. "I'm a son of a sea cook for carrying sail—and when I speak you're all to look sharp," he warned. "Anybody who doesn't 'll get his head blown off."

The crew gave each other desperate looks. Not only had they been shanghaied but the *Wanderer* had escaped with only the barest of provisions. Food was scarce. Some of the water, it turned out, was contaminated. None of the crew had clothing beyond what was on their backs. There were no oilskins to protect them from squalls, no bedding even, for the bunks. And although Martin had loaded up his cabin with muskets, boarding pikes, and pistols, the ship's crew lacked a chronometer, a nautical almanac, and even a chart of the Western Ocean.

Martin had a fix for that, however. Spotting distant sails, Martin ordered the *Wanderer* to pursue what turned out to be the *Troy,* a slow-sailing brig out of Boston. Outracing her, and sending a charge of grapeshot across the *Troy*'s bow for good measure, the *Wanderer* forced the *Troy* to come into the wind and stall. Clambering aboard, Martin made light conversation with the astonished captain—obtained a chart of the Florida coast, a copy of Blunt's *Coast Pilot,* and a nautical almanac—and then left the seaman, with shaking knees—and five dollars in gold.

Now, thanks to a strong breeze and a favorable northeasterly set in the current, the *Wanderer* swiftly crossed the Atlantic, arriving in two weeks at the tiny island of Flores, about a thousand miles from the northwest coast of Africa. While at sea, Martin had ordered the crew to paint out the name *Wanderer,* replacing it in bright red letters with *William.* Martin also discovered a clearance for Havana in the captain's cabin—left from Lamar's previous trip—and promptly had it doctored to read *Smyrna,* as in Smyrna, Turkey. Now she was the *William,* voyaging legitimately from Savannah to Smyrna. Martin also changed his name in the paperwork to George D. Walker, and ordered the crew to sign with fake names as well.

No sooner had the *Wanderer* come into the little port town of Santa Cruz, than Martin rowed ashore and presented himself to the British consul. The ship had been through a harrowing storm, he explained. Martin, who had already outfoxed the cautious Lamar, now fooled the consul as well: The British official was soon introducing Martin around to the locals; several merchants soon offered credit, and presently, food, blankets, new spars, and a flock of live chickens were sent aboard the *Wanderer.* Two of the island's prettiest young prostitutes, Anna Felice and her friend Mariana Jose, arrived aboard as well, one taking up quarters in the captain's state room and the other bedding down in the mate's berth.

By now, the *Wanderer* had become Santa Cruz's most salacious place of amusement. The crew drank and danced to the tune of a squeeze-box. The cook amused himself with revolver practice, shooting the daylights out of a broom. Santa Cruz's chief pilot and custom-house officer soon abandoned their offices and moved aboard, partaking in the fun. While still at sea, the *Wanderer*'s crew had sworn themselves to mutiny at the earliest opportunity. But now, in the tranquil paradise of Flores, with its lushly greened volcanic slopes and neat white cottages, they changed their minds.

But then Captain Martin's luck suddenly changed. Rumors began to leak back into town that Martin's pedigree was not what it was cracked up to be. The merchants began to fear for the credit they had so freely extended. And so—at the same time that the *Wanderer* trial in

Savannah was calling witnesses to the stand—the *Wanderer*'s crew in Santa Cruz were watching Captain Martin row excitedly toward them in the dinghy. Gaining the deck, Martin shouted for all hands to make sail. Looking to the shore, the crew saw an angry mob gathering on the beach, fists shaking and eyes searching for boats to launch out after the *Wanderer*. At that, the crew abruptly dropped 45 fathoms of chain and the ship's best anchor into the bay and hauled away. When the first mate asked what he should do with the officials from Santa Cruz, who were still aboard, Martin replied, "Throw the damned old carrion of a custom-house man overboard, but keep the pilot and the other two— they're sailors."

Once again, the *Wanderer* was off. As she headed out to sea, Martin stumbled back down to his cabin, got gloriously drunk on more champagne, and made love to Anna Felice, who, according to the records, was "woefully seasick" during the entire ordeal.

While the *Wanderer* plunged through the sea, the trial in Savannah continued.

"I seen the largest man there somewhere before," said Clubb, as the proceeding began the following morning. The lighthouse keeper pointed a thick finger at Brown. "I couldn't say where or when. I might have seen him on Jekyll Island or on board the *Wanderer*. I can't imagine where else I would have seen him."

"Very good. Now tell the court how you came to meet Captain Corrie," said Ganahl.

"Captain Cook—or Corrie—came to me at the Jekyll beach lighthouse. He wanted me to pilot the *Wanderer* in. He insisted on me going out that night as he was out of water and provisions."

"And did you?"

"I went out the next morning between five and six o'clock and piloted the *Wanderer* up the Little Satilla River."

"Please tell the court what you saw there," said Ganahl.

"I was informed that there were 413 Negroes on board. I saw one dead. He was thrown overboard at daylight. I saw about 40 on the aft part of the vessel."

"And what condition were they in?"

"Some was sick but most of them appeared well. Like I said, the Negroes was bundled together on board like pigs. But they wasn't manacled or nothing. They was free to roam the vessel. Some had blankets and pieces of cloth tied around them."

"With whom did you speak?"

"Well, I had very little conversation with Corrie until after the Negroes was landed. He stayed in the cabin. Afterwards he appeared to have gas enough to talk. Mostly, though, I spoke to Mr. Brown who gave my orders to the crew."

Standing for the cross-examination, Owens sought to whittle away at Clubb's credibility.

"You aren't really a commissioned pilot, are you?" he asked Clubb.

"I was a lighthouse keeper."

"Why, then, did you bring in the *Wanderer*?"

"Because I think it's the duty of all lighthouse keepers to help in cases of distress. They didn't offer me nothing. Well, they didn't pay me yet. Mr. Henry du Bignon was supposed to pay me."

"How much did you charge them?"

"Five hundred was the charge. They gave me a note two or three days after the landing."

"And so you had an agreement?"

"No agreement was made. Well, Trowbridge said that $500 is too much. A large price to charge. I told him I thought it was too little. But the du Bignons, they said they would be responsible to me for the amount."

"What is the usual charge?"

"Fifty dollars is the usual charge."

"And so why would you charge $500?"

"I charged $500 because it was a money-making business, and I was kind to them, and I thought they ought to pay me well."

Owens smiled. "I see."

"Do you believe the Negroes you saw on the *Wanderer* were Africans?" he asked Clubb.

"Sure I believe they was African Negroes."

"Do you know that transporting Africans is a violation of the law?"

"No."

"Really, sir?"

"Two or three days later, I heard that bringing in the *Wanderer* was a violation of the law."

"And how did that make you feel?" asked Owens.

"After I heard it was a violation of the law," said Clubb, hesitating, "I thought I should be paid well for it."

"I see," said Owens. "And you were. No further questions."

After a short recess, the clerk called the next witness, Chatham County jailer, Charlie Van Horn. Horn related how he had been awakened by Marshal Stewart with orders to bring the African boys to the magistrate's office, where he found Charles Lamar waiting to claim them, and how the magistrate finally turned the boys over.

"And so, with that you just turned over the Africans?" asked Ganahl.

"I knew such writs could be issued," replied Van Horn. "I thought that everything was legally fixed."

Ganahl put his hand to his chin and thought for a moment.

"Now, Mr. Van Horn," he said, approaching the witness, "tell me about the auction of the *Wanderer*. Specifically Mr. Lamar's . . ."

"Objection," Owens shouted, jumping up. "Irrelevant to this case . . ."

Justice Wayne motioned the two lawyers over to the bench. "Where are you going with this?" Wayne asked Ganahl. Ganahl leaned forward. "I have already connected Lamar and Tucker with the *Wanderer*; the *Wanderer* with the slave trade; and the persons at the bar with the *Wanderer*," he whispered. "I want to tie Lamar even more closely with the *Wanderer* by showing that he had possession of the Africans at the auction of the *Wanderer*." Wayne considered the request, and then ruled that the question could be asked—but that the court would determine the propriety of the answer.

"Mr. Van Horn," Ganahl started again, "will you state whether you were present at the sale of the *Wanderer*, and if so, what you heard Mr. Lamar remark?"

"I cannot say positively," replied Van Horn. "I was not near enough to hear what Lamar said—though I heard him say something." Van Horn hesitated. "I know what it was. But I didn't hear it for myself."

"What was it that you heard?" asked Ganahl.

"Objection!" Owens cried out. "Hearsay."

"Sustained," Wayne replied.

Ganahl bit his lip in frustration. Turning to the clerk, who nodded, Van Horn was told to step down.

The trial continued for several more days. Among the other witnesses called to the stand were Marshal Gordon, who testified about finding the Africans dancing around the fire on Jekyll Island, and Marshal Ross, who described finding the two Africans aboard the train in Macon. George Cheever, a customs inspector, told the jury how he brought Captain Corrie's trunk from the *Wanderer* to the custom house. Inside he found a logbook and charts, which had been used to make calculations of latitude and longitude. With these, he said, he was able to precisely trace the course of the *Wanderer* from the time she sailed out of Charleston up to her return. Hugh Davenport, who worked for the port of Savannah, testified that he had carefully examined the *Wanderer* and, in the forecastle, had found brackets that had been used to build the slave deck below the main deck. He had also measured the yacht carefully. Based on her size, standard practice would have permitted her to carry 116 passengers. Had she carried 500, he said, each of them would have had four feet in length and a foot in width in which to survive.

On the final day of testimony, Ganahl called Dr. William Hazelhurst to the stand. Ganahl saved Hazelhurst for last because the doctor, of all the witnesses, had the greatest bearing of honesty and integrity.

"I was in Brunswick and was sent for by Mr. du Bignon to go to Jekyll Island," Hazelhurst said, gazing at Ganahl with a keen intelligent air. "Mr. du Bignon did not mention the object of the call, but I suspected what it was for. I saw some Negroes there that I took to be Africans. Judging from all I saw there I should testify that they were not American Negroes."

"Dr. Hazelhurst, please tell us the conditions you saw when you reached the island."

"There were about forty of them, of whom about ten were sick. One died, how many more, I don't know," he replied. "They were sick with diseases of diarrhea and skin. The first was brought about by insufficient and bad food, the second by an impure state of the blood."

"And what, in your opinion, were the causes of these illnesses?"

"It was very probably impure and confined air, insufficient food, and the want of cleanliness."

"Sir, were you paid for this visit?"

"I was employed by Henry du Bignon, but didn't charge any bill to anyone. I went there in the way of business, but I don't know whether I will be paid or not."

"And again, sir, do you believe the Negroes you saw were Africans?"

"In my judgment, yes, those Negroes that I was called to see were Africans."

"And why do you believe that?"

"Because I had occasion to speak to them through an interpreter."

"And who was that?"

"He is an old African. He and the Negroes seemed to understand one another."

"And who is this old African?"

"His name is Jack. He's my Negro. He is employed by John du Bignon. His wages are paid out of proceeds of the sales of cotton from the du Bignon family, which is composed of John, Henry, and Catherine du Bignon."

Ganahl walked past the witness and stood before the jury.

"Sir, do you have any connection yourself to the du Bignon family?"

"Yes, my wife is Catherine du Bignon."

"Thank you. No other questions."

Several witnesses, of course, never took the stand: Henry du Bignon, John du Bignon, Richard Aiken, Nelson Trowbridge, and, of course, Charles Lamar. All of them refused on the grounds that their testimony might incriminate them. And so, following four days of discourse, Ganahl announced the prosecution's case closed. Owens rose next and stated that the defense would not present any witnesses of their own. The trial would now move to the closing arguments, and then to the deliberations of the jury.

The following day, November 21, the court met to hear the final arguments.

Ganahl rose and strode to a shaft of light that fell halfway between the judge's bench and the jury box. He read each of the indictments charging each of the prisoners with piracy, under the 1820 statute. "In each case," he told the jurors, "we have proven through clear evidence each of the issues: The American character of the yacht *Wanderer;* the ownership in whole or part by William C. Corrie; the date of her sailing from Charleston to Trinidad, and thence to the coast of Africa; her departure from the Congo River on the 19th of October; her arrival at Jekyll Island, straight as the wind could blow her, on the 28th of November, 1858; the disembarkation of the Africans at Jekyll; and the complicity of the prisoners that today sit at the bar in all these transactions, as testified to by several witnesses."

Now he stepped forward toward the jurors. "The case before you is of vast moment, in which great issues are involved," he said solemnly. "This is the first case in the history of this country, even the world, of this kind. And on that account, not only are the eyes of the honorable court and the spectators assembled here upon us, but the eyes of the country and the world."

Ganahl studied each face as he spoke. "You stand here as twelve independent Southern jurors," he continued. "And I thank God that no men are amongst us who preach a higher law than the constitution and laws of the country. It was the glory of the South that she had always been true; that, in that compact, we gave and received certain rights and privileges; that, in that sacred compact, we made the bargain and agreement under which these men are tried for their lives. Let the South stand by her bargain, then, and abide by her oath. This, gentlemen of the jury, is the great question that you must decide in its entirety. May God be with you in that pursuance."

Ganahl returned to his seat.

Now Owens rose and, before addressing the jury, turned his attention to Justice Wayne. "The questions of which I shall ask Your Honor to charge the jury are few," he said. "I first ask this court to charge the jury as to the ownership of the vessel, and that the registry of a vessel is *not* a proof of ownership." Owens then cited several legal precedents to support that view. "I further ask that the court charge the jury that *possession* of a vessel by a captain is not a proof of ownership. Otherwise, in real estate, the possession of a plantation would intimate the title vested in the overseer; as the possession of the horses and carriage of a gentlemen would indicate that it belong to the coachman, both of which positions are false.

"The second point of which I desire the court to charge the jury," Owens continued, "is that the prisoners must be proven to be of the ship's company or crew, and that in the language of the law, *passengers* are not responsible for the acts of the company's company or crew." He again cited precedent. "My address to the bench on the law has ended," Owens concluded. "And I cannot close my remarks at this time without thanking your honor for the patience and impartiality of which you have conducted this important case. I am keenly alive to the great responsibility resting upon me in my professional character as an advocate of those prisoners, charged with a crime, the penalty annexed to which is blood."

Owens now turned to the jury. He began his remarks by noting that in the early days, when Georgia was still a colony, the founding fathers of the Republic had created a "false philosophy," which drove slavery from the social compact. "Laws were established which declared the slave trade a social wrong, and this country submitted, this country yielded," Owens remarked. "Years elapsed and an institution which God permitted and Saul had sanctified, an institution from which the God of the Egyptians drew labor and which the God of the Jews had ratified, is now held in disrepute by a large portion of the world. During the last forty years a change has come over the spirit of our dream, and the scepter is passing away from us."

Now, said Owens, the jurors had the opportunity to "meet the question in open day," to do "what their forefathers *should have done*" when the question of slavery was subsumed in the making of the Constitution. If, back then, the question had been asked of twelve Southern jurors, rather than the Republic's fathers, Owens declared, "The question would have been answered—and the issue made, *with the sword.*" The image hung in the air, above the jurors.

Now Owens turned to the details of the case. "The prosecution has presented the slenderest of evidence to support its case," he said. "No connection had been proved between the prisoners and the *Wanderer*. It has been necessary to bring a *tailor* to describe the prisoner's breeches— and a *barber* to examine his beard. They must certainly have been ubiquitous. A witness saw them on the deck of the ship. On the island. On the highway." His gaze fell over the jurors. "And on this kind of testimony three quiet citizens have been incarcerated for twelve months in the common jail. They have been a spectacle for all eyes during five days in yonder dock. Are my clients to be hanged to sustain a theory?" He shook his head in disgust.

"You have heard the charges and the testimony to support them," he said, resting his hands on the railing before the jury box. "It is now for you to consider of your verdict, that you may do it with regard as well to the rights of the prisoners as to the state." He turned and pointed to the three men in the dock. "The lives of fellow beings are suspended on the issue. To us they have committed the trust of their defense. And whether they shall henceforth walk the earth in sunlight, or molder in dishonored graves, is dependent upon how we may perform our office."

There was complete silence in the courtroom. Every eye followed Owens as he paced to the center of the room. "But it is a greater and graver element than that at stake—for us as well as them," he said, pausing reflectively. "There are social theories that have come to battle in this world. The one takes its stand and finds its embodiment in the forms and constitution of the North. The other stands in the forms and embodiment we find in the constitution of the South. Which may be right is perhaps to be determined now.

"The North, to be sure, has power. They have the power to pass what laws they please, and they have passed them. They have circumscribed our institution; they have restricted it to certain latitudes; they have precluded it from vacant territories. They have abolished the trade of slaves in the District of Columbia; they are preparing to suppress and abolish the trade between the States." His voice hardened. "And they have passed a law that is now the object before us for enforcement. To bring it to enforcement is the last remaining step at which aggression trembles." Owens looked at the jurors and his voice rose. "But, gentlemen, it is our hope that no such question will occur; it is our hope and confidence that the proof is not sufficient to sustain the charges in this indictment."

He turned to where Brown, Rajesta, and Arguirir were sitting. "It is only to commend these friendless strangers to your favor, and to induce you to yield them kindly of what is indeed their right. It is to yield them the benefit of every reasonable doubt." He let that statement hang for a long moment, and then said in a low, trembling voice. "For if you do not, the same bolt that lays them low will pass through them—and piercing, will quiver in the very vitals of this country.

"Thank you."

Outside the courtroom, beneath the open windows, a cheer rose from the throng.

The following morning Henry Jackson presented the closing argument for the prosecution. It was another of his great orations—four and a half hours to Owens's forty-five minutes. One newspaper reporter put it well: "He wove into a close web all the crude surmises, the minute facts, the positive evidence, the far-fetched inferences, the remote particles of occurrence—everything in fact, bearing remotely or nearly, closely or irreverently on the matter, and—adorning it was an occasional glitter of imagery and mingling in periodical appeals and lectures to the jury—he flung the woof over the prisoners. . . ."

His oratory finished, Jackson fell back into his chair, grasping his throat in what seemed to be a spasmodic fit. "Brandy!" cried Justice Wayne, jumping up. "Bring the man some brandy!"

That afternoon, Justice Wayne was again before the jury, and in no un-certain terms urged them to convict the prisoners. "Using only the books and calculations of the yacht's captain," Wayne said, "Mr. Cheever has traced the course of the ship with most circumstantial accuracy, making the vessel's voyage, as he had estimated it, agree with the log book, and proving, by the perfect agreement of the chart on which he had lined the calculated course with the chart belonging to the ship, the fidelity of his estimations." This alone, Wayne said, should prove the voyage of the vessel.

As for the identity of the prisoners, Wayne argued that the three had been seen with the *Wanderer* in Charleston; then they had disappeared—from July to November of 1858—and then suddenly reappeared, with the *Wanderer,* in November 1858. On Jekyll Island, meanwhile, Harris, Clubb, and Christie had more than adequately identified the defendants.

Finally, Wayne told the jury that it was not its job to validate the law, or even the punishment. Its job was to look solely at the evidence. But, he promised, in an unusual bargain, if they would return a verdict of guilty, he would personally uphold any recommendation for mercy that they would attach. Now, he said, the final deliberation was in their hands.

Following his final words, the judge excused the jury to begin its deliberations. Brown, Rajesta, and Arguirir were taken back to their cells, and now the city waited for whatever verdict would come. It was 4 o'clock in the afternoon. It would be a long night in Savannah.

Ganahl sat on the back porch with his family. Jackson had dinner with Justice Wayne. Owens went down to the river and was seen in the twilight of evening speaking with Charles Lamar. The Reverend Charles Jones, whose son would be elected mayor of Savannah the following year, had written a few days earlier to his wife, who was out of town, tending to their new grandchild: "A lonely walk. Discovered Venus, just falling into the tops of the trees, brilliant as a diamond. Tea. Read the Wanderer trial as reported in the Republican. And now, I will write up my letter to my dear wife . . ."

Now, as the trial ended, he added, "Glad to hear that you are all well, and the baby, too, and that sleep visits you again. The charge of Judge Wayne to the jury when they were impaneled is a noble one. I wish it was printed in a pamphlet form and circulated to the whole state. It does the judge honor. The speech of Judge Jackson I sincerely hope will be at the pains of writing out; and if printed, it may go far to correct public sentiment and fix the hand of infamy upon the miscreants who have escaped, to the disgrace of the state, the just vengeance of the law. It is abominable. I am glad that they are indicted. Would that some of the principles that go at large could be laid hold of! We can only pray that Justice may not fall in the streets."

Later that night the city was largely deserted. Only the fire guard up in the Exchange Building's tower remained awake, as were some of the seamen in the brothels and bars down by the river.

The following morning people began to gather around the Custom House, some sitting on the steep steps out front, others in the vestibule. Another group gathered in the alley behind the big building, on Bay Lane. Looking up to the window that faced south, they could see the jurors, sequestered on the second floor.

Rumors flew as to the progress of the jury. The *Savannah Daily Morning News* was wagering that the jury would split, causing a mistrial. Then came the news. The jury was ready to reconvene: Following twenty hours of deliberations, the court bailiff notified the court that the jury had reached a verdict.

People jumped to their feet and poured into the courtroom again. The stairways quickly filled. Outside, on the grassy areas surrounding the building, a crowd gathered, and after the admonishments of a few among them, hushed so that they could hear the proceedings. Inside, everyone took their seats. The prisoners filed in impassively and sat down, with two constables behind them. Then the entire assembly rose again as first Justice Wayne, and then the jurors, filed in.

"The prisoners will rise," said the bailiff. Brown, Arguirir, and Rajesta got to their feet.

"Members of the jury, are you all agreed upon a verdict?" Wayne asked.

The foreman of the jury stood.

"We have, Your Honor," he said.

Justice Wayne nodded. "Do you find the prisoners in the dock guilty or not guilty?"

There was a hesitation; the assembly held its breath.

"We the jury," he replied, "find the defendants not guilty as charged."

A wave of emotion swept through the courtroom. Ganahl fell back in his seat, his face pale. Jackson stood motionless, stunned. Brown was shaking Owens's hand furiously. Nelson Trowbridge had come up and grasped him by the shoulder. Then a wave of spectators pushed forward to congratulate Owens. Ashen-faced, Wayne slammed down his gavel, remanding Brown, Rajesta, and Arguirir back to the Chatham County Jail on a lesser indictment of holding the Africans. The courtroom doors burst open, and the spectators poured down the stairs. The reporters ran back to their offices, and soon their telegrams had crossed the nation and made their way to Europe.

The words of the *New York Times,* spoken months earlier, now seemed ominously prescient: *For if they fail to hang the men who engaged in it— if their officials are so lax, or their juries so perjured, as to permit this trade to be carried on with impunity, in face of all our laws against it—they will suffer all the consequences of an actual complicity in the proceeding itself . . . the entire population of the North will wage upon it a relentless war of extermination.*

Perhaps that's why the verdict was taken so quietly in the South. There were no parades, no public rejoicings. "We cannot say the public expectation has been disappointed in this result," was all the *Savannah Republican* could muster the following morning. It was as though the outcome of the trial was merely another step toward a war that was increasingly inevitable.

Eight days later, John Brown was hanged. "The telegraph brings us the intelligence that John Brown, the notorious horse thief, murderer, insurrectionist and traitor, expiated his guilt on the gallows at Charleston, Va. yesterday at 12 o'clock . . ." said the *Savannah Daily Morning News* on the morning of December 3. "We can almost imagine that we hear the howl of the abolition hosts of the North as the telegraph, with a lightning flash, diffuses among them the news of the martyrdom of their Saint Ossawatomie. The church bells of New England are tolling his knell, and the three thousand preachers of the Gospel of abolition, with their millions of fanatical disciples, are piously bewailing his death. Well, let them howl."

John Brown had ridden out to the scaffold in a wagon, sitting on his own coffin. Hooded, he had dropped fifteen inches to the end of the rope and his hands had quivered. As he swung in the light breeze, silence had spread over the assemblage. Then the voice of a Virginia militiaman cried out: "So perish all such enemies of Virginia! All such enemies of the Union! All such foes of the human race!"

But it was Southern fanaticism that concerned the North. Said the *New York Times,* "We have our fears that the sober judgment of the majority may be over-ruled and overridden by the hot-headed fanaticism of the resolute and reckless minority—those who seem to have complete and scarcely disputed sway in the politics of the Southern states . . . Like any bully, the radicals could have been subdued by any reasonable show of force. But the forces of moderation were in disarray—or had been driven into silence. The hotspurs would have their day."

Indeed, the hotspurs in the South were gaining ground. And their day soon would come.

18

CHARLESTON

IN JANUARY, the biggest event in Savannah was the weeklong series of horse races at the Ten Broeck course. The most popular of these was the saddle race, in which a Pickaway filly, a bay mare, and a chestnut colt were entered. At the word "Go," the three dashed off in fine style, the filly ahead, and the other two neck and neck. The horses maintained the same relative position until they neared the quarter stretch, when the chestnut colt began to gain on the bay horse and soon passed him, coming in three or four lengths ahead of the bay and about as much behind the filly.

As the crowd leapt to its feet and cheered, no one had a bigger smile on their face than Charles Lamar, who had leaned over the railing, waving his cap in his hand, shouting happily. Indeed, life was good. Lamar's plantation had hauled in a record crop, and cotton prices were at an all-time high. The Lamar rice mill was bulging with grain. And now, as the newly reelected president of the Savannah Jockey Club, here he was, presenting the Pickaway filly's owner with the winner's purse and a wreath of flowers.

The *Savannah Daily Morning News,* which had been restrained in its public support for Lamar before the trial, was now effusive. "We confess, we admire his enterprise and spirit," the paper gushed. "We would not hesitate a moment in voting for him to be Governor of Georgia. We want, in the South, teachers of the Lamar stamp."

Indeed, Lamar *was* putting his stamp on local activities. He was active, for instance, in the local Southern Rights Vigilance Association. This group spent its time tar and feathering Northerners and running dissidents "suspected of uttering or entertaining sentiments hostile to slavery" out of town on a rail.

But Lamar didn't have a great interest in seeking a local office, or even the governorship. It was politics on the *national* level that caught his attention. In three months, the Democratic Party would hold its convention in Charleston. Stephen A. Douglas was considered the Democratic Party's best chance. Douglas had beaten Abraham Lincoln in the Illinois Senate race two years earlier, and he was the Democratic Party's best bet to beat Lincoln again in the 1860 presidential contest.

Many Georgians favored Douglas. But not Lamar—nor any of the other radical fire-eaters. They realized that a Douglas victory might just hold the Union together, and for them, that was a terrible thing. A win by Lincoln, on the other hand, would cause South Carolina to secede, which would probably ignite a general secession among the Southern states. It was exactly what Spratt had wanted—the first step toward a slave-owners' republic, in which the fire-eaters would dominate the land. It's what William L. Yancey, the great orator and radical fire-eater, had wanted as well. "We shall fire the Southern heart, instruct the Southern mind, give courage to each other," Yancey had promised, "and at the proper moment, by one organized, concerted action, we can precipitate the Cotton States into a revolution."

But how could the fire-eaters thwart Douglas and assure the election of a Republican? They concluded that the best strategy would be to force a "slave code" onto the Douglas political platform. The measure, penned by Yancey, stated that slave property would be entitled to the same rights as any other form of property, in the territories *and on the high seas.* This not only confirmed an extension of slavery nationally, but the reopening of the African trade. If Douglas accepted the measure, he would undoubtedly drive away his Northern supporters, and lose the election to Lincoln. But if he *didn't* support the plank, which was far more likely, then the fire-eaters would walk out of the Democratic convention, causing the Democratic Party to splinter. Either way, they figured, the Democratic Party would be mortally wounded, Lincoln would win, and the fire-eaters' revolution would be under way.

The rub, however, was that for all their bluster, the fire-eaters really didn't have much support in the South. When Yancey had run for the Senate in Alabama just two years earlier—on the same proslavery platform—not only did he fail to win, but he came in a distant third. Yancey was a superb orator—his commanding presence and velvety voice had won audiences nationwide. So his defeat had nothing to do with the delivery. It had to do with the *content:* The good citizens of Alabama simply did not like his message of African slave trading and violent revolution.

Georgia fire-eaters were in a similar fix: They could depend on the support of the wealthy plantation owners, who needed slaves, and the city business owners, who required the commerce generated by slaves. But in the cool northern mountains of Georgia, most of the farmers and small-town merchants had no stake in slavery at all, and even less interest in disbanding the Union over it. Many of them wanted America's unity preserved, and they happened to like the Democratic Party and the pro-Union message of Stephen Douglas. Even in Savannah, 95 percent of the whites were not slaveholders, a statistic that alarmed the planter elite.

To get their revolution rolling, then, the fire-eaters needed to act fast. The first part of the strategy was to win the support of the small farmers and mountain people in the South through a campaign of fear. They did this through cleverly written pamphlets, distributed by the hundreds of thousands around the South, and rallies and speeches extending to the most remote hilltops and mist-shrouded valleys, where the pro-Union, pro-Douglas Southerners were most likely to live. "So soon as the slaves are at liberty, thousands of them would leave the cotton and rice fields in the lower parts of our State, and make their way to the healthier climate in the mountain region," Georgia governor Joseph Brown warned at one of these rallies. "We should have them plundering and stealing, robbing and killing in all the lovely valleys of the mountains." He added: "The poor honest laborers of Georgia can never consent to see slavery abolished, and submit to all the taxation, vassalage, low wages, and downright degradation which must flow," the governor asserted. "They will never take the Negro's place; God forbid."

The second part of the strategy involved a minor piece of fraud and intimidation. In Georgia, the state Democratic Party, which had many Douglas supporters in its ranks, had called for a convention in March in which delegates for the upcoming National Democratic Convention would be chosen. Rather than submit to that, the fire-eaters rigged up an earlier convention, one in which they knew they could assemble a majority. It was a naked grasp for power, but the fire-eaters went for it.

Fortunately, a fast-thinking correspondent for the *Augusta Dispatch* scribbled down what ensued as the fire-eaters announced their resolution at the state capitol:

"But December 8 is not enough time for people to meet and elect their delegates," stuttered one representative, noting that one week would not give delegates from the northern mountains and valleys time to attend. "The masses—the great backbone of the party—will be excluded," he exclaimed.

"Duly noted," responded the fire-eater at the podium.

"The election of the delegates to the Charleston Convention is the business of the people—not of their representatives in the General Assembly," argued another.

"Duly noted," he responded again.

"Your fine Democratic legislators have their price, sir, and could be readily bought over to support any candidate," cried another.

From the podium came an icy stare.

"This is not democracy—this is a palace coup!" shouted the fourth. He felt a heavy hand fall upon his shoulder.

On December 8, the early convention was held, and a slate of fire-eating delegates was endorsed. A few more political maneuvers were required, but in the end, the radicals beat the majority into a minority, and took the power from the moderates in the state.

"There is a deep, sullen, desponding state of feeling among our people who really desire the perpetuation of the Union," despaired James Nisbet, the editor of the *Augusta Daily Constitutionalist*. "They see the Republican party under the control of extreme men and the Democratic Party at the South pushed to the extreme policy by Ultralists, and they fold their hands and say, 'All is lost.'" Indeed, all was lost for Douglas, for similar coups were under way in Alabama, Texas, and Florida. It was not the first time in history that a group of radicals had overwhelmed the will of a weak and unfocused majority, nor would it be the last.

The fire-eaters had won their civil war in the Deep South, at least temporarily. Now they were ready to take their divisive tactics to the Democratic National Convention in Charleston, where they would need to break up the Democratic Party's support throughout the South. Charles Lamar was ecstatic. He could taste the sweet fruit of disunion already.

On April 23, 1860, Democratic delegates from the across the nation poured into Institute Hall, near downtown Charleston, where some three thousand wooden chairs had been screwed down to the floor, awaiting the rowdy throngs. As the carriages rolled in, and the delegates streamed from the railway cars and down the gangplanks of the paddle wheelers, bands played and spectators with political signs lined their paths. The Douglas men took over Hibernia Hall, a two-story building with two big meeting halls and a multitude of offices, as well as the Mills House nearby. They pumped both full of cigar smoke and confidence, assuming that their man would win.

The Southern rights supporters, meanwhile, took over the Charleston House, with the fire-eaters in full force. There was a mixture of opinion between them, to be sure, but all the luminaries were in attendance: Spratt and Yancey, were there, of course, as was Louisiana's John Slidell, Georgia's William B. Gaulden, Ethelbert Barksdale, editor of the *Jackson Mississippian*, Alfred Iverson of Georgia, Clement Clay of Alabama, Louis T. Wigfall of Texas. There was Robert Barnwell Rhett, editor of the *Charleston Mercury*, and rabid Edmund Ruffin. Not all of the Southerners there were ready for disunion. Some, like Jefferson Davis, Howell Cobb, and even African slave trade advocate Gaulden thought the union might still survive. But in the end, they were the powder keg that would soon send the nation hurtling into civil war.

For the next several days, in a convention filled with delegates and spectators, the Democratic Party attempted to find a compromise platform.

The speeches were impassioned, the debate sincere, but as the days passed, the prospects for agreement became increasingly slim. Meanwhile, at night, the fire-eaters took over Charleston. It was their town, after all, the cradle of their revolution, the birthplace and the burial grounds of the great John C. Calhoun. Gathering around flaming barrels of pine resin, firecrackers and rockets sizzling and crackling all around, the fire-eating orators were in their prime, proclaiming Southern rights and secession.

Beside one blazing barrel of pine resin, one could find William B. Gaulden, Georgia's prominent domestic slave trader. "The African slave trade brings a heathen and worthless man here, makes him a useful man, Christianizes him, and sends him and his posterity down the stream of time to join in the blessings of civilization!" Gaulden exclaimed, as the crowd about him roared its assent. "Besides," he laughed, "I can buy better Negroes in Africa for $50 apiece than those for which I had to pay $1,000 to $2,000 a head in Virginia!"

"I'm from Indiana, and I'm in favor of it," shouted one man in the crowd. "I want to go to Africa to buy a savage and introduce him to the blessings of civilization and Christianity!" Another man jumped forward. "When you do," he interrupted gleefully, "you can get one or two recruits from New York to join you!" The man from New York looked familiar— in fact it was Marshal Rynders, from the Port of New York. And standing right next to Rynders was another familiar face: William C. Corrie. "Last night Col. Gaulden took a benefit, and the crowd, or a large portion of it, seemed wonderfully delighted by the performance," the *Savannah Republican* noted. "*Captain Corrie,* of the Wanderer, was standing by his side while he was speaking, and seemed wonderfully charmed by the discourse."

On the fifth day of the convention, late in the afternoon, while the rain was smashing down outside, Yancey arose and, to a thunderous ovation, took the stage. To continued applause, Yancey said that the South had come to the convention to defend her constitutional rights. "Ours is the property invaded; ours are the institutions which are at stake," he stated. "Ours is the peace that is to be destroyed; ours is the honor at stake— the honor of children, the honor of families, the lives, perhaps, of all— all of which rests upon what your course may ultimately make into a great heaving volcano of passion and crime, if you are enabled to consummate your designs. Bear with us, then, if we stand sternly upon what if yet that dormant volcano . . ." Yancey's oratory brought the Southern delegates to their feet, shouting themselves hoarse.

As Yancey descended from the stage, he was followed by Senator George E. Pugh of Ohio. Pugh's comments were tinged with sarcasm and disparaged the Southerners' concerns. Must the Democratic Party become the tool of three hundred thousand slaveholders? he asked acidly. Did the South really think the North would endorse, upon its recommendation, the continuation and expansion of slavery? "Gentlemen of the South," he declared caustically. "You mistake us—you mistake us. We will not do it!

The vote on the Democratic platform came a few days later. Yancey had already dropped the reopening of the slave trade from his proposed slave code: It was too bitterly debated, even in the South at this time, he had pragmatically decided, and had better wait. But Yancey's measure still demanded official recognition of slavery as a national institution. Instead, the convention delegates voted for a platform that had been shaped by the Douglas men. That platform did not endorse national slavery; rather suggesting that the issue be left up to the U.S. Supreme Court.

When the final vote on the last clause of the minority report was announced, and the chair confirmed that it was carried, the dropping of a pin might have been heard in the convention. Said one observer: "Every man, woman and child within the vast hall in which the delegates assembled seemed aware that a great crisis had arrived, and that events were about to occur in which the deepest interest of American citizens were involved."

The silence was broken by Leroy Walker of Alabama, the gaunt

Southerner who was Yancey's most trusted aide. Walker, in a few brief words, explained why his colleagues in the South could not accept the platform, and why, under the circumstances, the Alabama delegation deemed it their duty to withdraw from the convention.

No sooner had Walker resumed his seat than William F. Barry, of Mississippi, rose to his feet and declared that his state had also resolved to withdraw. Next came the ex-governor of Louisiana, who declared that he and his delegates had also resolved to withdraw. The chairmen of the delegations from South Carolina, Florida, Arkansas, and Texas announced that they, too, would leave. The spectators and other delegates looked on, stunned. Tears ran down a few cheeks. They were seeing, before their eyes, the Union dissolving.

But not everyone was unhappy. That night, Charleston celebrated wildly. There were fireworks and bands playing deep into the night. For many of the Southern fire-eaters, this was Independence Day, the day their revolution would begin.

Charles Lamar was delighted. He, along with his cousins Henry G. Lamar and John B. Lamar, had helped break up the Democratic Party in Georgia, dissolving its remains into the fiery, prosecessionist Southern Rights Party. "We shall have disunion, certain, if Lincoln is elected!" Lamar wrote excitedly to his father. "I hope Lincoln is elected—*I want dissolution*—and have, I think, contributed more than any man South for it," he bragged.

19

LAMAR TRIAL

A FEW weeks after the end of the Charleston convention, Lamar was back in Savannah, sitting in the dock at the Federal courthouse, looking bored, working a toothpick through his teeth, and greeting people who came by. He wasn't the only defendant in court that day. Henry du Bignon, Richard Aiken, Nelson Trowbridge, and John Tucker were there as well. All of them were charged with having taken illegal possession of the Africans after they had been landed on Jekyll.

Lamar wasn't particularly concerned. After all, Brown, Rajesta, and Arguirir had been acquitted. Now, who in Savannah would have the nerve to testify against Charles Lamar?

That was the challenge facing Hamilton Couper, the federal prosecutor in the case. Couper, thirty, had a particular connection to Lamar. His father, James Hamilton Couper, had been on the *Pulaski* with the Lamar family, and like Charles and Gazaway, was one of the few survivors.

Couper's first witness was John Boston, the Savannah customs collector. Boston had defied Lamar two years earlier, refusing to give him clearance for the *Rawlins*. Now the customs collector was meek. Had Boston ever heard Lamar make any remarks about the African slave trade? Couper asked. Boston replied that he didn't want to say anything in which his "recognition was not perfectly clear." Couper asked a few more questions; Boston replied evasively, noting that he "was sorry to have had anything to do with this matter." As a witness, Boston was useless.

Next came Van Horn, the jailer who had taken a pummeling from Lamar. In the heat of that melee, Couper asked, had Lamar mentioned that he owned the *Wanderer,* or the Africans? Van Horn squirmed uncomfortably in his chair and finally said that he couldn't remember much of the incident, other than that Lamar apologized some time later. "It was sort of an apology," Van Horn explained. "Such an apology as he generally makes."

Couper called a few other witnesses to the stand, but the others were equally unresponsive. Couper realized the case was lost. "Further perseverance in these prosecutions, I am convinced, are utterly useless," he said in a telegraph to Attorney General Black, requesting permission to file a nolle prosequi (permission not to prosecute), in all of the remaining cases. Permission was granted: On May 28, 1860, at 5 P.M., the federal case against Charles Lamar and his friends was over.

Following the acquittals, champagne undoubtedly flowed at some private parties, but there was no public celebration. "The abrupt termination of these trials was the subject of much remark on the street," noted the *Savannah Republican.* "But in view of the disturbance they have created in our community—often arraying friend against friend and the utter hopelessness of a conviction in the end—we believe all were gratified with the result." The paper added: "If Africans are to be imported, we hope to Heaven that no more will be landed on the shores of Georgia."

Meanwhile, Attorney General Black was making one last effort to get his hands on Corrie. On instructions from President Buchanan, he ordered Magrath to enter a nolle prosequi in the case. The strategy was that Corrie, once freed from South Carolina, could be moved to Georgia. Once again, Magrath flatly refused. A U.S. president could order a nolle prosequi to *terminate* a case, Magrath explained in his decision, but the chief executive had no precedent for issuing a nolle prosequi to *move* a case from one jurisdiction to another. In other words, Mr. President, no. Corrie would remain in Charleston.

Not only that, said Magrath. "I always thought, and the most careful consideration has strengthened the conviction, that there exists a misinterpretation of the Act of Congress of the 15th May, 1820," Magrath wrote. There were two problems, he said. First, the Act of 1820 does not mention slave trading *by name* as piracy. Second, even if the Act of 1820 were applicable, it prohibits the importation of persons who are *free*. But are Africans, penned in a barracoon awaiting transportation, free? Magrath wrote that that presumption would be very hard to prove.

To the horror of many Northerners, Magrath was clearly playing the nullification card created by John C. Calhoun thirty years earlier. Corrie "struts the streets of Charleston amidst the caresses of applauding thousands," roared Massachusetts senator Henry Wilson, "shielded from a felon's doom by the monstrous perversions of the laws of the land by a faithless, if not by a perjured judge."

Magrath's decision demonstrated the widening gap between North and South: While the Northern press condemned Magrath unsparingly, not a single Southern newspaper condemned Magrath's decision. The *Savannah Daily Morning News* even offered applause: "The judge's decision certainly does great credit to the bench, whose independence he vindicates, and to himself, for the ability he displays." The British were watching the proceedings closely as well. British consul Bunch noted that Magrath's nullification of federal law was a clear sign that the bonds holding the United States together were coming apart.

But with Magrath's heels dug firmly in, Buchanan and Black realized that the case was over. Further efforts on their part would only make sectional tensions worse. When James Conner, the U.S. attorney in Charleston who was prosecuting the case, telegraphed Black for further instruction, he received no reply. Taking Black's silence as a sign that the attorney general had given up, Conner went on record, absolving himself from further responsibility. Then he discharged the grand jury. That was it. Corrie, the smooth-talking Southern gentleman, was free.

———

There was still one major conspirator unaccounted for: J. Egbert Farnum. While all the activity had centered on the conspirators in the South, Farnum had been left free, hobnobbing at his favorite restaurants in New York and hanging out with his lobbyist friends in Washington. Henry Jackson tried to get the New York authorities to arrest him, but they wouldn't. This upset Jackson so much that he went to President Buchanan. Buchanan, in turn, gave Jackson the authority to get Farnum himself.

Jackson did so, calling on none other than Isaiah Rynders, the lawman who had cleared the *Wanderer* from the Port of New York, to make the arrest. Rynders arrested Farnum at Farnum's favorite hangout, the St. Nicholas Hotel in Manhattan, and brought him before Judge Samuel Rossiter Betts. Betts signed a warrant of extradition and sent Farnum, on December 10, 1859, back to Savannah in handcuffs.

Now Lamar and his associates were in serious trouble. Rumors were going around that Farnum had been willing to turn state's evidence for $7,000 and immunity. Farnum did have a big mouth. He'd not only bragged about the *Wanderer* to the press, but he'd apparently told the whole story to Edwin Ward Moore, the former commander of the Republic of Texas Navy.

In April, Farnum went on trial in Savannah on federal piracy charges. The usual witnesses were trotted out, who said very little—and then came Commander Moore, a star witness if there ever was one. Moore, bold and erect, and completely unintimidated by Charles Lamar, told the jury all the details as told him by Farnum. On the morning of May 27, the case against Farnum concluded. The odds for conviction seemed excellent.

But once again, Lamar stepped into the breach. On May 1, Deputy Jailer Peter Luddy had just locked Farnum into his cell for the night and was returning to the front of the jail when Lamar and seven or eight colleagues (including Brunswick mayor Carey Styles, who would later found the *Atlanta Constitution*) approached him in the hallway. "Peter, old boy, we want the keys," one of them said pleasantly. At first Luddy thought they were kidding, but when he saw their drawn revolvers he realized otherwise. As the men grabbed for the keys, a skirmish ensued.

Luddy's collar was torn and his pocket ripped off. As soon as Farnum was sprung, the group hurried off to the Pulaski House, the finest hotel in town, at the northeast corner of Bull and Bryan Streets.

There they were having a good time, when, at about 9 o'clock that night, U.S. Attorney Couper happened by. Hearing the undisguised ruckus, Couper ran for help, returning within minutes with Luddy, a deputy marshal, and a few friends. Bursting into the room with revolvers drawn, Couper and the others declared that they had come to arrest Farnum. Lamar's group pulled out their revolvers. Styles told Couper to keep his hands off Farnum. Couper replied that he was taking the prisioner in. Bloodshed was imminent. Then one of the party suggested that the arrest be postponed until morning. Couper, badly outnumbered, agreed. The next morning, though, Couper didn't find Farnum at the jailhouse. Couper sent the word around that unless Farnum was back fast, his bail would be revoked. Shortly after two that afternoon, Farnum returned and was put back in his cell.

It was a memorable night on the town, but moreover an instructional night for Farnum, who learned who really controlled things in Savannah, and what fate might well await him if he ever testified against Charles Lamar.

Lamar struck again on May 22, as Moore, alone, walked down the stairs leading from the courtroom following his testimony.

"Commodore Moore," Lamar said, stepping in front of him. "My friend, Mr. Farnum says that your testimony, from beginning to end, is one —— —— lie, and I endorse what he says." The crowd that usually accompanied Lamar gathered around Moore, growling its assent. Moore, looking coolly down his nose at Lamar, took out his memorandum book, and said to Lamar, "Will you kindly give me your name, Sir?"

Lamar replied in a most excited manner: "My name is C. A. L. Lamar, and right here is the place to settle this difficulty."

"No, this is not the place to settle this difficulty," Moore replied calmly. "You are armed and I am not. You are surrounded by your friends and I am friendless." Then he looked sharply at Lamar. "But you may rest assured that this difficulty will be settled and in a most satisfactory manner."

Moore then suggested that any of the crowd members that endorsed Mr. Lamar's sentiments should provide their names as well. A writer for the *Savannah Daily Morning News* was present and reported, "There was dead silence."

Now Joseph Ganahl came tripping down the stairs, and ran immediately over to Moore. "Commodore, just show this crowd that you are ready to put daylight through them and they will leave you alone." Moore did just that, challenging Lamar to a duel.

At daybreak the following morning, as the fog was lifting off the ground at Screven's Ferry, the place on the South Carolina side of the Savannah River where honor was traditionally restored, Lamar and Moore met. U.S. Attorney Hamilton Couper served as Moore's second, and defense attorney John Owens serving as Lamar's second. A surgeon accompanied the group and, as was the custom, was told to turn his back so that he would not witness what was, after all, a criminal act.

The dueling pistols were removed from the rosewood case that held them. Gunpowder and lead balls were rammed down the muzzles. The seconds drew for positions. Moore, an excellent marksman, remarked that he would not kill Lamar—since Lamar was the cousin of Mirabeau Lamar, the former president of the Republic of Texas—but merely drill Lamar through his right shoulder. Lamar offered no similar consideration for Moore.

The two men each took their twelve paces. Then they turned and faced each other. Moore fired first. At the explosion, Lamar's eyes flew wide open. His pistol discharged, the shot careening wildly off course. As the smoke cleared, Lamar took an unsteady step forward. He had not been hit, but Moore was dumbfounded. He looked quizzically down at his pistol. Then he saw the mistake: His second had forgotten to return the ramrod to its place beneath the barrel, which had lightened the pistol and caused the bullet to pass clean over Lamar's shoulder, an inch higher than intended.

As the seconds rushed forward to the men to press for an amicable resolution, as tradition required, Owens's first apology was to Moore for Lamar's egregiously poor aim. Lamar, indignant, interjected that he had intended to shoot wide all along. Nevertheless, Lamar offered something of an apology—that his language had been used under excitement and misapprehension, and that he now withdrew and regretted it. Lamar extended his hand and Moore took it. But the commodore deserved the last word, and he got it: "You are a lucky man, Mr. Lamar," said Moore, holding up his weapon. "This ramrod was out of my pistol."

But the battle in the courtroom was still unresolved. Lamar had hired attorney S. Yates Levy to defend Farnum. Levy realized he couldn't dispute the evidence that was laid down by Moore, so he took another tack: Levy told the jurors that the U.S. Constitution has no powers to punish offenses except where specifically given to the Congress. Even in these cases, he said, the penal nature must be construed *strictly*.

Yates then explained to the jury that if slavery in the states is recognized by the Constitution—and it certainly was—then the Constitution should certainly recognize it *there*—the Congo. If it then recognizes slavery here, and slavery there, slaves on both sides must be recognized equally as merely property. Thus, said Levy, "Negro property peaceably and lawfully acquired, whether in this country or elsewhere, where slavery is recognized is regarded merely as a chattel . . . in the absence of these rights, therefore they stand in the same position as a bale of silks, or a case of shoes, and it would be absurd to enact that the introduction of such chattel into this country should be a crime."

At the conclusion of the trial on June 4, Justice Wayne delivered another impassioned charge to the jury, reminding them of the horrors of the African slave trade, and of the contribution of Southern men to its prohibition. The jury deliberated for thirty hours, and came back split (a later count showed ten to two for acquittal). With the nation sliding rapidly toward civil war, attempting another trial was useless. The following day, Justice Wayne dismissed the grand jury. Farnum was released.

Out of the entire *Wanderer* episode, in fact, only one charge stuck. Lamar was convicted, along with Styles and two other of his friends, of springing Farnum from jail. The group received $250 fines and thirty-day jail sentences, which Lamar was able to serve at home.

When an unidentified congressman tried to needle Lamar, by sending him a letter with the address *IN JAIL,* Lamar fired off an angry request to U.S. Senator Lucius Q. C. Lamar, of Mississippi, another
illustrious cousin, asking him to arrange a duel. "I am *not* in jail," wrote
Lamar, "and the damned Government has not the power to put and
keep me there. I am in my own rooms, over my office, and go home
every night and live like a fighting cock at the expense of the Government; for we notified the Marshal, at the beginning, that unless he fur-
nished us, we would not stay with him, but dissolve all connection that
exists or might exist between us."

Lamar then offered some prophetic words: "I can whip the Government any time they make the issue, unless they raise a few additional reg-
iments." It was a boast that he would soon have the opportunity to prove.

On November 20, 1860, Georgia's legislators formally resolved "that
the election of Abraham Lincoln . . . ought not to be submitted to," and
that "we respectfully suggest to the legislature to take immediate steps
to arm and organize the militia of the state." A few days following Lincoln's election, Lamar penned a letter to his father. "I do not agree with
you about the mode and manner of action; we must go out promptly,"
Lamar wrote on November 26, 1860. "We have for ten years been calling upon the abolition states to repeal their laws. I am opposed to any
further calls—it would take too much time, and force us to live for a
time, at least, under Lincoln's rule, which I shan't do."

Not everyone in Georgia agreed with Lamar's sentiments, however.
Many citizens, particularly those in central and north Georgia, were not
ready to spring into disunion at the election of the Republican president. "We do not intend to submit to the decision of the secession
movement which has been taken out of the hands of the People and has
fallon into the hands of Dimegougs and office seekers, pick pockitts and
vagrants about towns and cities . . ." said one leader from mountainous
north Georgia, warning that he had the names of 2,500 volunteers who
were "gest as willing as you ever seen mountain boies" to use the "point
of the bayonet and the mussel of the musket" to stay in the Union.
"The people of Cherochee want to stay in the union," he continued, "so

I hope you will let us go in peace and we will set up for our celves and still remain in the union."

The prospect of a civil war within Georgia, and probably throughout the South, didn't bother Lamar, however. "If Georgia doesn't act promptly, we, the military of Savannah, will throw her into Revolution, and we will be backed by the Minute Men all throughout the state," he wrote his father. "We do not care for what the world may approve of. We know we are right and we'll act regardless of consequences."

Indeed, many young men of the South were now seen wearing a blue cockade—which designated them as secessionists. Others wore black glazed caps with the letters M.M.—Minute Men—emblazoned in red letters. Those who resisted secession were called Submissionists, Abolitionists, and Lincolnites. "We are in the midst of a revolution," Attorney General Black wrote dolefully. "It is fruitless to argue now the causes that produced it or whether it be a good or bad thing . . ."

One by one, the moderate leaders of the South—those who had promoted the Union in the face of the radical secessionists—were sucked into the wildfire: Howell Cobb; Savannah mayor Charles C. Jones; Henry R. Jackson; George Mason of Virginia; Jefferson Davis of Mississippi; James Hammond of South Carolina; Judah Benjamin of Louisiana; Robert E. Lee, among many others.

Even Gazaway Lamar, despite his earlier pro-Union standings, was now a secessionist. His first acts were to attempt to ship thousands of muskets south and to begin to finance the new confederacy by brokering millions in Confederate bonds to New York investors.

On December 20, 1860, South Carolina voted itself out of the Union. Two weeks later, Georgia's delegates gathered to determine whether Georgia should stay in the Union or not. The following day, Georgia governor Brown announced that secession had been passed "overwhelmingly." Later, he admitted that the vote had actually been close—50,243 votes for secession and 37,123 against. A more recent analysis places the vote at 42,744 to 41,717 against. On the basis of about one thousand votes, then, and some of those probably fraudulent, "Georgia" left the Union.

The cannon on Capitol Square in Milledgeville boomed at about 2 o'clock, signaling the secession of Georgia. Celebrations swept through the state. Soon Savannah's proud militias—the Chatham Artillery, the Savannah Volunteer Guards, Republican Blues, Georgia Hussars, Irish Jasper Greens, German Volunteers, the Oglethorpe Light Infantry, the DeKalb Guards, and other units—marched off to war. "We quarreled with them [the fire-eaters] *then* because we saw their cause would destroy the union," the *Augusta Daily Constitutionalist* said anxiously. "We thank them *now* that it did."

Awaiting the Georgia fighters, of course, would be Manassas, Richmond, Sharpsburg, Fredericksburg, Gettysburg, the Wilderness, Murfreesboro, Chicamauga, Kennesaw, Atlanta, Franklin, Nashville, and Columbus, battles that would draw the last of their blood.

20

THE WANDERER

ON DECEMBER 24, 1860, two weeks after John Brown's body was lowered into its grave in North Elba, New York, the *Wanderer* turned up unexpectedly in Boston, Massachusetts. She was torn and battered. Said the *Boston Traveller:*

> As this vessel is the wonder of the day—the representative of a great principle, the principle of reviving the slave trade—everything relating to her must be of interest. She now lies at the south side of Union Wharf, with sails unbent, foretopmast down, and jib-boom unshipped, in charge of two men, who guard her, watch-and-watch, repelling all attempts to board her. Yesterday and today she has been visited by crowds of all classes, from the moneyed to the money-less, and crowds will probably visit her tomorrow and the next day. . . .

To trace the *Wanderer*'s path to Boston, one must pick up at the port of Santa Cruz, where she had escaped the wrath of the merchants there.

Once out to sea, the notorious Captain Martin ordered his crew to head for the slave coast of Africa. He had plans for his seasick lover, Anna Felice, who was still aboard, and her friend Mariana Jose, but not pleasant ones: When they got to Africa he would trade the ladies for slaves. He figured he could get about one hundred Africans for each of them.

Ten days of hard sailing and the *Wanderer* had made Port de Lago, on the island of Madeira. There, Martin spotted a British warship, and fearing a boarding, took off to sea again. By now the crew was ready to revolt. They just needed the opportunity, and they found it at the end of November, upon sighting a French vessel, the *Jeannie,* of Marseilles. Martin fired a charge of grapeshot to bring her to.

As Martin and a few other crewmen rowed over to the *Jeannie,* the first mate aboard the *Wanderer* exclaimed, "Boys, I'm going to take this vessel back to the United States. Are you with me?" The crew shouted, "Yes," the foresail was raised, and she was off. As they passed the *Jeannie,* they could see Captain Martin in the fore rigging, cursing and shaking his fists furiously at them.

Dressed only in rags, the men nearly froze as they ran across the North Atlantic. But finally the *Wanderer* reached Fire Island, then bounced north to Gay Head, then Tarpaulin Cove, and finally arrived at Union Wharf in Boston—where she immediately drew a curious crowd. The U.S. marshal immediately impounded the *Wanderer,* and despite the heroics of the crew in securing their freedom, they—and even the ladies—were hauled off to spend Christmas Eve in jail.

For the next several months, Charles and Gazaway fought a legal battle with the government for the return of the *Wanderer.* Finally, upon submitting bonds equal to the appraised worth of the now-battered yacht ($5,940), the Lamars were permitted to bring her back to Savannah. The following year, Lamar sent the *Wanderer* to Havana, with Nelson Trowbridge, to find a buyer. None appeared, but in the spring of 1861, a customer was found in New Orleans.

On the way to New Orleans, the yacht's new commander put in at Key West. There, she was spotted and detained by the U.S. Navy. "Sir," read the message from the Union officer aboard to the secretary of the Navy, "I have the honor to report to you that the notorious Wanderer arrived in this port April 5th, from Havana." He continued, ". . . armed with one long 24-pounder, and with a crew of 25 men, this vessel may be disastrously destructive to our shipping in the West Indies, and there was a general feeling of relief expressed among shipmasters in Havana when it was learned that I had seized the *Wanderer*."

He added, "While aware that I have no legal grounds for detaining the vessel, I do not feel justified in permitting her to escape to the rebels, and the only way in which that result can be prevented is by the U.S. Government becoming purchasers . . ." Instead of paying for her, though, the government simply seized the *Wanderer,* making her over into a Union gunboat. In that capacity, she was credited with capturing two schooners and two sloops during the Civil War. After the war, the government sold her at auction at Key West.

The new owner was a captain from Maine, who sent her battered body up and down the Northeast coast, hauling cargo. Now rapidly deteriorating, she next fell into the hands of a captain who used her to carry limes and coconuts—finally running her aground in foul weather. The *Wanderer* was repaired, and this time, sold to S. S. Scattergood, of Philadelphia. Now she carried fruit between Philadelphia and the West Indies. In January 1871, she made her last cruise, coming ashore in a brutal gale on Cape Maisi, at the eastern end of Cuba. There, following a life more controversial than Captain Rowland could ever have anticipated when he created her, the *Wanderer* sank ignominiously beneath the sea and settled her bones into the sand forever. Although rumors of other slaves smuggled ashore persisted into the time of the Civil War, none of these episodes were ever proven true. The *Wanderer* remains the last confirmed cargo of African captives to America.

Farnum quickly retreated North following the voyage of the *Wanderer*. Before Farnum was returned for trial secessionist Edmund Ruffin ran into him outside the U.S. Senate chambers. Farnum declared that he had been arrested and was going to Savannah to be tried as a pirate. "He seemed in very good spirits," Ruffin remarked, "and expressed the very confident hope that they would not hang him in Savannah—in which I accorded."

As soon as his trial had ended, Farnum returned North to his usual antics. A few months later the *New York Times* reported that Farnum "made himself conspicuous in the barroom of the St. Nicholas Hotel, drawing a pistol on a guest, who pulled a pistol on him in return. Many of the witnesses wanted to 'see the fun out,' as they termed it, and among others, threw obstacles in the way of the policeman. Meanwhile, Farnum, in the confusion, effected his escape."

When the war came, Farnum served in the Union army, commanding a regiment at Fredericksburg. Rising to the rank of colonel, he took over a brigade at Chancellorsville and fought at Gettysburg. In 1866, he was brevetted brigadier general for his war service and, ironically, considering his participation in slaving, became a collector for the shamelessly corrupt Port of New York—and was then elevated to the lucrative position as New York City's Inspector of Customs. When he died in 1870, at the age of forty-seven, a regiment of the national guard Zouaves, resplendent in red hats, red trousers, and ceremonial jackets, carried the wreath-topped coffin from his home on Stuyvesant Street. Four white horses pulled the hearse through the city to Greenwood Cemetery in Brooklyn, where the Governor's Island band awaited the signal to play the appropriate dirge.

As soon as South Carolina had seceded from the Union, Leonidas Spratt was dispatched to Florida as South Carolina's official "Ambassador of Secession," there giving such a fiery, tightly reasoned speech—proclaiming the South a slave republic—that the delegates cheered and voted Florida out of the Union as well. Later, as a "special correspondent" of the *Charleston Mercury,* Spratt sent celebratory dispatches home from the Battle of Manassas. He was subsequently appointed judge advocate-general on General Longstreet's staff.

Following the war, Spratt made a subdued living as a lawyer in Charleston and Richmond, his eloquence contained to such expositions as "The Charleston City Debt" and "The Blue Ridge Railroad." His final years were spent at his home on Talleyrand Avenue in Jacksonville, Florida, where, in the end, he rarely left his room. There, one afternoon, his dreams of a slave republic died with him.

On October 5, 1903, Spratt's obituary appeared in the back pages of the *Florida Times-Union,* set ingloriously between an advertisement for Gorham Silver Polish and Baird's Hardware. Only the obit writer seemed to be impressed, for his eulogy sounded as though he were playing taps for some long-lost cause. "Peacefully," he wrote, "as one who falls into restful slumber after labors well done, the end came yesterday to the long and useful career of Col. Leonidas William Spratt, one of the most prominent citizens of Jacksonville and a distinguished Southerner whose part in the history of his native and adopted states will ever have a place of honor. . . . Col. Spratt belonged to that typical class, whose virtues are being more and more revered by the modern generation—the Southern Gentleman of the old school. In courtesy, keen humor, and a high sense of honor and chivalry, he realized the ideal."

William Corrie also disappeared quite rapidly into the mists of history. No record is to be found of any Civil War service. Following the conflict, though, Corrie was back in Charleston, although in what seemed to be a transitory state: In 1866, he lived at the Charleston Hotel; in 1867 and in 1868 moved down the street to the Pavilion Hotel; in 1869 to a residence at 53 Meeting Street. In 1870, puffy, vomiting, and still drinking heavily, he died at the Mills House Hotel of kidney failure. He was fifty-two.

Many years after the *Wanderer* trials, Henry Rootes Jackson, who had returned following the war to the practice of law, would write: "No resident of Savannah can have forgotten what a period of peculiar excitement it was, nor what were the labors, and even the personal exposure of the District Attorney, Mr. Ganahl, in whom the government never had a braver man, more efficient or indefatigable officer."

Yet Ganahl resigned from the U.S. government following the acquittals of Brown, Arguirir, and Rajesta, apparently shaken by what he had seen as a gross miscarriage of justice. He moved his family to Augusta in 1860, and, when the war came, served as a surgeon and rose to the rank of major. Following that, he resumed his law practice in Augusta.

Friends often urged Ganahl to seek higher office, but surrounded by his wife and five children, and the recognition, as the Augusta papers put it, "for his vigorous prosecution of the celebrated *Wanderer* case," he was content to maintain his anonymity. On occasion, the righteous indignation that filled him during the *Wanderer* trial rose to the surface, however. In 1880, for instance, he spoke out against former Georgia governor Joseph E. Brown, who had been a leading fire-eater before the war, and after the war, a true friend to the Northern carpetbaggers and opportunists who came south to exploit the land. Ganahl, in a speech that laid out the villainous hypocrisy of Brown, remarked, "He forced the bitter cup of humiliation to our lips, and we drank it to the dregs." Ganahl died in Augusta on September 8, 1900.

When the war came, Charles Lamar formed his own company—"The Lamar Rangers" (later designated the Seventh Battalion Georgia Infantry and finally 61st Georgia Infantry). Lamar's men elected him lieutenant colonel and he commanded the defenses at Jekyll Island. Six months later, however, Lamar turned the command over to his old friend Carey Styles and joined his father and Georgia governor Joe Brown in the blockade-running business. At that task Lamar excelled, and soon had five steamships running Yankee lines. On December 14, 1863, Lamar was aboard one of those steamers when it wrecked off Wilmington, North Carolina, and he once again nearly died at sea.

When Sherman captured Savannah, Lamar's blockade-running activities ceased, and he turned back to combat, returning to battle as a colonel of the 25th Regiment, Georgia Cavalry. His commander this time was none other than his old nemesis, Howell Cobb, who now wore the bars of a Confederate general (Henry Rootes Jackson was also fighting nearby, as a brigadier general in the Confederate army).

On April 16, 1865, Union and Confederate troops met in the woods outside Columbus, Georgia. The war had actually ended eight days earlier—Lee had already surrendered to Grant at Appomattox. Rumors of the peace had spread to the troops in Georgia, but many still clung to the cause. Now they were locked in a furious night battle, the faces of the combatants illuminated by the blue flashes of artillery. Somewhere in the midst of the battle were General Cobb and Colonel Charles Lamar. As the rebels retreated across the Chattahoochee River, the Yankees poured over them. Cobb and about six hundred other Confederates retreated to Macon, where they surrendered three days later. But Lamar never got there.

"Dear Brother," Aunt Rebecca, who had survived the *Pulaski* sinking, wrote Gazaway Lamar on May 1, 1865:

> *You will have heard before this reaches you of the untimely death of dear Charlie. He had participated in the defense of Columbus and had acted very gallantly. But after the retreat he became separated from his friends, was ordered to surrender, which he did, ordered to dismount, which he did. He was then asked for his side-arm, and he had just replied that he had none when some foolish fellow shot off a pistol nearby. The Yankee, having his already cocked, and supposing that Charlie had fired, shot him dead.*

"The flower of our family is gone," agonized Gazaway. The old man was in jail now. He had helped the governor of Georgia purchase ten thousand muskets that were shipped South. He had printed millions of dollars in Confederate bonds. He had started and maintained a blockade-running operation as well. Then, on May 1, 1865, two weeks after Lincoln's assassination, Union soldiers burst into his home in Savannah, seized his books and records, and hauled Lamar off in chains. Now he sat in the Old Capitol Prison in Washington, suspected in the assassination of Lincoln (for which he was never charged and was eventually set free).

"My health is broken and I may not see you again," Gazaway wrote to Rebecca from his cell, "but I hope we can meet where the Yankees cease from troubling us, and the weary are at rest."

Rebecca had written that Charles Lamar had been shot without a firearm at his side. And yet, would Lamar die so dishonorably? Would he willingly drop his beloved Adams .44 revolver—with *C.A.L. Lamar* coursing its barrel in flowing script—into the red Georgia mud? It seems improbable, out of character.

Indeed, it was: On November 12, 1891, a headline in the *Savannah Morning News* read, "MRS. C. A. L. LAMAR DEAD." Noted that paper: "She was married to one of the best-known men in Savannah of his day—C. A. L. Lamar . . . He was at Columbus when General Wilson entered the town. Refusing to surrender as the Federals charged across the bridge over the Chattahoochee River, he was killed."

Refusing to surrender. Indeed, that was the true end of Charles Lamar. Following the surrender at Appomattox, most of the rebel soldiers had thrown down their arms. Gazaway Lamar, sensing the futility of the struggle, had signed the loyalty oath to the Union—and had urged Charles to do so as well. But not Charles Augustus Lafayette Lamar. As the Yankees poured across the Franklin Street Bridge into Columbus, the ghost of John C. Calhoun fluttered over his head.

"In a few minutes the fighting was hand to hand," Confederate soldier Pope Barrow recalled later. "A Federal cavalryman, whose horse had been shot from under him, stepped in front of Black Cloud, the horse Col. Lamar was riding, seized the bit with his left hand, and threw up his carbine with his right, and called on Lamar to surrender. Quick as lightning, Lamar plunged his spurs into his horse's sides and tried to run over his opponent. At that instant—as the horse reared and plunged above the soldier—he fired, and at the crack of the carbine Lamar fell lifeless to the ground."

A swarm of blue coats followed the cavalryman over the bridge. As they raced forward, one of them bent hurriedly over the body of Lamar, grasping his revolver and gold watch. Then the soldier pressed on, his eyes aglow with the flames that had begun to envelope the city of Columbus ahead. Charles Lamar was eventually returned home, to be interred at the Laurel Grove Cemetery in Savannah.

In his annual message to Congress on December 3, 1860, President Buchanan had stated, "It is with great satisfaction that I communicate the fact that since the date of my last annual message, not a single slave has been imported into the United States in violation of the laws prohibiting the African slave trade. This statement is founded upon a thorough examination and investigation of the subject."

Furthermore, the president had ordered the African Squadron considerably beefed up. By the winter of 1860, the American contingent on the African coast consisted of eight vessels with 97 guns and 11 howitzers, with another four vessels with 16 guns and 9 howitzers, near Cuba.

Still, it took the Lincoln administration to deal slave trading the final blow. On April 10, 1862, Abraham Lincoln asked the U.S. Senate to ratify a treaty between the United States and Britain. The treaty, noting the failure of efforts to stop the slave trade, offered reciprocal rights of search and the right of immediate condemnation upon the sight of any suspicious item. The British were delighted, but the Americans were still sensitive to the British dominance of the seas. The Senate approved Lincoln's measure, as required by the Constitution, but behind closed doors in an executive session. Nothing leaked out to the press, or even to the *Congressional Globe*. Still, with that resolution, the African Squadron got its teeth back.

The Lincoln administration shut down the slave trade in other ways as well. It established special courts in New York, Sierra Leone, and the Cape of Good Hope, under the authority of both a British and an American judge, that could convict slavers immediately, and send them to jail without appeal. On November 6, 1861, Captain Nathaniel Gordon of the slaver *Erie* came before one of these courts in New York City, and was convicted of piracy. An appeal to President Lincoln was denied, and three months later the native of Portland, Maine, was hanged. Gordon was the first—and only—North American ever to be hanged for slave trading under the act of 1820.

Lincoln also ordered a clean up of the Port of New York. In six months, five ships were seized and four slavers convicted, more than ever before. In 1859, the *New York Courier* called for the removal of the corrupt Marshal Rynders, based on his performance in the *Wanderer* case. Rynders, in turn, wrote that he was blameless, that the U.S. attorney had ordered her release. In 1860, Rynders was indicted by a grand jury, on charges of bribery in the release of the slaver *Storm King* from New York harbor. The case disappeared into the depths of the city court system, however—"has the case been settled, or laid on the shelf?" questioned the *New York Times* the following year—leaving Rynders to walk away, a free man.

Following the war, the Spanish government, which had encouraged Cuba's robust slave trade for decades, finally ended it. The move was purely pragmatic: Having fought a war to stop slavery, the United States would not hesitate to dismantle Cuba's slave economy itself, and take the island as well. It was the Emancipation Proclamation, though, that broke the back of America's slave trade, and the passing of the Thirteenth Amendment to the U.S. Constitution that finally ended it in the United States forever. As W. E. B. DuBois noted, "The Thirteenth Amendment legally confirmed what the war had already accomplished, and slavery and the slave trade fell at one blow."

And what epitaph should be chiseled into the tomb of the fire-eaters? As the Civil War was entering its final year, Horace Maynard, a legislator from East Tennessee, offered this fitting summation: "One of the most obvious and striking facts is the utter falsehood of those who inaugurated this terrible reign of anarchy and misrule," he wrote. "When they told us the Northern men were a race of cowards, and would not fight, they probably believed it; when they assured us that one Southern man was the equal in a fight of five Yankees, or abolitionists, as they contemptuously and indiscriminately call all Northern troops, they may have believed that; when they declared that all we of the South had to do was to show a bold front, and the North would back down, their past experience may had led them to believe this also; when they urged forward the volunteers, with the prospect of seizing Washington in a few weeks, and thence passing swiftly on through Philadelphia, to plunder the vaults of Wall Street, and the stores of Broadway, it is by no means certain that they did not indulge in such delusions . . ."

He continued: "Indeed the ignorance of this lordly and insolent oligarchy is equaled only by its ineffable baseness. I say oligarchy, for it is known that the men who concocted, and who do now control the thing they call the Southern Confederacy, are not as numerous, in point of fact, as the figures on a chessboard. It is eminently a closed corporation, and was so intended to be. The men who compose it are, for the most part, the same clique well known for years in this city as claiming exclusive jurisdiction over the Democratic Party, and assuming such absolute authority over 'the South,' that even now a great many people suppose there are no other persons of consequence . . .

"There are those within the sound of my voice who can testify to their utter perfidy, who have been the victims of their want of principle, and whose self-respect has suffered from their insolent and overbearing demeanor. . . . To hesitate, to doubt, to hold back, to stop, was to call down a storm of wrath that few men had the nerve to encounter, and still fewer the strength to withstand. Not only in the political circles, but in social life, their rule was inexorable, their tyranny, absolute."

This, indeed, is a fitting epitaph for the fanatics who helped drive the nation to war.

But there is one more story to tell.

21

Cilucangy

CILUCANGY PEERED through the narrow slats of the slave pen, where he had been imprisoned for two weeks. His chest still ached in the place where the hot iron had pressed itself, smoking, against his flesh.

He dreamed his way back to his village, Cowany, deep in the mountainous country beyond the Congo. He dreamed of the chief, Mfotila, who had stood before the straw house, very tall. Cilucangy was only a boy then, holding his mother's hand, and this was before the men with tattooed foreheads had taken him away, crying, and the village had been burned and his mother slain.

There was a stirring in the enclosure, where others, like him, bore brands on their chests and gnashed their pointed teeth and cried. Next to him was a little girl, named Mabiala, and an older girl, Manchuella, who rocked Mabiala sadly in her arms. Zow Uncola, another boy, who came from a village far to the east, where the water dripped out of the rising sun, slept with his head in her lap. Suddenly, Tahro, one of the older boys, leapt up. The men with the strange tongues were approaching. They spoke loudly. Everyone jumped to their feet.

The door of the enclosure was swung open and Cilucangy fell forward. He stumbled through the forest and then out into the scrub with the others, and when they came to the beach, Cilucangy was alarmed to see a ship hanging offshore, a sinister form above the sparkling water. His arms were bound in leather thongs and he struggled to get in the long canoe, and then they were rowed out to the ship. As Cilucangy was hauled aboard, he looked up into the blue eyes of Corrie, with the darker visage of Farnum behind, and then he was forced with the others into the slave deck below.

For forty-two nights he rocked against the bodies of his fellow captives in the underdeck of the *Wanderer,* and during the day was led up to the deck, where a bucket of salt water was thrown over his body before he was given something to eat. Many of the others died. The Portuguese men aboard would throw them over the rail. Just when their water and their food were almost gone, they came to a shoreline that Cilucangy felt looked very much like the one he had left, with low scrub and twisted trees. They were taken off the ship and fed. Finally, with fresh food having been eaten, and before a vast roaring fire set on the beach, he could straighten his twisted limbs and, in a stiff, slow, hobbling motion, dance.

Eventually they were herded onto another ship, this one with a frightening fire aboard that spit white clouds. They were taken up a narrow river and, once again, unloaded. They were put that night in a house, and slept nearly on top of one another on the crowded floor. A doctor came and looked at them. Cilucangy remembered that the doctor took them to a cornfield. The corn was still green, but they were hungry, and they fell upon it like locusts and consumed it all.

In 1857, John F. Tucker, a friend of Charles Lamar's, bought a large plantation upriver from Savannah. Much of its nineteen hundred acres lay along the Savannah River. It was low country, where rice could be grown. The tract had several one-room shacks for the slaves, each with its own chimney made of stucco and sticks, and a brick mill for shelling the rice. At the end of the plantation road, on the bluff overlooking the river, was a white plantation home, with four smooth pillars gracing its broad entrance.

In December of 1857, shortly after Tucker had helped Lamar bring

the Africans up the Savannah River from Jekyll Island, he placed a
$53,650 mortgage on his plantation so that he could buy one hundred
of them.

Now, in the cold December light, the Africans were brought before
him. He picked several and then, it seems likely, he spotted Cilucangy.
The boy had soft, intelligent eyes and high cheekbones. Tucker nodded,
and a Portuguese handler parted the boy from the others. Cilucangy was
brought to the plantation, and put to work. Before long, the skill that
his mother had taught him—basket weaving—made him a favorite, and
he was relieved of the heavier chores.

By the time that Sherman's army had passed through Georgia, Tucker's
plantation was in ruins. The main house had been burned to the ground,
and the rice fields, left unplanted, soon filled with weeds and was worthless. Tucker's mortgage was foreclosed upon, and the land was taken
away from him. But Cilugangy had no place to go. He clung to the
wreckage of the South, for it was the only place he had.

Eventually the plantation fell to George A. Keller, an experienced
planter, who had won many prizes at the Chatham and Effingham
County fairs. Keller offered the former slaves tenant houses, wages of
about 40 cents a day, and a garden plot. Cilucangy stayed, and when the
state fair came around, he would sell his baskets. One time, he wove a
complete house from straw, like the one he remembered the chief standing in front of many, many years before.

He was Ward Lee now, to many people. He wore a soft flannel dress
coat, a checked vest, a white shirt with high rounded collars, a black tie,
and even a watch chain and watch. He even voted now: A white man
told him if he voted for Hopkins, he would own the piece of ground
that he worked. So he went into a room with the other freed slaves,
where he pointed his finger to the ceiling, as he was told to do, and then
took hold of a pen, with which he made a scratch in a book.

In 1908, when an anthropologist from the University of Chicago
came to speak with him, he told his story and posed proudly for a pho-
tograph with other *Wanderer* survivors who lived nearby, such as Pucka
Geata (Tucker Henderson) and Tahro (Romero).

He married and had four children. They moved, with some of the others, up the Savannah River. Ward Lee seemed satisfied. But one night he began to dream of his mother again, and the chief and the straw house. The next week he had a notice printed, which he circulated in town:

> *Please help me. In 1859 I was brought to this country when I was a child. I cannot say just what age I was then, but I was aroused by the spirit—and I trust it was the spirit of God—on last May. One year ago it was revealed to me to go back home to Africa, and I have been praying to know if it was God's will, and the more I pray the more it presses on me to go, and now I am trying to get ready, if God be with me, to go back to Africa as soon as I can get off to go. And now I beg every one who will, please help me. I will be glad of whatever you will give me. . . . I am bound for my old home if God be with me, white or black, yellow or red. I am an old African. Ward Lee.*

Lee passed away ten years later, without ever returning to Africa. Two of his sons bought a farm nearby. Then several members of the family began to migrate North. Lee's grandson, William, moved to Brooklyn and started a car wash there. Others began to move farther out on Long Island. In the 1980s, Lee's great-great-granddaughters, Sharon Sansaverino and Sheryl Valenti were named the Doublemint Gum Twins, and their smiling faces were seen on billboards and in advertisements across America. Today, the family counts teachers, lawyers, and guidance professionals among its members.

Not far from the Uniondale exit of the Long Island Expressway sits a red brick house with white shutters and a tidy front yard. There Margret Higgins, the great-granddaughter of Ward Lee, can look around during a family reunion and see their success. The family will always honor the courage and resiliency of Ward Lee. And they won't forget him. The little boy on Higgins's knee, after all, is not just Alexander Valenti, her grandson. His full name is Alexander *Cilucangy* Valenti.

Forty-five minutes on the Long Island Expressway from the Higgins home is the village of East Setauket. At Fox's True Value Hardware you turn left onto Shore Road. Down the hill, past split-rail fences and elegant eighteenth- and nineteenth-century homes, lies Setauket Harbor, with a flock of Canadian snow geese settling in at its golden rim. Today, the vessels that rest along the waterfront in their snowy cradles sport names like *Majac, C-Breeze,* and *Quality Times II.* But one hundred fifty years ago, this was the site of the William Joseph Rowland shipyard— the spot where the keel for the *Wanderer* was laid in the winter of 1857.

You walk across the frozen ground, trying to picture the *Wanderer* rising there. You can almost hear the cries of the workmen and the hollow chunk of the adzes as they bite into the wood. A man with a cigarette dangling from his lip pokes his head out of a window nearby and eyes you curiously. The windchill is now near zero. Your pen is frozen, and the ink no longer flows. There are lessons to be learned from it all. And perhaps a reason for hope as well.

Notes

1. EARLY SAVANNAH

4   Savannah's colonial past: Charles Hardee, *Reminiscences and Reflections of Old Savannah* (privately printed, 1928), 63; portions published in *Georgia Historical Quarterly* (hereafter *GHQ*) 12 (1928).

5   *fire wagons*   Hardee, *Reminiscences,* 59.

5   *"The first thing"*   Mills Lane, *Savannah Revisited: History and Architecture* (Savannah: Beehive Press, 2001), 46.

5   *"Long limbs were thrown out"*   Hardee, *Reminiscences,* 65.

6   *"Southern people have one"*   Lane, *Savannah Revisited,* 46.

6   Manufacturing: Richard W. Griffin, "The Origins of the Industrial Revolution in Georgia: Cotton Textiles," *GHQ* 42 (1958): 358–65; Richard H. Haunton, "Savannah in the 1850s" (Ph.D. diss., Emory University, Atlanta, 1968), 5.

6   Railroads: Haunton, "Savannah in the 1850s," 5; Hardee, *Reminiscences,* 83.

7   *"As the people were coming"*   Walter J. Fraser Jr., *Savannah in the Old South* (Athens: University of Georgia Press, 2003), 229.

7   *Georgia's banks "will"*   *Augusta Chronicle,* November 4, 1834.

7   *"Having a day or two since"*   *Savannah Daily Georgian,* June 13, 1838.

8   Agrarian Ideal: Norris Preyer, "Why Did Industrialization Lag in the Old South?" *GHQ* 55 (1971): 383.

8   *Georgia's founder, James*   Rodney M. Baine, *The Publications of James Edward Oglethorpe* (Athens: University of Georgia Press, 1994), xiv, 165.

8   *But when cotton prices slumped*   Robert R. Russell, *Economic Aspects of Southern Sectionalism, 1840–1861* (NY: Russell & Russell, 1960), 35, 58; R. H. Shryock, "The Early Industrial Revolution in the Empire State," *GHQ* 11(2) (1927): 123.

9   *New York's best hotels*   Philip S. Foner, *Business & Slavery: The New York Merchants and the Irrepressible Conflict* (Chapel Hill: University of North Carolina Press, 1941), 1.

9   *"The 'gay season' in New York"*   *Savannah Daily Morning News* (hereafter *Savannah News*), December 16, 1858.

9   *And if one had missed the luminaries*   Fraser, *Savannah in the Old South,* 209.

9   *That idea soon caught on*   Shryock, "The Early Industrial Revolution," 109.

10   *they offered a series of toasts*   John McCardell, *The Idea of a Southern Nation: Southern Nationalists and Southern Nationalism, 1830–1860,* (NY: W. W. Norton, 1979), 98, 102.

10   *"Gentlemen, The Aquatic Club"*   E. Merton Coulter, "Boating As a Sport in the Old South," *GHQ* 27(2) (1943): 238.

11   Gazaway Lamar's background: Thomas R. Hay, "Gazaway B. Lamar, Confederate Banker," *GHQ* 37(2) (1953): 89; Hardee, *Reminiscences,* 53; William Harden, *Recollections of a Long and Satisfactory Life* (Savannah: Review Printing Co., 1934), 52; Alexander C. Brown, "The John Randolph: America's First Commercially Successful Iron Steamboat," *GHQ* 36(1) (1952): 33; William M. Robinson, *History of Gazaway B. Lamar* (NY: *Dictionary of American Biography,* 1933).

11   *Savannah needed a "rail road"*   Hardee, *Reminiscences,* 53; Thomas Gamble, *A History of the City Government, 1790–1901* (City of Savannah, 1900), 175.

11   *At the time . . . Laurel Howard*   Harden, *Recollections,* 53; Brown, "The John Randolph," 34.

12   The *John Randolph*: Brown, "The John Randolph," 34.

12   *"As might have been expected"*   *Augusta Daily Constitutionalist,* August 15, 1834.

13   *Augusta's city dignitaries*   *Augusta Chronicle,* August 16, 1834.

2. THE *PULASKI*

14   *"No expense has been spared"*   *Savannah Daily Georgian,* April 11, 1838.

15   *Back in 1819, William Scarbrough*   Robert G. Albion, *The Rise of New York Port, 1815–1860* (NY: Charles Scribner's Sons, 1939), 314.

15   *the following ad appeared*   *Savannah Daily Georgian,* June 12, 1838.

16 *"The engines"*   *Savannah Daily Georgian,* April 11, 1838; Robert W. Groves, "The Wreck of the Steam Packet Pulaski" (1955), 5, Pulaski file, Library, Georgia Historical Society, Savannah.

18 The *Pulaski* wreck: Accounts drawn from Rebecca Lamar McLeod, "Account of the Loss of the Steamer Pulaski," *GHQ* 3(1) (1919): 63; James Hamilton Couper, "Account of the Wreck of the Pulaski," Pulaski file, Library, Georgia Historical Society; Groves, "The Wreck of the Steam Packet Pulaski," 25.

24 *"Awful Steamboat Disaster"*   *Savannah Daily Georgian,* various accounts, June 21–July 20, 1838.

24 *"We confess that we have"*   *Savannah Daily Georgian,* June 22, 1838.

25 *When Rebecca regained*   McLeod, "Account of the Loss of the Steamer Pulaski," 63.

25 *On July 13, 1838*   *Savannah Daily Georgian,* July 14, 1838.

26 *Gazaway left Savannah*   Hay, "Gazaway B. Lamar, Confederate Banker," 93.

26 *one relative wrote*   Hay, "Gazaway B. Lamar, Confederate Banker," 92.

3. LATER SAVANNAH

27 Charles Lamar: Tom H. Wells, "Charles Augustus Lafayette Lamar, Gentleman Slave Trader," *GHQ* 47 (1963): 160; Tom H. Wells, *The Slave Ship Wanderer* (Athens: University of Georgia Press, 1967), 2; Ana Lee Prieto, "Charles A. L. Lamar: Southern Gentleman and Owner of the Slave Ship *Wanderer,*" 13, Lamar file, Library, Georgia Historical Society.

28 *"I remember well seeing him"*   Harden, *Recollections,* 10.

28 Lamar's personality: Winfield M. Thompson, "Historic American Yachts: The Slave Ship *Wanderer,*" *The Rudder* 15 (February 1904): 54; Wells, "Charles Augustus Lafayette Lamar," 166; Wells, *The Slave Ship Wanderer,* 3.

28 Savannah's growth: *Savannah News,* March 12, 1851; Fraser, *Savannah in the Old South,* 256–57; Haunton, "Savannah in the 1850s," 30, 132.

28 *A few houses from Lamar*   Harden, *Recollections,* 10.

29 *Lamar could be the sprightly*   "Some of the Boys of Dr. White's School," Savannah *News,* April 6, 1884.

29 Lafayette: Hardee, *Reminiscences,* 55. (Note: Mirabeau Lamar was put in charge of guiding General Lafayette through Savannah and probably guided him into Lamar's baptism.)

29 New industry: Haunton, "Savannah in the 1850s," 132; Fraser, *Savannah in the Old South,* 249, 251.

29 freight cars: Haunton, "Savannah in the 1850s," 135.

30 *Exclaimed the* Savannah   Haunton, "Savannah in the 1850s," 10, quoting the *Savannah Evening Journal,* November 12, 1852.

30 *Yet for all of the appearance*   Shryock, "The Early Industrial Revolution," 378.

30 The South's economic rank: Russell, *Economic Aspects of Southern Sectionalism,* 58–60, 227–30.

31 New York's grip on commerce: Robert G. Albion, *Square-Riggers on Schedule: The New York Sailing Packets to England, France, and the Cotton Ports* (Hamden, CT: Archon Books, 1965), 52; Albion, *The Rise of New York Port,* 96–118; Haunton, "Savannah in the 1850s," 120.

31 *"With plenty of money in assets"*   Haunton, "Savannah in the 1850s," 138.

32 Gazaway's new career: Hay, "Gazaway B. Lamar, Confederate Banker," 93–97.

32 *Charles had seen how the New York newspapers*   Foner, *Business & Slavery,* 1–12; Albion, *Square-Riggers on Schedule,* 73–76; Albion, *The Rise of New York Port,* 119.

32 Northern influences: Foner, *Business & Slavery,* 3.

32 *"New York City, like a mighty"*   Foner, *Business & Slavery,* 10.

33 *Who conducts our commerce*   *The Cause of the South: Selections from DeBow's Review, 1846–1867,* Paul F. Paskoff and Daniel J. Wilson, eds., (Baton Rouge: Louisiana State University Press, 1982), 183; Foner, *Business & Slavery,* 10.

33 Charles Lamar's anger: Edmund Ruffin, *The Diary of Edmund Ruffin,* vol. 1, introduction and notes by William K. Scarborough (Baton Rouge: Louisiana State University Press, 1972), 386; Clement Eaton, *The Freedom-of-Thought Struggle in the Old South* (NY: Harper & Row, 1964), 36; Ronald T. Takaki, *A Pro-Slavery Crusade: The Agitation to Reopen the African Slave Trade* (NY: The Free Press, 1971), ix, 73–81; George Francis Dow, *Slave Ships and Slaving* (Mineola, NY: Dover Publications, 2002), 14; Avery O. Craven, *The Growth of Southern Nationalism* (Baton Rouge: Louisiana State University Press, 1981), 392; Allen Nevins, *The Emergence of Lincoln,* vol. 2 (NY: Charles Scribner's Sons, 1952), 141.

33 *On the appointed day*   Coulter, "Boating As a Sport in the Old South," 240.

34 *It was why*   *Savannah News,* March 10, 15, 1859 and February 10, 1859.

35 *"What would New York's"*   Foner, *Business & Slavery,* 4.

35 Northern workers: Dennis Rousey, "From Whence They Came to Savannah," *GHQ* 79 (1995): 311; Haunton, "Savannah in the 1850s," 50.

35 Crime: Richard Haunton, "Law and Order in Savannah, 1850–1860," *GHQ* 56(1) (1972): 2.

36 Lamar had no use for the North: Russell, *Economic Aspects of Southern Sectionalism*, 206–209.

4. THE FIRE-EATERS

37 Calhoun's cause: Manisha Sinha, *The Counterrevolution of Slavery: Politics and Ideology in Antebellum South Carolina* (Chapel Hill: University of North Carolina Press, 2000), 19.

38 *The English traveler* Eaton, *The Freedom-of-Thought Struggle*, 50.

38 The fire-eaters: Takaki, *A Pro-Slavery Crusade*, 10–16, 125–30; Sinha, *The Counterrevolution of Slavery*, 126; Ulrich B. Phillips, "The Course of the South to Secession: The Fire-Eaters," *GHQ* 22(1) (1938): 41.

38 *"At the conclusion of the speech"* Eaton, *The Freedom-of-Thought Struggle*, 51.

38 Edmund Ruffin: *Diary of Edmund Ruffin*, vol. 1, xiii, xvi, 588; Bertram Wyatt-Brown, *Southern Honor* (NY: Oxford University Press, 1982), 35.

39 *Slavery was not "a necessary evil"* Eaton, *The Freedom-of-Thought Struggle*, 62, 155–56.

39 Biological argument: Paskoff, *The Cause of the South*, 31; Craven, *The Growth of Southern Nationalism*, 258.

40 *Yancey was an alcoholic* Takaki, *A Pro-Slavery Crusade*, 15; Wyatt-Brown, *Southern Honor*, 359; Robert B. Rhett, *A Fire-Eater Remembers*, William C. Davis, ed. (Columbia: University of South Carolina Press, 2000), xvi.

40 *"I love Glory"* Takaki, *A Pro-Slavery Crusade*, 91.

40 Sensitivity: Wyatt-Brown, *Southern Honor*, 44; McCardell, *The Idea of a Southern Nation*, 281; Takaki, *A Pro-Slavery Crusade*, 87.

40 Sir Walter Scott: Eaton, *The Freedom-of-Thought Struggle*, 49; Takaki, *A Pro-Slavery Crusade*, 18.

40 *Charles Lamar knew it well* "A Slave-Trader's Letter-Book," *The North American Review* 143, 360 (November 1886), 448; Haunton, "Law and Order in Savannah," 13.

40 *the final memorial* Eaton, *The Freedom-of-Thought Struggle*, 140–47, 156.

41 Spratt's background: Takaki, *A Pro-Slavery Crusade*, 1–9; Sinha, *The Counterrevolution of Slavery*, 140; Harvey Wish, "The Revival of the African Slave Trade in the United States, 1856–1860," *Mississippi Historical Review* 27 (1941): 570; Herbert Wender, *Southern Commercial Conventions, 1837–1859* (Baltimore: Johns Hopkins Press, 1930), 230; *Savannah News*, December 28, 1858.

41 *Spratt had another great accomplishment* Russell, *Economic Aspects of Southern Sectionalism*, 124–50.

42   *"When the South gets ready"*   *Federal Union* (Milledgeville, GA), reprinted in *Savannah News,* May 20, 1858.

42   Spratt's African slave trade manifesto: Takaki, *A Pro-Slavery Crusade,* 23–40; McCardell, *The Idea of a Southern Nation,* 135–40; David M. Potter, *The Impending Crisis* (NY: Harper & Row, 1976), 395; L. W. (Leonidas W.) Spratt, "Speech Upon the Foreign Slave Trade Before the Legislature of South Carolina," December 14, 1858, printed in the *Savannah News,* December 28, 1858, and reprinted by Steam-Power Press, Columbia, SC, 1858; Spratt, "Philosophy of Secession, A Southern View" (Charleston, SC: 1861).

42   American slave trade: Daniel P. Mannix, *Black Cargoes: A History of the Atlantic Slave Trade, 1518–1865* (NY: Viking Press, 1962), 54; Takaki, *A Pro-Slavery Crusade,* 3.

42   *In one sale*   *Savannah News,* December 12, 1858.

43   Machiávellian motives: Russell, *Economic Aspects of Southern Sectionalism,* 181, 216; Nevins, *The Emergence of Lincoln,* 160;

43   *Even Abraham Lincoln had said*   Carl Sandburg, *Abraham Lincoln: The Prairie Years,* vol. 2 (Charles Scribner's Sons, 1945), 165, 181, 202.

43   *But a suprising number*   Wish, "The Revival of the African Slave Trade," 573; Russell, *Economic Aspects of Southern Sectionalism,* 213; American Anti-Slavery Society, *Annual Report for the Year Ending May 1, 1859* (NY: American Anti-Slavery Society, 1860), 37; McCardell, *The Idea of a Southern Nation,* 135; Potter, *The Impending Crisis,* 396.

5. THE *RAWLINS* AND *COBDEN*

45   *A recent pay raise*   Carol Wells, "William Postell, Adventurer," *GHQ* 57 (1973): 390.

45   *By now the convention*   Wender, *Southern Commercial Conventions,* 208; Russell, *Economic Aspects of Southern Sectionalism,* 143, 214–19.

46   The first *Rawlins* attempt: *Savannah News,* July 18, 1857; Telegram, Howell Cobb to John Boston, July 16, 1857, Records of the Office of the Secretary of the Interior Relating to the Suppression of the African Slave Trade and Negro Colonization, 1854–1872, Record Group (RG) 48, Microfilm (M) 160, United States National Archives.

47   Financial dealings of Cobb: Letters, Howell Cobb to Lamar, *GHQ* 5(2) (1921): 44.

47   *"I am loathe to trouble you"*   "A Slave-Trader's Letter-Book," 450.

47   *"Discharge him"*   "A Slave-Trader's Letter-Book," 451.

47   *"I am anxious to have you"*   "A Slave-Trader's Letter-Book," 452.

48   *On June 18, Gilley*   Carol Wells, "William Postell, Adventurer," 390; Tom Wells, *The Slave Ship Wanderer,* 6.

48 *"Sir: I informed you"*   Telegram, Howell Cobb to Collector of Customs, New Orleans, March 1, 1858, Records of the Office of the Secretary of the Interior Relating to the Suppression of the African Slave Trade, National Archives.

48 *Three revenue cutters*   Warren S. Howard, *American Slavers and the Federal Law, 1837–1862* (Berkeley: University of California Press, 1963), 142.

49 *"When it was known"*   *New York Times* (hereafter *NYT*), September 10, 1858, 3.

50 *"You remember our conversations"*   John Lamar to Mary Ann Cobb, June 12, 1858, and Gazaway B. Lamar to John Lamar, October 16, 1858, Howell Cobb Papers, Hargrett Rare Book and Manuscript Library, University of Georgia, Athens; Wells, *The Slave Ship Wanderer*, 5.

50 *"I was astonished"*   "A Slave-Trader's Letter-Book," 449.

51 Shipping emigrants: *NYT,* June 23, 1858, 2.

51 *This, added Lamar,*   Charles A. L. Lamar, "The Reply of C.A.L. Lamar of Savannah, Georgia, to the Letter of Hon. Howell Cobb, Secretary of the Treasury of the United States, Refusing a Clearance to the Ship *Richard Cobden*" (Charleston: Steam Power Press, 1858); *Savannah News,* June 9–10, 1858; William L. Mathieson, *Great Britain and the Slave Trade, 1839–1865* (NY: Octagon Books, 1967), 151.

51 *"I have been abridged of my proper right,"*   Lamar, "The Reply of C.A.L. Lamar of Savannah."

52 *"He is a gone sucker"*   "A Slave-Trader's Letter-Book," 456.

52 *"I can show you"*   "A Slave-Trader's Letter-Book," 452.

6. JOHNSON'S *WANDERER*

53 Shaping the *Wanderer*: The Boston Traveller (pseud.) "The Private Yacht Wanderer, Arrival of the Runaway at Boston," December 24, 1859, in the *NYT,* December 26, 1859, 8; *NYT,* June 11, 1858, 4; Peter Carnahan, *Schooner Master: A Portrait of David Stevens* (Chelsea, VT: Chelsea Green Publishing, 1989), 6; Douglas Phillips-Birt, *The History of Yachting* (NY: Stein and Day, 1974), 34.

54 *Rowland had arrived*   Edwin Adkins, *Setauket: The First Three Hundred Years* (NY: David McKay, 1955), 85; *Bicentennial History of Suffolk County* (Babylon: Budget Steam Press, 1885), 78.

54 Rowland's background: Thompson, "Historic American Yachts," 53.

56 The *America*: John Parkinson, *The History of the New York Yacht Club: From Its Founding Through 1973* (NY: New York Yacht Club, 1975), 559; David Shaw, *America's Victory: The Heroic Story of a Team of Ordinary Americans, and How They Won the Greatest Yacht Race Ever* (NY: The

Free Press, 2002), 56; Royal Yacht Squadron, America's Cup Jubilee Regatta, Information Leaflet No. 4, www.rys.or.uk/da/11668.

57   Death of Steers: Parkinson, *The History of the New York Yacht Club,* 12, 39; Shaw, *America's Victory,* 227; *NYT,* June 11, 1859.

57   The *Wanderer*'s proportions: Thompson, "Historic American Yachts," 53.

58   Building a wooden ship: Carnahan, *Schooner Master,* 36, 54; Basil Greenhill, *The Evolution of the Wooden Ship* (NY: Facts on File Press, 1988), 88; H. Cole Estep, *How Wooden Ships Are Built: A Practical Treatise on Modern American Wooden Ship Construction* (Cleveland: Penton Publishing, 1918), 34.

59   Conditions of workmen: Greenhill, *Evolution of the Wooden Ship,* 88.

60   Launching ceremony: Shaw, *America's Victory,* 222.

60   *"She has long topmasts"*   *NYT,* June 11, 1858

60   *"The interior," noted*   *Harper's Weekly,* January 29, 1859, 70.

61   First cruise: *NYT,* August 13, 1857.

63   Voyage southward: *Brooklyn Daily Eagle,* March 8, 1858, 3.

64   *"The admiration for her fine"*   *NYT,* June 11, 1858

7. CORRIE'S *WANDERER*

66   Edgar's background: Parkinson, *The History of the New York Yacht Club,* 15, 28.

68   *Corrie had succeeded*   *NYT,* June 11, 1858, 4.

68   *"A high-toned"*   Thompson, "Historic American Yachts," 54.

68   *Added the* New York Times   *NYT,* June 11, 1858.

68   Corrie's social whirl: *NYT,* April 9, 21, 1858; May 6, 1858, 2.

69   *"I understand that"*   Laura A. White, "The United States in the 1850s As Seen by British Consuls," *Mississippi Valley Historical Review* 19 (1933): 525. See also Consul Robert Bunch, Charleston, SC, to Earl of Malmesbury (Minister of Foreign Affairs), December 16, 1858, and January 3 and 20, 1859, in Class B, Correspondence with British Ministers and Agents in Foreign Countries, and with Foreign Ministers in England, Relating to the Slave Trade, British Foreign Office Collection 541, Confidential Print Series, Vol. 13, microfilm (Wilmington, DE: Michael Glazer and Scholarly Resources, 1977).

69   Farnum's background: *Harper's Weekly,* May 28, 1857, 332.

69   *The* Albany Statesman   *Albany Statesman,* reprinted in the *NYT,* December 17, 1858, 2.

69   Harper's Weekly *ran*   *Harper's Weekly,* May 23, 1857.

69   *"I appeal to every officer"*   *NYT,* April 14, 1857.

70   Trip to Port Jefferson: *NYT,* June 11, 1858; Thompson, "Historic American Yachts," 54.

71   Slave ships in New York City: Howard, *American Slavers and the Federal Law*, 49–52; American Anti-Slavery Society *Annual Report for the Years Ending May 1, 1858* (NY: American Anti-Slavery Society, 1859), 183; *Journal of Commerce*, June 30, 1856; American Anti-Slavery Society, *The Anti-Slavery History of the John Brown Year, Annual Report for the Year Ending May 1, 1860* (NY: American Anti-Slavery Society, 1861), 24.

71   Description of slave trade conversation drawn from: "The Slave Trade in New York," *Continental Monthly* 1 (January 1862): 86–91; *Charleston Mercury*, reprinted in the *NYT*, August 22, 1859, 6; *New York Herald*, April 1, 1857, 4; London *Times*, July 3, 1860, 9; *New York Daily Tribune*, June 5, 1860, 4; Howard, *American Slavers and the Federal Law*, 50.

73   *When the elections are over*   "The Slave Trade in New York," 87.

73   *"Few of our readers"*   W. E. B. Du Bois, *The Suppression of the African Slave Trade to the United States of America, 1638–1870* (Baton Rouge: Louisiana State University Press, 1965), 178, quoting the Journal of Commerce, 1857.

73   *"We are informed"*   American Anti-Slavery Society, *Annual Report for Year Ending May 1, 1859* (NY: American Anti-Slavery Society, 1860), 24.

74   Judge Betts: Howard, *American Slavers and the Federal Law*, 98–99, 156–69; *Appleton's Cyclopedia of American Biography, 1887,* edited by Virtual American Biographies, 2001, www.Virtualology.com.

74   *"The traders engaged"*   *New York Daily Tribune*, June 5, 1860, 4.

75   *At dawn*   *NYT*, June 11, 1858. 4; Thompson, "Historic American Yachts," 55.

75   *During the revolution*   Bill Bleyer, "Shipshape in Suffolk," in "Long Island: Our Story," Newsday Online, www.newsday.com.

76   The *Wanderer* back in New York: *NYT*, June 11, 1858; Thompson, "Historic American Yachts," 55.

76   On board the *Wanderer*: *NYT*, June 11, 12, 1858; *Harper's Weekly*, January 29, 1859.

78   *"Boys, that's the whole story"*   *NYT*, June 12, 1858.

78   *Mystery of the Yacht Wanderer*   *NYT*, June 11, 1858.

79   *"If thine enemy"*   *NYT*, June 12, 1858, 4.

80   Farnum's brawl: *NYT*, June 16, 1858, 4.

80   Reception in Charleston: *NYT*, July 8, 1858, 4.

80   Filling the tanks: *Savannah Republican*, January 10, 1859, reprinted in the London *Times*, February 2, 1859.

81   Leaving Charleston: *NYT*, July 8, 1858, 4.

81   In Trinidad: *NYT*, July 8, 1858, 4.

81   *The* Viper *was one of*   Alan R. Booth, "The United States African

Squadron, 1843–1861," *Boston University Papers in African History,* vol. 1 (Boston: Boston University Press, 1964), 115.

81   The African Squadron on the other side: Howard, *American Slavers and the Federal Law, 1837–1862,* 41–43; Hugh G. Soulsby, *The Right of Search and the Slave Trade in Anglo-American Relations, 1814–1862* (Baltimore: Johns Hopkins Press, 1933), 102–104, 138–140. See also *Instructions to the African Squadron, Message from the President of the United States,* March 1, 1859, 35th Congress 2d Session, House Ex. Doc. 104; and *African Slave Trade, Message from the President Transmitting a Report from the Secretary of State in Reference to the African Slave Trade,* December 6, 1860, 36th Congress, 2d Session., House Exec. Doc 7.

82   *For all this*   W. E. F. Ward, *The Royal Navy and the Slavers: The Suppression of the Atlantic Slave Trade* (NY: Pantheon Books, 1969), 150.

82   The "calcined" town: *NYT,* May 24, 1859, 1.

8. INTO AFRICA

83   *She flew*   *Lithographs of Pennants and Private Signals of the New York Yacht Club* (NY: New York Yacht Club, 1890).

83   *Beneath those emblems*   Ship's documents, *Wanderer* Yacht folder, Black History Collection, Manuscript Division, Library of Congress; Wells, *The Slave Ship Wanderer,* 10.

84   Kroomen: Mannix, *Black Cargoes,* 16, 48.

84   Nearing the factory: Dow, *Slave Ships and Slaving,* 4.

85   *"Arrived at Punta"*   Log Book of the Slave Ship *Wanderer* in *Wanderer* (Ship) Records Special Collections, Department, Woodruff Library, Emory University.

85   Descriptions of factory drawn from: Robert W. Shufeldt, "The Secret History of the Slave Trade," *New York Evening Post,* February 7, 1861, 1, reprinted in *The Journal of Negro History* 55(3), No 3 (1970), 218–35.

86   History of the factory: Dow, *Slave Ships and Slaving,* 2; Mannix, *Black Cargoes,* 76.

87   *"It's all evolved into"*   Shufeldt, "The Secret History of the Slave Trade"; Ward, *The Royal Navy and the Slavers,* 150; Howard, *American Slavers and the Federal Law,* 18.

88   Slave trader drawn from: Mannix, *Black Cargoes,* 76–77, 249; Mary H. Kingsley, *Travels in West Africa* (London and NY: Macmillan, 1897), 20; Shufeldt, "The Secret History of the Slave Trade," 1; Dow, *Slave Ships and Slaving,* 3, 7.

89   *"I was aboard a brig"*   Dow, *Slave Ships and Slaving,* xxxi.

90 Africa excursion drawn from: Kingsley, *Travels in West Africa,* 48, 73, 76, 94, 188; Mannix, *Black Cargoes,* 219, 220, 251; Donald R. Wright, "Matthew Perry and the African Squadron," reprinted in *America Spreads Her Sails: U.S. Seapower in the Nineteenth Century,* Clayton R. Barrow, ed. (Annapolis: Naval Institute Press, 1973), 88; J. Taylor Wood, "The Capture of a Slaver," *Atlantic Monthly,* vol. 86, no. 516, October 1900), 12.

91 Meeting the HMS *Medusa*: *NYT,* Dec. 18, 1858.

92 *"In compliance with Section 6"*   Commander William Bowden, RN, to Secretary of the Admiralty, September 15, 1858, no. 243, Class A, Reports from British Naval Officers Relating to the Slave Trade, in *Irish University Press Series of British Parliamentary Papers, Slave Trade* (Shannon: Irish University Press, 1968–1971), vol. 45.

93 *She was the* Margate   Phillips-Birt, *The History of Yachting,* 44; Carnahan, *Schooner Master,* 100; Shaw, *America's Victory,* 163.

94 *"September 26: Gave"*   Log Book of the *Wanderer.*

9. OUT OF AFRICA

95 Conover: Howard, *American Slavers and the Federal Law,* 132–35.

96 The *Cumberland*: USS *Cumberland* (1843–1862), U.S. Department of the Navy, Naval Historical Center, Photographic Section, Online Library of Selected Images, U.S. Navy Ships, www.history.navy.mil/index. html.

96 Leisurely schedule: Earl of Malmesbury (Minister of Foreign Affairs) to Lord Lyons (Envoy to the U.S.), May 6, 1859, no. 263, Class B, Correspondence with British Ministers and Agents in Foreign Countries, and with Foreign Ministers in England, Relating to the Slave Trade, in *Irish University Press Series of British Parliamentary Papers, Slave Trade,* vol. 45; *New York Herald,* December 15, 1858, 1; *NYT,* May 24, 1859, 1.

97 *On that late summer afternoon*   *New York Herald,* December 15, 1858, 1.

97 The *Vincennes*: USS *Vincennes* (1826–1867), Online Library of Selected Images, U.S. Navy Ships, www.history.navy.mil/index.html.

97 Totten: Howard, *American Slavers and the Federal Law,* 139–41.

98 *"As soon as your ship"*   Captain Thomas A. Conover, USN, to Commander Benjamin J. Totten, USN, October 7, 1858, in Africa Squadron, 1843–1861, Letters Received by the Secretary of the Navy from Commanding Officers of Squadrons, RG 45, M 89, Naval Records, National Archives.

98 *But before Totten*   *New York Herald,* December 15, 1858, 1.

99 *Rufus Soule* affair: Described in correspondence of Captain Conover, USN, to Commander Totten, USN, posted December 10, 1858, Africa Squadron, Letters Received by the Secretary of the Navy; see also Com-

modore Charles Wise, RN, to Rear-Admiral Sir F. Grey, RN, November. 3, 1858, no. 249, Class A, Reports from British Naval Officers Relating to the Slave Trade," in *Irish University Press Series of British Parliamentary Papers, Slave Trade,* vol. 45.

100 *"Sir," Totten wrote*   Commander Totten, USN, to Captain Conover, USN, December 10, 1858, Africa Squadron, Letters Received by the Secretary of the Navy.

101 Signaling shore: Dow, *Slave Ships and Slaving,* 288–92; Commodore Wise, RN, to Secretary of the Admiralty, October 28, 1858, ADM 1/5694, Class A, Reports from British Naval Officers Relating to the Slave Trade, in British Foreign Office Collection 541, Confidential Print Series, microfilm, vol. 13, 772.

101 Slave market: Description drawn from Rev. William De Loss Love, "The Reopening of the African Slave Trade," *The New Englander* 18 (February 1860): 90; Theodore Canot, *Captain Canot, Twenty Years of an African Slaver, Being an Account of his Career and Adventures,* Brantz Mayer, ed. (NY: D. Appleton and Co., 1854), 13; Amos J. Beyan, "Transatlantic Trade and the Coastal Area of Pre-Liberia," 1995, 3–5, at www.LiberianForum.com; Wood, "The Capture of a Slaver," 3; Dow, *Slave Ships and Slaving,* 10, 137, 205.

102 Barracoon: Wood, "The Capture of a Slaver," 3.

103 Canoes: Dow, *Slave Ships and Slaving,* 64.

103 The Kroomen: Isobel (Mrs. David C.) Gill, *Six Months in Ascension: An Unscientific Account of a Scientific Expedition* (London: John Murray, 1878), Ch. 21; Beyan, "Transatlantic Trade and the Coastal Area of Pre-Liberia," 3.

104 *Some slavers were*   Mannix, *Black Cargoes,* 105.

104 Approach of the *Vincennes*: *NYT,* May 24, 1859, 1.

105 *A few years earlier, the U.S.S.* Porpoise   Wood, "The Capture of a Slaver," 3.

106 *The* Wanderer *was flying*   *NYT,* May 24, 1859, 1; Howard, *American Slavers and the Federal Law,* 146; Captain Conover, USN, to Secretary of the Navy, December 13, 1858, Africa Squadron, Letters Received by the Secretary of the Navy.

106 Near-collision: *NYT,* May 24, 1859.

106 *Indeed, one of the old salts*   *NYT,* May 24, 1859.

107 Voyage of a slave ship drawn from: Wood, "The Capture of a Slaver"; Dow, *Slave Ships and Slaving,* 144, 297, 306, 311; Canot, *Captain Canot, Twenty Years of an African Slaver,* 15; Love, "The Reopening of the African Slave Trade," 90.

108 *"All persons are warned"*   *Savannah News,* November 23, 1858.

10. JEKYLL ISLAND

110 *Just before dawn*   Events detailed from newspaper accounts beginning December 13, 1858, and from subsequent reports of trial testimony beginning November 14, 1859, in the *Savannah Republican, Savannah News,* and *Charleston Mercury.*

115 *By the time*   Savannah, Georgia, 1858–1859, *City Directories of the United States Through 1860,* microfiche (New Haven: Research Publications, 1984).

117 *He took off fast*   *Savannah News,* November 19, 1859.

117 Ganahl's background: *Savannah News,* September 9, 1900, 3; Joseph Ganahl file, Library, Georgia Historical Society.

118 *"Dear Sir, Your communication"*   Joseph Ganahl to Woodford Mabry, December 12, 1858, Letters Received from Georgia, 1809–1870, United States Attorney General, Entry 9, RG 60, Department of Justice, National Archives, Archives II, College Park, MD.

119 *"Is the slave-trade reopened?"*   *New York Herald,* December 13, 1858.

121 *The* Savannah Republican *noted*   *Savannah Republican,* December 13, 1858.

122 *Cautioned the* New York Times   *NYT,* December 17, 1858, 4.

122 *The* Brooklyn Eagle *seemed to agree*   *Brooklyn Daily Eagle,* December 17, 1858, 2.

123 *the* Albany Statesman   *Albany Statesman,* December 15, 1858, reprinted in the *NYT,* December 17, 2.

11. EARLY EVIDENCE

125 *In early January*   Marion (AL) *Commonwealth,* reprinted in the *NYT,* January 12, 1859, 3; *NYT,* December 30, 1858, 3; Kenneth M. Stampp, *The Peculiar Institution: Slavery in the Ante-Bellum South* (NY: Vintage Books, 1989), 75, 101.

126 Africans in Montgomery: *Atlanta Daily Intelligencer,* December 24, 1858; Montgomery *Daily Confederation,* reprinted in the *New York Herald,* January 5, 1859; *Savannah News,* January 8, 1859.

128 *That night Gordon and a friend*   Account drawn from trial testimony reported in the *Savannah News,* November 14–24, 1859; Wells, *The Slave Ship Wanderer,* 35.

129 Price's clothing store: *New York Herald,* January 5, 1859; *Savannah Republican,* December 13, 1858, and January 1, 1859; Savannah, 1859, *City Directories.*

131 Summoning John Owens: *Savannah News,* November 19, 1859.

132 *Henry Rootes Jackson*   E. Merton Coulter, "The Speech of Henry R.
Jackson," *GHQ* 50 (1966): 366; *The Wanderer Case, The Speech of Hon.
Henry R. Jackson,* ca. 1886–1891 (Atlanta: Care Franklin Printing Co,
1891).

12. THE HEARING

134 The hearing: Events drawn from accounts and testimony reported by *Savannah Republican,* December 20, 1858–January 3, 1859; *Savannah
News,* December 20, 1858–January 3, 1859; *Augusta Daily Constitutionalist,* December 20, 1858–January 3, 1859; and *New York Herald,* January 3–4, 1859.

134 During the remainder of the hearing: Reportage of the hearing, *Savannah
Republican* and *Savannah News,* December 17–20, 1858.

142 Clubb held a gun: *Savannah News,* November 14, 1888.

142 *"I returned this morning from Augusta"*   "A Slave-Trader's Letter-Book,"
456.

142 *On January 28, 1859, Lamar*   "A Slave-Trader's Letter-Book," 457.

143 Lamar's concerns: C. A. L. Lamar to Gazaway B. Lamar, January 14,
1859, Charles A. L. Papers, 1857–1865, Special Collection 400,
Woodruff Library, Emory University.

143 Reaction of the press: *Charleston Daily News,* December 9, 1858, re-
printed in the *New York Herald,* December 13, 1858, 4; *Macon State
Press,* reprinted in the *Savannah News,* December 18, 1858; *Natchez Free
Trader,* reprinted in the *Savannah News,* January 22, 1859.

143 *said the* Edgefield Advertiser   *Edgefield* (SC) *Advertiser,* reprinted in
the *NYT,* December 31, 1858, 1; *Southern Presbyterian Review* 11 (April
1859); *Montgomery Advertiser,* December 28, 1858, reprinted in the *National Era,* January 13, 1859.

144 *"The Southern press is practically a unit"*   *NYT,* January 1, 1859.

144 *"It will be quite useless to urge"*   *NYT,* December 28, 1858.

146 *He heard a rustling*   *Savannah News,* November 12, 1891, 5.

13. THE PRESIDENT

146 Buchanan: Philip S. Klein, *President James Buchanan* (University Park:
Pennsylvania State University Press, 1962), 12, 333.

147 Lincoln's humor: Sandburg, *Abraham Lincoln: The Prairie Years,* vol. 2, 306.

147 *On December 16, 1858*   *Journal of the Senate of the United States,* 35th
Congress, 2d Session, December 16, 1858, 58, and January 7, 1859, 115.

148 *"With every day's mail that reaches us"*   *NYT,* December 24, 1858.

148 Black: William N. Brigance, *Jeremiah Sullivan Black: A Defender of the Constitution and the Ten Commandments* (Philadelphia: University of Pennsylvania Press, 1934), 46.

149 Buchanan's position on slave trade: Nevins, *The Emergence of Lincoln,* 47.

149 *"There is a small but vigorous party"* *NYT,* December 28, 1858.

150 *"We all look to the Federal Administration"* *NYT,* December 28, 1858.

150 *"When Mr. Jackson was here"* Jeremiah S. Black, Attorney General of the U.S., to Joseph Ganahl, U.S. Attorney, Savannah, January 31, 1859, in Letterbook 5, Letters Received 1809–1863, United States Attorney General, Entry 10, RG 60, National Archives, Archives II.

151 *It was with some sense of confidence, then* Presidential Message on Landing of Barque Wanderer on Coast of Georgia with Cargo of Africans, January 12, 1859, 35th Congress, 2d Session, Senate Ex. Doc. 8; *Message of the President on Importation of Africans into Georgia,* February 15, 1859, 35th Congress, 2d Session, House Ex. Doc. 89.

153 Lamar claiming African boy: *Savannah News,* December 25–29,1858; Wells, *The Slave Ship Wanderer,* 36–37; Joseph Ganahl, U.S. Attorney, Savannah, to Attorney General Black, December 25, 1858, Letters Received from Georgia, 1809–1870, United States Attorney General, Entry 9, RG 60, National Archives, Archives II; Savannah, 1860, *City Directories.*

153 *If he made a sound* Savannah News, December 28, 1858; Joseph Ganahl, U.S. Attorney, Savannah, to Attorney General Black, December 25, 1858.

153 *A short time later* New York World Telegram, April 2, 1859, 1; *Savannah Republican,* reprinted in the *NYT,* March 28, 1859, 1; Wells, *The Slave Ship Wanderer,* 43; arrests of Aiken and others in U.S. District and Circuit Court Records, Southern District-Georgia, RG 21, National Archives, Southeast Region, Atlanta.

154 Marshal Ross story: Wells, *The Slave Ship Wanderer,* 36.

155 *When Van Horn and the two Negroes* Savannah Republican, reprinted in the *NYT,* March 15, 1859, 8.

156 *"Some of our citizens were taken aback"* Savannah News, reprinted in the *New York World Telegram,* April 9, 1859, 6.

157 *On January 26, 1859* The United States v. The Yacht Wanderer, United States District and Circuit Court Records, Southern District-Georgia, RG 21, National Archives, Southeast.

158 *No sooner had he finished* NYT, March 21, 1859; *Providence* (RI) *Daily Journal,* March 21, 1859, reprinted in the *Brooklyn Daily Eagle,* March 24, 1859, 2.

158 *The crowd roared* Providence Daily Journal, March 21, 1859, reprinted in the *Brooklyn Daily Eagle,* March 24, 1859, 2.

159 *"Mr. Lamar said that"* NYT, March 21, 1859, 4.

159 *Henry J. Raymond*   Francis Brown, *Raymond of the Times* (NY: W. W. Norton, 1951), 80.

160 *"You may search the country"*   *NYT,* March 22, 1859, 4.

160 *"The above comes to us"*   *NYT,* March 22, 1859, 4.

161 Raymond-Lamar joust: "A Slave-Trader's Letter-Book," 457–58.

162 *Lamar accused a visitor*   *NYT,* March 22, 1859, 4; *Savannah News,* March 29–30, 1859.

162 *"It will, no doubt"*   *NYT,* April 5, 1859, 4.

162 *"In my notice for the meeting"*   Notice reprinted in *Augusta Daily Constitutionalist,* January 19, 1859.

162 *"We unhesitantly advocate"*   *Savannah Republican,* reprinted in the *New York World Telegram,* May 1, 1859, 4; True Bill against Lamar, January 1859, U.S. District and Circuit Court Records, Southern District-Georgia, RG 21, National Archives, Southeast.

163 *Even when Deputy Marshal McRae*   *Augusta Daily Constitutionalist,* April 16, 1859; *Savannah Republican,* reprinted in the *NYT,* April 22, 1859, 2; *NYT,* April 20, 1859; *Savannah News,* March 12, 1859.

163 *"Lamar is a dangerous man"*   *The Children of Pride: A True Story of Georgia and the Civil War,* Robert M. Myers, ed. (NY: Popular Library, 1972), 250.

163 *Lamar was feeling confident*   *New York World Telegram,* April 30, 1859, 4.

163 *Successful Surgery*   *NYT,* April 23, 1859, 9; Fraser, *Savannah in the Old South,* 309.

14. THE BRITISH

165 *"I must acquaint your Lordship"*   Consul E. Molyneux, Savannah, to Earl of Malmesbury, March 1 and 5, 1859, Class B, Correspondence, in *Irish University Press Series of British Parliamentary Papers, Slave Trade,* vol. 45.

166 *evil empire*   Howard, *American Slavers and the Federal Law,* 9–13.

166 *Said he: "The occasional"*   Harrel E. Landry, "Slavery and the Slave Trade in Atlantic Diplomacy, 1850–1861," *Journal of Southern History* 27 (1961) 201.

166 *Who can doubt but that*   Don E. Fehrenbacher, *The Slaveholding Republic: An Account of the United States Government's Relations to Slavery* (NY: Oxford University Press, 2001), 167.

166 *What a farce is the*   *New York Herald,* February 7, 1859, 2.

166 Buchanan's view: Benjamin Moran, *The Journal of Benjamin Moran, 1857–1865,* Sarah A. Wallace and Frances E. Gillespie, eds. (Chicago: University of Chicago Press, 1948–1949), xxi–xxiii.

167 *Now vessels that*   Landry, "Slavery and the Slave Trade in Atlantic Diplomacy," 199.

167 *newspapers demanded blood*   Fehrenbacher, *The Slaveholding Republic,* 185; White, "The United States in the 1850s As Seen by British Consuls," 531.

167 *"In my letter"*   Commodore Wise, RN, to Secretary of the Admiralty, October 28, 1858, ADM 1/5694.

168 British debates: Mathieson, *Great Britain and the Slave Trade,* 155–160; Fehrenbacher, *The Slaveholding Republic,* 185.

168 *Said British foreign secretary*   Mathieson, *Great Britain and the Slave Trade,* 156.

169 *The London* Times, *after*   Soulsby, *The Right of Search,* 165; London *Times,* June 15, 1858.

169 *"The termination of that for which"*   Mathieson, *Great Britain and the Slave Trade,* 156; Fehrenbacher, *The Slaveholding Republic,* 186.

169 *"It must be a source of sincere"*   *Annual Message of the President,* December 4, 1860, 36th Congress, 2d Session, Senate Ex. Doc. 1.

170 Slave trading becomes big business: Mathieson, *Great Britain and the Slave Trade,* 161–63; Ward, *The Royal Navy and the Slavers,* 160; Howard, *American Slavers and the Federal Law,* 52.

170 *"The Spanish company was like"*   Howard, *American Slavers and the Federal Law,* 55.

171 *"Mr. — or as he styles himself"*   White, *"The United States in the 1850s As Seen by British Consuls,"* 525; Consul Bunch, Charleston, to Earl of Malmesbury, December 16, 1858.

172 Yacht Club bans *Wanderer: NYT,* February 8, 1859, 4; Thompson, "Historic American Yachts," 114.

173 Magrath decision: Sinha, *The Counterrevolution of Slavery,* 169, 172; *Savannah News,* May 21, 1859; Andrew G. Magrath, "The Slave Trade Not Declared Piracy by the Act of 1820," *"The United States vs. William C. Corrie.* Presentment for Piracy," Opinion, Hon. A. G. Magrath, District Judge, U.S. Circuit Court, District-South Carolina, April 19, 1860 (Charleston, SC: S. G. Courtney & Co, 1860); also published as *U.S. v. Corrie,* Circuit Court, District-South Carolina, April 19, 1860, *Federal Cases,* vol. 25, 658 (Case 14,869, 1860).

173 *"The forthcoming book"*   *Charleston Mercury,* reprinted in *Savannah News,* September 14, 1859.

173 *"Expelled by the New York"*   *NYT,* October 14, 1859.

15. VICKSBURG

176 *Later that afternoon*   Wender, *Southern Commercial Conventions,* 228; *Savannah News,* May 18, 1859.

176 The Vicksburg convention: Description drawn from Wender, *Southern Commercial Conventions,* 228; Spratt, "Speech Upon the Foreign Slave Trade"; Sinha, *Counterrevolution of Slavery,* 149; *Savannah News,* December 28, 1858.

177 *"There is* honor"   Takaki, *A Pro-Slavery Crusade,* 204, quoting from *DeBow's Review.*

183 Opposition of Henry S. Foote: Description drawn from *NYT,* May 19, 1859, 4; Craven, *The Growth of Southern Nationalism,* 108; William Catton and Bruce Catton, *Two Roads to Sumter* (NY: McGraw-Hill, 1963), 87; Takaki, *A Pro-Slavery Crusade,* 198; Michael P. Johnson, *Toward a Patriarchal Republic: The Secession of Georgia* (Baton Rouge: Louisiana State University Press, 1977), xx–xxi.

184 *"The ultra pro-slavery men"*   New York Herald, May 14, 18, 1858.

184 Press reaction: (New Orleans) *Daily Picayune,* May 20, 1859; *Memphis Enquirer,* reprinted in the *Savannah Republican,* May 23, 1859; *Savannah Republican,* May 19, 1859.

185 *"There is one little"*   *NYT,* June 10, 1859, 4.

16. TRIAL, PART I

189 Martin steals *Wanderer: The United States of America, by Information, versus the Schooner Wanderer, and Cargo,* Circuit Court of the United States in Admiralty, United States District Court, District-Massachusetts (Boston: Prentiss & Deland, 1860), at American Memory, the Library of Congress: memory.loc.gov/ammem/index.html; Thompson, "Historic American Yachts," 238.

189 Justice Wayne: Alexander A. Lawrence, *James Moore Wayne: Southern Unionist* (Chapel Hill: University of North Carolina Press, 1943), 128, 160; American Anti-Slavery Society, *The Anti-Slavery History of the John Brown Year,* 28.

190 John Brown: Potter, *The Impending Crisis,* 380.

191 *"It was an attempt by white men"*   Sandburg, *Abraham Lincoln: The Prairie Years,* vol. 2, 201.

191 *a second wave*   Robert Penn Warren, *John Brown: The Making of a Martyr* (Nashville: J. S. Sanders & Co., 1993), 394, 417.

191 *The Tremont Temple*   *NYT,* November 23, 1859, 5; Nevins, *The Emergence of Lincoln,* 98.

191 *Massachusetts governor John A. Andrew*   Warren, *John Brown,* 416.

191 *"The South Must Prepare"*   Savannah News, November 17, 1859.

191 *Had anyone in the courtroom*   Nevins, *The Emergence of Lincoln,* 20–23; George F. Milton, *The Eve of Conflict: Stephen A. Douglas and the Needless War* (Boston: Houghton Mifflin Co., 1934), 370.

192 *"Mr. Foreman and gentlemen"*   The trial testimony was reported by the *Savannah News,* the *Savannah Republican,* and the *Charleston Mercury,* November 14–24, 1859, from which this dialogue is drawn.; see also, *The Charge of Mr. Justice Wayne of the Supreme Court of the United States, given on the Fourteenth Day of November, 1859, to the Grand Jury of the Sixth Circuit Court of the United States, for the Southern District of Georgia* (Savannah: E. J. Purse, 1859); also published as *The Charge of Judge Wayne, Federal Cases,* vol. 30 (Case 18,269a, 1859).

195 Justice Wayne's views: Lawrence, *James Moore Wayne,* 143, 156–159; Catton, *Two Roads to Sumter,* 134.

17. TRIAL, PART II

206 Martin's *Wanderer: The United States of America, by Information, versus the Schooner Wanderer and Cargo;* Thompson, "Historic American Yachts," 238.

216 *"Bring the man some brandy"*   Robert Myers, *The Children of Pride,* vol. 2 (NY: Popular Library, 1977), 355.

217 *"A lonely walk"*   Myers, *The Children of Pride,* 352, 358.

219 *"The telegraph brings us the intelligence"*   *Savannah News,* December 3, 1859.

219 *Hooded, he had dropped*   *The Diary of Edmund Ruffin,* vol. 1, 370.

219 *"So perish all enemies"*   Warren, *John Brown,* 439.

220 *"We have our fears"*   *NYT,* April 22, 1859, 4.

18. CHARLESTON

221 Cotton prices are high: Russell, *Economic Aspects of Southern Sectionalism,* 204–205.

222 Lamar: *Savannah News,* January 10, 17, 1860.

222 *"We confess, we admire"*   From an editorial in *The Empire State,* Griffin, GA, reprinted on the top of the front page of the *Savannah News,* April 22, 1859.

222 Vigilante group: *Savannah Republican,* December 30, 1859; Johnson, *Toward a Patriarchal Republic,* 19.

222 *"We shall fire the Southern heart"*   Craven, *The Growth of Southern Nationalism,* 327.

222 Yancey's slave code: Sinha, *Counterrevolution of Slavery,* 197; Nevins, *The Emergence of Lincoln,* 128, 207; Milton, *The Eve of Conflict,* 371.

223 Fire-eaters' unpopularity: Milton, *The Eve of Conflict,* 397; Fraser, *Savannah in the Old South,* 284.

223 *To get their revolution rolling*   Johnson, *Toward a Patriarchal Republic,*
     86, 92; Craven, *The Growth of Southern Nationalism,* 321–23.

224 *The second part of the strategy*   Milton, *The Eve of Conflict,* 398, 413,
     423; *Augusta Daily Constitutionalist,* November 24, 25, 27, December 6,
     9, 10, 1859; *Savannah News,* December 9, 1859; *Savannah Republican,*
     March 16, 1860; Craven, *The Growth of Southern Nationalism,* 321–23.

224 *had beaten the majority into a minority*   Milton, *The Eve of Conflict,*
     413; Craven, *The Growth of Southern Nationalism,* 323–27.

225 *"There is a deep, sullen"*   Milton, *The Eve of Conflict,* 398.

225 *It was not the first time*   Nevins, *The Emergence of Lincoln,* 129.

225 Charleston Convention: Description drawn from Murat Halstead, *Three
     Against Lincoln: Murat Halstead Reports the Caucuses of 1860,* William B.
     Hesseltine, ed. (Baton Rouge: Louisiana State University Press, 1960), 7;
     Sinha, *Counterrevolution of Slavery,* 200–207; Milton, *The Eve of Conflict,*
     428.

226 Marshal Rynders appears among fire-eaters: American Anti-Slavery Society,
     Annual Report for the Year Ending May 1, 1861 (NY: American Anti-Slavery
     Society, 1862), 126.

226 Corrie appears next to Rynders: *Savannah Republican,* April 28, 1860;
     American Anti-Slavery Society, *Annual Report for the Year Ending May 1,
     1861,* 126.

227 *"Ours is the property invaded"*   Halstead, *Three Against Lincoln,*
     52–54; Nevins, *The Emergence of Lincoln,* 217; Craven, *The Growth of
     Southern Nationalism,* 329–32.

227 *"Gentlemen of the South"*   Halstead, *Three Against Lincoln,* 54.

227 Yancey puts slave trade issue under the carpet: Sinha, *Counterrevolution of
     Slavery,* 179–82; Wish, "The Revival of the African Slave Trade," 587;
     Takaki, *A Pro-Slavery Crusade,* 228–30.

227 *Said one observer, "Every man"*   *The Constitution,* Washington, D.C.,
     reprinted in the *Savannah News,* May 12, 1860.

228 *No sooner had Walker*   Halstead, *Three Against Lincoln,* 83; Potter, *Im-
     pending Crisis,* 1848–1861, 410.

228 *He, along with his cousins*   Letter of Adella Lamartine Estes, Gazaway
     B. Lamar Papers, 1822–1910, Hargrett Rare Book and Manuscript Li-
     brary, University of Georgia, Athens.

228 *"We shall have disunion"*   Charles A. L. Lamar Papers; *Savannah News,*
     December 24, 1858, and September 28, 29, 30, 1859.

19. LAMAR TRIAL

229 James Couper: James Hamilton Couper file, Library, Georgia Historical
     Society.

229 Boston and Van Horn testimony: *Savannah News,* May 29, 1860.

229 Case ends: *Savannah Republican,* reprinted in the *Charleston Daily Courier,* May 30, 1860; Wells, *The Slave Ship Wanderer,* 59; General Records of the Department of Justice, Georgia, 1811 to 1870, RG 60, National Archives, Southeast; *Savannah News,* May 29, 1860; *NYT,* May 29, 1860, 5.

230 Magrath ends Corrie case: *Charleston Mercury,* April 13–14, 1860; American Anti-Slavery Society, *Anti-Slavery History of the John Brown Year,* 28; *U.S. v. William C. Corrie,* Opinion, April 19, 1860.

231 Reaction to Corrie: Sinha, *The Counterrevolution of Slavery,* 170–73.

231 *"The judge's decision"*   *Savannah News,* April 21, 1860.

231 *The British were watching*   United States Consular, Charleston, Consul Bunch, Savannah, to Earl of Malmesbury (British Minister of Foreign Affairs), May 3, 1860, FO 84, Vol. 1112, from "Records of the British Foreign Office, 1780–1948," Microfilm, Photostats, and Transcripts of Originals in the Public Record Office, in the Manuscript Division, Library of Congress, Washington, D.C.

232 Pursuing Farnum: *NYT,* May 8, 1860, 8.

232 Jailbreak: Wells, *The Slave Ship Wanderer,* 69; *NYT,* May 7–8, 1860; *Charleston Mercury,* May 4, 1860; *Savannah Republican,* May 3, 1860.

234 Duel with Moore: *Savannah News,* May 25, 1860 and November 12, 1891; *NYT,* May 30, 1860, 4; Thomas Gamble, *Savannah Duels and Duelists, 1733–1877* (Spartanburg: Reprint Co., 1974), 150.

235 Yates defense of Farnum: *Savannah News,* May 10, May 22–27, 1860.

235 Lamar's single conviction: *U.S. v. C. A. L. Lamar,* May 8, 1860, U.S. District and Circuit Court Records, Southern District-Georgia, RG 21, National Archives, Southeast.

236 *"I am not in jail"*   "A Slave-Trader's Letter-Book," 460.

236 *"I do not agree with you"*   Charles A. L. Lamar to Gazaway B. Lamar, November 26, 1860, Gazaway B. Lamar Papers.

236 Northern Georgians resist: Johnson, *Toward a Patriarchal Republic,* xxi, 158; Sinha, *The Counterrevolution of Slavery,* 135.

237 *"If Georgia doesn't act"*   Charles A. L. Lamar to Gazaway B. Lamar, November 26, 1860, Gazaway B. Lamar Papers.

237 Revolt spreads: Eaton, *Freedom-of-Thought Struggle,* 383.

237 *"We are in the midst"*   Jeremiah Sullivan Black, Biography Resource Center (Farmington Hills, Mich.: The Gale Group, 2004); Johnson, *Toward a Patriarchal Republic,* 122.

238 The moderates fall into line: Sandburg, *Abraham Lincoln: The Prairie Years,* vol. 2, 378; Russell, *Economic Aspects of Southern Sectionalism,* 182; Catton, *Two Roads to Sumter,* 250.

238 Governor Brown calls for secession: Johnson, *Toward a Patriarchal Republic,* 63; Russell, *Economic Aspects of Southern Sectionalism,* 232.

238 *"We quarreled with them"*   Donald E. Reynolds, *Editors Make War; Southern Newspapers in the Secession Crisis* (Nashville: Vanderbilt University Press, 1970), 176.

20. THE *WANDERER*

239 *"As this vessel is the wonder"*   *Boston Traveller,* reprinted in the *NYT,* December 26, 1859, 8.

240 Martin's end: *The United States of America, by Information, versus the Schooner Wanderer, and Cargo;* Thompson, "Historic American Yachts," 238.

240 *The following year, Lamar sent*   *NYT,* December 31, 1860, 1; *Brooklyn Daily Eagle,* November 30, 1861, 2; Thompson, "Historic American Yachts," 242–43.

241 The end of the *Wanderer:* William M. Robinson, *The Confederate Privateers* (New Haven: Yale University Press, 1928), 196; Thompson, "Historic American Yachts," 341–43; Wells, *The Slave Ship Wanderer,* 84–85; United States Office of Naval Records and Library, *Official Records of the Union and Confederate Navies in the War of the Rebellion,* series I, vol. 16, (Washington: U.S. Government Printing Office, 1903), xx and various paging, 530–800.

241 Farnum's new career: *The Diary of Edmund Ruffin,* vol. 1, 268–70; Stewart Sifakis, *Who Was Who in the Civil War* (NY: Facts on File Press, 1988), 212; *Appleton's Cyclopaedia of American Biography,* James G. Wilson and John Fiske, eds. (NY: D. Appleton and Co., 1896), 412; *Brooklyn Daily Eagle,* September 19, 1860, 2.

241 *A few months later*   *NYT,* September 28, 1860, 8.

242 *When the war came*   *NYT,* May 16, 20, 1870.

242 Spratt: William J. Casey, "Leonidas W. Spratt," August 14, 1953, filed at South Carolina Historical Society, Charleston, SC; also Spratt pamphlets, Charleston, SC, Library Society; *Florida Times-Union,* Jacksonville, FL, October 5, 1903.

243 Corrie's demise: Charleston, South Carolina, 1860–1870, *City Directories of the United States 1860–1901* (New Haven: Research Publications, 1984); Death Card for William C. Corrie, Charleston, SC, Public Library.

243 Ganahl's life: *The Wanderer Case, The Speech of Hon. Henry R. Jackson; Augusta Daily Constitutionalist,* September 9, 1900; Hardee, *History of Savannah,* 432; Joseph Ganahl file, Library, Georgia Historical Society. Also, *Address of Hon Joseph Ganahl Before the Alumni Society, University of Georgia* (Athens: Southern Banner Power Press, 1878).

244 *When the war came, Charles Lamar*   James P. Jones, "Wilson's Raiders Reach Georgia: The Fall of Columbus," *GHQ* 59 (1975): 313; John A. Cobb, "Civil War Incidents in Macon," *GHQ* 7 (1923): 282; "Lamar's Rangers," from Compiled Service Records of Confederate Soldiers Who

Served in Organizations from the State of Georgia, Microfilm 266, RG
109, War Department Collection of Confederate Records, National
Archives.

245 *"Dear Brother"* Gazaway B. Lamar Papers.

245 *"The flower of our family is gone"* Gazaway B. Lamar Papers.

245 Gazaway Lamar: Hay, "Gazaway B. Lamar," 122; Edwin Coddington,
"The Activities of a Confederate Business Man," *The Journal of Southern
History* 9(1) (February 1943): 106; Brent Hughes, "Banking on the Con-
federate Cause," *Washington Times*, May 23, 1998.

245 Charles Lamar died fighting: *Savannah News*, November 12, 1891; *The
Confederate Veteran Magazine* 3 (1895): 130.

246 Buchanan finds no further violations of slave trade act: Annual Message of
the President of the United States, 36th Congress, 2d Session, December
4, 1860.

246 Buchanan adds ships to African Squadron: Soulsby, *The Right of Search*,
154.

247 Lincoln requests treaty with British: Howard, *American Slavers and the
Federal Law*, 60–61; Soulsby, *The Right of Search*, 172; *Message of the
President of the United States to the Senate and House of Representatives,
June 10, 1862, transmitting a copy of a treaty for the suppression of the
African slave trade between the United States and her Britannic Majesty, and
correspondence which preceded the conclusion of the instrument*, 37th Con-
gress, 2d Session, Senate Ex. Doc. 57, 1–15.

247 Only slave trader to die: Howard, *American Slavers and the Federal Law*,
90, 200–205.

247 Rynders faces removal: American Anti-Slavery Society, *Annual Report for
the Year Ending May 1, 1861*, 132; *NYT*, November 19, 1860 and January 17, 1861, 6; Howard, *American Slavers and the Federal Law*, 167.

247 Spain ends Cuban slave trade: Ward, *The Royal Navy and the Slavers*, 226.

248 The Thirteenth Amendment: Du Bois, *The Suppression of the African
Slave Trade*, 191–93.

248 Fire-eaters' epitaph: "Speech of the Hon. Horace Maynard of Tennessee
in the House of Representatives, January 31, 1863," 37th Congress, 3d
Session, reprinted in the pamphlet "The African Slave Trade," (Philadelphia: Charles Sherman Sons, 1863).

21. CILUCANGY

250 Cilucangy: Charles J. Montgomery, "Survivors from the Cargo of the
Negro Slave Yacht Wanderer," *American Anthropologist* 10 (1908): 611.

251 John Tucker's purchase of *Wanderer* slaves: Georgia Writers' Project, Savannah Unit, "Drakies Plantation," *GHQ* 14 (1930): 230.

252 *He was Ward Lee now*   Montgomery, "Survivors from the Cargo of the Negro Slave Yacht Wanderer," 614; *Savannah News,* April 18, 1868.

253 *Please help me*   Montgomery, "Survivors from the Cargo of the Negro Slave Yacht Wanderer," 621.

253 *Lee's grandson, William, moved*   Joye Brown "The *Wanderer, a Long Island Family Searches for Its Past*" in "Long Island: Our Story," Newsday Online, www.newsday.com.

254 Where the *Wanderer* was built: Adkins, *Setauket,* 85; *Bicentennial History of Suffolk County,* 78.

BIBLIOGRAPHY

Adkins, Edwin. *Setauket: The First Three Hundred Years, 1655–1955.* NY: David McKay, 1955.

Albion, Robert. *The Rise of New York Port.* NY: Charles Scribner's Sons, 1939.

——. *Square-Riggers on Schedule.* Hamden, CT: Archon Books, 1965.

American Anti-Slavery Society. *The Anti-Slavery History of the John Brown Year, Annual Reports for the Years Ending May 1, 1858, 1859, 1860, 1861.* NY: American Anti-Slavery Society, 1859, 1860; NY: Greenwood Publishing Group, 1969.

Baine, Rodney. *The Publications of James Edward Oglethorpe.* Athens: University of Georgia Press, 1994.

Bicentennial History of Suffolk County. Babylon, NY: Budget Steam Press, 1885.

Brigance, William. *Jeremiah Sullivan Black: A Defender of the Constitution and the Ten Commandments*. Philadelphia: University of Pennyslvania Press, 1934.

Brown, Francis. *Raymond of the Times*. NY: W. W. Norton, 1951.

Carnahan, Peter. *Schooner Master: A Portrait of David Stephens*. Chelsea, Vermont: Chelsea Green Publishing, 1989.

Catton, William, and Bruce Catton. *Two Roads to Sumter*. NY: McGraw-Hill, 1963.

Craven, Avery. *The Growth of Southern Nationalism*. Baton Rouge: Louisiana State University Press, 1981.

Crenshaw, Ollinger. *The Slave States in the Presidential Election of 1860*. Baltimore: Johns Hopkins Press, 1945.

Dow, George. *Slave Ships and Slaving*. Mineola, NY: Dover Publications, 2002.

Du Bois, W. E. B. *The Suppression of the African Slave Trade to the United States, 1638–1870*. Baton Rouge: Louisiana State University Press, 1965.

Eaton, Clement. *The Freedom-of-Thought Struggle in the Old South*. NY: Harper & Row, 1964.

Estep, H. Cole. *How Wooden Ships Are Built: A Practical Treatise on Modern American Wooden Ship Construction*. NY: W. W. Norton/ Penton Publishing, 1918.

Fehrenbacher, Don. *The Slaveholding Republic: An Account of the U.S. Government's Relations to Slavery*. NY: Oxford University Press, 2001.

Foner, Philip. *Business & Slavery: The New York Merchants and the Irrepressible Conflict.* Chapel Hill: University of North Carolina Press, 1941.

Fraser, Walter. *Savannah in the Old South.* Athens: University of Georgia Press, 2003.

Gamble, Thomas. *A History of the City Government, 1790–1901.* City of Savannah, 1900.

———. *Savannah Duels and Duelists, 1733–1877.* Spartanburg: Reprint Company, 1974.

Gill, I. *Six Months in Ascension.* London: John Murray Co., 1878.

Greenhill, Basil. *The Evolution of the Wooden Ship.* NY: Facts on File Press, 1988.

Halstead, Murat. *Three Against Lincoln: Murat Halstead Reports the Caucus of 1860.* Edited by William Hesseltine. Baton Rouge: Louisiana State University Press, 1960.

Harden, William. *Recollections of a Long and Satisfactory Life.* Savannah: Review Printing Company, 1934.

Howard, Warren. *American Slavers and the Federal Law, 1837–1862.* Berkeley: University of California Press, 1963.

Jackson, Harvey. *Forty Years of Diversity.* Athens: University of Georgia Press, 1984.

Johnson, Michael. *Toward a Patriarchal Republic: The Secession of Georgia.* Baton Rouge: Louisiana State University Press, 1977.

Johnson, Vicki. *The Men and the Vision of the Southern Commercial Conventions.* Columbia: University of Missouri Press, 1993.

Kingsley, Mary. *Travels in West Africa.* London: Macmillan, 1897; Washington, D.C.: The National Geographic Society, 2002.

Klein, Philip. *President James Buchanan.* University Park: Pennsylvania State University Press, 1962.

Kolchin, Peter. *American Slavery.* NY: Hill and Wang, 1993.

Lane, Mills. *Savannah Revisited: History and Architecture.* Savannah: Beehive Press, 2001.

Lawrence, Alexander. *James Moore Wayne: Southern Unionist.* Chapel Hill: University of North Carolina Press, 1943.

Mannix, Daniel. *Black Cargoes: A History of the Atlantic Slave Trade, 1518–1865.* NY: Viking Press, 1962.

Mathieson, William. *Great Britain and the Slave Trade.* NY: Octagon Books, 1967.

Mayer, Brantz, ed. *Twenty Years in the Slave Trade* (by Captain Canot). NY: Appleton, 1854.

McCardell, John. *The Idea of a Southern Nation.* NY: W. W. Norton, 1979.

McCash, June. *The Jekyll Island Cottage Colony.* Athens: University of Georgia Press, 1998.

McPherson, James. *Battle Cry of Freedom.* NY: Oxford University Press, 1988.

Milton, George. *The Eve of Conflict: Stephen A. Douglas and the Needless War.* Boston: Houghton Mifflin Co., 1934.

Moran, Benjamin. *The Journal of Benjamin Moran, 1857–1865.* Edited by Sarah Wallace and Francis Gillespie. Chicago: University of Chicago Press, 1948–1949.

Myers, Robert. *The Children of Pride*. Vol. 2. NY: Popular Library, 1977.

Nevins, Allen. *The Emergence of Lincoln*. NY: Charles Scribner's Sons, 1952.

Parkinson, John. *The History of the New York Yacht Club: From Its Founding Through 1973*. NY: New York Yacht Club, 1975.

Paskoff, Paul, and Daniel Wilson, eds. *The Cause of the South*. Baton Rouge: Louisiana State University Press, 1982.

Phillips-Birt, Douglas. *The History of Yachting*. NY: Stein and Day, 1974.

Potter, David. *The Impending Crisis*. NY: Harper & Row, 1976.

Reynolds, Donald. *Editors Make War: Southern Newspapers in the Secession Crisis*. Nashville: Vanderbilt University Press, 1966.

Rhett, Robert. *A Fire-Eater Remembers*. Edited by William Davis. Columbia: University of South Carolina Press, 2000.

Robinson, William. *The Confederate Privateers*. New Haven: Yale University Press, 1928.

Ruffin, Edmund. *The Diary of Edmund Ruffin*. Vol 1. Introduction and notes by William Scarborough. Baton Rouge: Louisiana State University Press, 1972.

Russell, Robert. *Economic Aspects of Southern Sectionalism, 1840–1861*. NY: Russell & Russell, 1960.

Sandburg, Carl. *Abraham Lincoln: The Prairie Years*. 2 Vols. NY: Charles Scribner's Sons, 1945.

Shaw, David. *America's Victory*. NY: The Free Press, 2002.

Sifakis, Stewart. *Who Was Who in the Civil War*. NY: Facts on File Press, 1988.

Sinha, Manisha. *The Counterrevolution of Slavery: Politics and Ideology in Antebellum South Carolina.* Chapel Hill: University of North Carolina Press, 2000.

Soulsby, Hugh. *The Right of Search and the Slave Trade in Anglo-American Relations.* Baltimore: Johns Hopkins Press, 1933.

Stampp, Kenneth. *The Causes of the Civil War.* NY: Simon & Schuster, 1991.

———. *The Peculiar Institution.* NY: Vintage Books, 1989.

Stick, David. *Graveyard of the Atlantic.* Chapel Hill: University of North Carolina Press, 1952.

Takaki, Ronald. *A Pro-Slavery Crusade: The Agitation to Reopen the African Slave Trade.* NY: The Free Press, 1971.

Thomas, Hugh. *The Slave Trade.* NY: Simon & Schuster, 1997.

Ward, W. E. F. *The Royal Navy and the Slavers: The Suppression of the Atlantic Slave Trade.* NY: Pantheon Books, 1969.

Warren, Robert Penn. *John Brown: The Making of a Martyr.* Nashville: J. S. Sanders, 1993.

Wells, Tom. *The Slave Ship Wanderer.* Athens: University of Georgia Press, 1967.

Wender, Herbert. *Southern Commercial Conventions, 1837–1859.* Baltimore: Johns Hopkins Press, 1930.

Wright, Donald. "Matthew Perry and the African Squadron." In *America Spreads Her Sails.* Edited by Clayton Barrow. Annapolis: Naval Institute Press, 1973.

Wyatt-Brown, Bertram. *Southern Honor.* NY: Oxford University Press, 1982.

INDEX